Wharton

Social Life in the Early Republic

Oakland Community College
Highland Lakes Library
7350 Cooley Lake Road
Union Lake, Michigan

SOCIAL LIFE IN
THE EARLY REPUBLIC

Mrs. Richard Gittings (Polly Sterett)
By Charles Willson Peale

SOCIAL LIFE
IN THE
EARLY REPUBLIC

BY

ANNE HOLLINGSWORTH WHARTON

AUTHOR OF "THROUGH COLONIAL DOORWAYS," "COLONIAL DAYS AND DAMES," "HEIRLOOMS IN MINIATURES," "A LAST CENTURY MAID," ETC.

WITH NUMEROUS REPRODUCTIONS OF PORTRAITS, MINIATURES, AND RESIDENCES

CORNER HOUSE PUBLISHERS
WILLIAMSTOWN, MASSACHUSETTS 01267
1970

FIRST PUBLISHED 1902

REPRINTED 1970

BY

CORNER HOUSE PUBLISHERS

Printed in the United States of America

PREFACE

NEW YORK, Boston, and the Southern cities, in the early years of the republic, possessed a characteristic and interesting social life. Philadelphia still held the place that she had won in Colonial days as a literary and social centre, but the new capital was the scene of a life more typically republican than that of any of these older towns.

During the first quarter of the last century men from the different States who had taken part in Revolutionary councils and congresses, those who had helped to win the battles of the republic and to frame its code of laws, were to be heard in the Senate and House or were to be met upon the streets of Washington, while women who had graced the drawing-rooms of Mrs. Washington in New York and Philadelphia passed through the doors of the new White House to pay their respects to Mrs. Adams, Mrs. Madison, and Mrs. Monroe. Among representative men and women from the centres of cultivation and refinement, North and South, there was a picturesque mingling of delegates from the recently admitted Border

States, all brought together in the closer relations that are only possible in a small city.

In the beautiful Washington of to-day, with its interesting, varied, kaleidoscopic life, it would be impossible to find a drawing-room like that of Mrs. Madison, Mrs. Edward Livingston, or Mrs. John Quincy Adams, in which all the great and little folk were to be met in one evening, as Mr. Josiah Quincy encountered them when he visited Washington in 1826. Many scattered centres of interest there are to-day, but no one centre towards which the rays of light focus, as in that earlier time when the mistress of the White House welcomed to her drawing-room Webster, Clay, Calhoun, Marshall, Story, Washington Irving, Sir Charles Bagot, Lord Ashburton, Father Richards, David Crockett, Matthew Lyon, the good Indian Pushmataha, "Eagle of the Choctaws," and his eulogist John Randolph.

One of the penalties incident upon advancing civilization is the passing away of the characteristic and individual features of society. After hearing an older Washingtonian say, when asked some question about Mr. Fillmore, that she "knew nothing about him or any of the modern Presidents," it occurred to the writer that it might be advisable to preserve for the generations to come a picture of the social life of the capital—an already fast-fading retrospect—while men and women are living who describe Webster, Clay, and Jackson as they appeared to them, or recall the quaint figures of Mrs. Alexander Hamilton and Mrs. Madison in old age, or the younger faces of Cora Livingston, Adèle Cutts, Mrs. Gardiner G. Howland, and Madame de Potestad.

To those who have aided her with personal recollections or valuable family papers and letters the author makes grateful acknowledgment, her thanks being especially due to Mrs. Samuel Phillips Lee, Mrs. Beverly Kennon, Mrs. M. E. Donelson Wilcox, Miss Virginia Mason, Mr. James Nourse and the Misses Nourse of the Highlands, to Mrs. Robert K. Stone, Miss Fanny Lee Jones, Mrs. Semple, Mrs. Julia F. Snow, Mr. J. Henley Smith, Mrs. Thompson H. Alexander, Miss Rosa Mordecai, Mrs. Harriot Stoddert Turner, Miss Caroline Miller, Mrs. T. Skipwith Coles, Dr. James Dudley Morgan, and Mr. Charles Washington Coleman.

A. H. W.

PHILADELPHIA, October, 1902.

CONTENTS

ILLUSTRATIONS

ILLUSTRATIONS

ILLUSTRATIONS

ILLUSTRATIONS

ILLUSTRATIONS

ILLUSTRATIONS

SOCIAL LIFE IN THE EARLY REPUBLIC

I

A SOCIAL EVOLUTION

"THE Bostonians unite simplicity of morals with that French politeness and delicacy of manners which render virtue more amiable," wrote Brissot de Warville, who visited the principal cities of America soon after the Revolution. In the New England city the observing Frenchman recorded that he discovered "neatness without luxury," and if in other cities and towns that he visited he found more luxury and perhaps less neatness, in all of them he met cultivated men, and women so charming that he frankly admitted that for beauty and conversational ability they compared favorably with those of any court in the Old World.

All visitors to America before and during the Revolution wrote with enthusiasm of the social life which they enjoyed in Boston, New York, Philadelphia, and the Southern cities. Instead of the rude and primitive life that might have been expected in a new country, they found here what they recognized as society in its best sense,—the meeting of men and women for rational intercourse and enjoyment without the extremes of luxury and license that were to be found in most capitals of Europe.

This early and rapid development of social life in the Colonies was largely due to the fact that they were English in character from Maine to Georgia. Despite the Dutch, Swedish, German, and other nationalities present in New York, Delaware, and in nearly all of the settlements, the dominant impression was made by the Anglo-Saxon, who, with all his reserve and apparent coldness, is a creature of social instincts, dependent upon the exchange of ideas and hospitalities, who carries his English habits and customs with him into the wilderness. Nowhere was this trait more emphasized than in the Southern Colonies, where men and women living upon remote plantations cheerfully jogged and jolted over miles of rough roads in order to assist at countryside dinners, dances, weddings, and christenings.

In the Northern and Middle Colonies the pleasures of society were chiefly confined to towns and cities, while in the South, although social life centred in certain towns, especially in such capitals as Savannah, Charleston, Williamsburg, and Annapolis, the joys of social intercourse extended to the countryside. During the hunting season the Virginian planter kept open house for weeks at a time, and his brother of Maryland was not slow in following his example. It is related of one of the patriarchal landholders of Maryland that, when importuned by his relatives to break the entail upon his estate, he replied, "If I divide it, I shall make as many fox-hunters as I make heirs."

In nothing were the English characteristics of the Southern settler more clearly shown than in his love of field sports. A Maryland chronicler writes of his countrymen, "On horses that seemed almost tireless, and with dogs like the horses, they sometimes chased Reynard across the eastern peninsula from the Chesapeake to the Atlantic. The return journey and the stops at hospitable mansions on the way took more time than the pursuit of the fox, and the whole expedition sometimes lasted a week."

In the early married life of the Washingtons at Mount Vernon there was scarce a day that the General did not record in his diary a visit or a dinner at some neighbors, or going with Mrs. Washington and the children to Mr. Fairfax's to stand godfather to one of his children, or fox-hunting with Colonel Bassett, Mr. Fairfax, and Jacky Custis, or coming home to find that a number of guests had arrived during his absence; so generous, indeed, was the hospitality of Mount Vernon that, although its master owned a hundred cows, he sometimes humbly confessed that he had to buy butter.

Nor was the life of Maryland and Virginia, with its fox-hunting and constant exercise of hospitality, entirely given over to pleasure. Plantation living, with its various open-air duties and diversions, seemed to offer abundant facilities for reading and study, and in the South there grew up a race of men familiar with the English classics as with those of Greece and Rome. If George Sandys entertained his leisure hours by translating Ovid upon the picturesque banks of the James, and the Southern gentleman was wont to form his language upon the writings of Addison, Pope, and Bolingbroke, there were also many who were so familiar with the pages of English jurists that they adapted the precepts found therein to the life of their own time, and when the casuistry of the mother country became intolerable, were ready to meet her arguments with wits sharpened upon English authorities.

The Duc de la Rochefoucauld, although he met many clever men and women in Philadelphia, New York, and Boston, did not hesitate to give as his opinion that in the South "A taste for reading was more prevalent among gentlemen of the first class than in any other part of America." Another discriminating traveller, Smyth, although impressed with the luxurious living in the beautiful country-seats along the James, and the fondness of their inmates for the chase, expressed much the same opinion with regard to the attainments of the

Southern gentleman. After meeting Mr. Charles Carroll of Carrollton, whom he calls "one of the richest inhabitants of the United States," and visiting the houses of Dr. James Murray, Governor Ogle, and many other hospitable citizens of Annapolis, the duke recorded to the honor of this city that "All that he had seen of its men and women led him to think it one of the places which a stranger would be most inclined to choose, if he did not catch the disease of the country, the thirst for speculation."

The division of the Southern Colonies into parishes established another meeting-ground between the county families of Virginia, Maryland, and the Carolinas. The Virginian, being of English ancestry, followed the religious usages of his fathers. Bishop Meade's history of the churches of Virginia furnishes a record of the leading families as well, those being days when temporal and spiritual interests contrived to jog along pleasantly together in the Old Dominion and in her sister Colonies. An amusing instance of the self-constituted importance of a Virginia parson is to be found among the traditions of St. George's Parish, Spottsylvania. One Mr. Thompson of this parish had made proposals of marriage to Lady Spotswood, relict of the governor. Being a lady of high degree, possessed of a title and broad acres, the widow expressed some doubt as to whether such a marriage would be suitable to one in her station in life, upon which the parson, nothing daunted, set forth with elaboration and at considerable length the advantages appertaining to his cloth. After expatiating upon the honor and dignity of his calling, as relating to the salvation of souls, beyond that of the greatest princes on earth, and like unto that of the blessed angels, and the Son of God Himself when he condescended to dwell among men, the reverend gentleman proceeded to strengthen his cause by the following outburst of eloquence and sarcasm:

> "From all which, it evidently appears, y^{t} in all Ages & Nations of ye World, whether Jews, Heathens, or Christians, great Honour & Dignity has been always conferred upon ye clergy. And when it is moreover declared y^{t} whosoever despiseth them, despiseth not Man but God. All which Titles shew y^{t} upon many accounts they stand called, appropriated & devoted to God himself. And therefore, if a Gentleman of this sacred and honourable character should be married to a Lady, though of ye greatest extraction & most excellent personal qualities (which I'm sensible you're endowed with,) can be no disgrace to her, nor her family, nor draw ye censures of ye world upon either, for such an action. And therefore Dr Madam, your argument being refuted you can no longer consistently refuse to consummate my happiness."

It may be unnecessary to state that the widow yielded to the persuasions of a lover who possessed the gift of tongues in so large a measure, and Lady

Spotswood became the wife of the Rev. John Thompson, who is described as a handsome and accomplished gentleman.

Whatever traces the antiquarian may discover of extravagance and luxury in Colonial capitals, there was in early times little danger of social life being dominated by the class of large wealth and aimless leisure that has later threatened its higher interests in our leading cities. In those strenuous days the leisure class was in too small proportion to be counted a factor in the life of the time. Few enjoyed wealth and leisure except those who rested from their labors; and if some of the magnates of old New York, Philadelphia, and Boston appeared upon the pages of the directories of their day as "gentleman," it was because a youth of well-ordered activity had earned them a right to such dignified and aristocratic repose.

Our ancestors, with a wiser and broader outlook upon life than that of a later time, evidently considered those who represented the intellectual and religious interests in the community quite as essential to the completeness of social intercourse as those who stood for material prosperity. The Duc de la Rochefoucauld observed that the leaders of society in Philadelphia were the great lawyers and merchants. There were also in this city eminent divines, honored for their character and attainments, and always a circle of scientific men, like David

Rittenhouse, the Hopkinsons, Bonds, Rushes, and Ellicotts, whose studies and original researches were encouraged by the Philosophical Society of which they were members. Mr. Adams wrote to his wife, from the capital, of dinners with the celebrated Dr. Priestley and other learned men, as well as of sumptuous entertainments at the Binghams and at the house of Robert Morris in the company "of other venerable old rakes, threescore years of age or a little over or a little under." If De Liancourt recorded that he had "seen balls on the President's birthday where the splendor of the rooms and the variety and richness of the dresses did not suffer in comparison with Europe," he and his compatriot, the observing De Chastellux, found many congenial companions among scholarly Philadelphians, while they were as much charmed by the cultivation and conversational powers of the women as by their beauty.

Mr. Richard Parkinson, an enthusiastic English agriculturist who visited America about 1798, when not absorbed in following the excursions of the Hessian fly or taking notes upon the superior treatment of timothy practised by Mr. Gittings, who had a large farm near Baltimore, found much to interest him in the social life of Maryland and Virginia. He recorded a delightful visit of some days at General Ridgely's country-seat, where he dined with the governor of Maryland and several members of the Assembly. Mr. Parkinson was hospitably entertained at Mount Vernon, where, in an interesting conversation with General Washington, the great man expressed himself freely with regard to the relative importance of several American cities. "Baltimore," he predicted, "would be the risingest town in America, except the federal city. Philadelphia would decline; but New York would always maintain an eminent commercial rank from its position—the frost not stopping the navigation so early, and sometimes not at all."

In view of subsequent developments, General Washington's predictions are not without interest. Many of the Southern towns, like those of the Northern Colonies, owed much of their social distinction to commercial prosperity, as wealth increased rapidly all along the seaboard. If Massachusetts boasted her merchant princes like the Dexters, Derbys, Hoopers, and Pepperells, and New York her successful Dutch traders, the planters of Virginia and Maryland were by no means averse to commerce as a convenient and lucrative method of exchanging the products of their plantations for those of other lands. Baltimore, which General Washington spoke of as a rising town, was already an important commercial centre, to which Georgetown was proving a formidable rival, as one-third of all the tobacco of Maryland was sent out from that port. Large quantities of furs and Indian goods were also exported in exchange for various commodities from Great Britain, and sugar, molasses, and rum from the West Indies.

Among the various Colonial cities and towns of greater or less importance socially, politically, and commercially, it is not strange, when a capital was to be chosen for the new federation of States, that the claims of many aspirants to this honor should have been presented. None north of New York or south of Annapolis were seriously considered. This latter gay little town felt that it had strong claims to political preferment, which its corporation, led by Mayor Samuel Chase, did not hesitate to set forth with emphasis. The Honorable Congress was duly reminded of the advantages of Annapolis, especially "its central situation to the Federal States, and the convenience of the members of Congress to repair thither by land or water: the facility of receiving and conveying intelligence to Europe and its remarkable healthiness and capacity of defence from any attack of an enemy: *being in the opinion of this corporation* the most eligible place in the United States for the residence of the Honorable Congress and their officers and foreign ministers." *

* Copied from Proceedings of the Corporation of Annapolis, 1783.

The relegating of the capital of the new republic to the banks of the Potomac, or the River of Swans, as the Indians had named it, was not accomplished without many heated discussions on the floor of Congress. It was while this question was under debate that Fisher Ames, of Massachusetts, doubted whether "the government would stand the shock of a selection which involved as many passions as the human heart could display."

The subject of the "Residence Bill," as it was called, was treated of in the diary of Honorable William Maclay, of Pennsylvania, with much acrimony and not a little dry humor. President Washington, who was one of the few persons whom Mr. Maclay was usually able to admire, came in for his full share of blame, because Mr. Maclay considered him to be too much under the influence of Mr. Hamilton, who, to the Pennsylvania Senator's mind, represented the arch-enemy of true Democracy. When Mr. Maclay realized that the location of the national capital was bound up with the Assumption Bill, and that the President had been inoculated with the "funding disease," he exclaimed in hot indignation, "Alas, that the affection—nay, almost admiration—of the people should meet so unworthy a return! Here are their best interests sacrificed to the vain whim of fixing Congress and a great commercial town (so opposite to the genius of the Southern planter) on the Potomac," etc.

According to Mr. Jefferson's statement in his "Anas," the site of the capital was not really decided in Congress, but over the Virginia statesman's dinner-table. It may have been to this dinner that Mr. Maclay referred when he wrote in his New York diary, July 20, 1790: "There was a dinner this day which I had no notice of, and never thought of such a thing." Mr. Jefferson, then Secretary of State, had recently returned from abroad. Colonel Hamilton met him in front of the President's house, and as the two walked up and down the street together, Hamilton explained to Jefferson the strained relations between the North and South. If, he argued, the North accepted the bill for the assumption of the domestic debt and secured the "residence of the capital" for a Northern city, Mr. Hamilton clearly saw before the country dangers and difficulties, even the secession of the Southern States; while, on the other hand, if the war debt of twenty millions were not assumed by the general government, it was feared that the Eastern or creditor States might secede from the federation. Plainly, a compromise was necessary in the opinion of the wise and far-seeing Hamilton. Mr. Jefferson pleaded ignorance of the matter, as he had been abroad. He would, he said, be pleased if Colonel Hamilton would dine with him the next day, meet a few Virginians, and discuss the question calmly over Madeira and punch. Like many other important matters, the site of the capital was decided over a glass of wine, and before the guests quitted the table the compromise was agreed upon,—in this case one that the nation has never had reason to regret. A bill was introduced, which promptly passed both Houses, by which "the President was authorized to appoint commissioners to survey, under his own direction, a district of territory, not exceeding ten miles square, at some place on the River Potomac, between the mouths of the Eastern Branch and the Conococheague."

When it was finally decided to place the capital on the Potomac, and the Northern members were appeased by the assumption of the war debt, whose obligations were heavier North than South, there was still something to be done in order to pacify Pennsylvania. This State, whose capital had been the scene of the most important civic events of the Revolution, and whose great financiers, Robert Morris and Thomas Willing, had supplied the Commander-in-Chief with the sinews of war, could not well be overlooked. Indeed, there had been good reason to expect a Pennsylvania town to be the site of the national government, as a bill had passed both Houses in September, 1789, locating the capital in a ten-mile square of the quaint and picturesque village of Germantown.* That this old German settlement should have been thus distinguished was no more remarkable than that Trenton, Harrisburg, Wright's Ferry, Lancaster, and various other unimportant inland towns should have been seriously considered as sites for the capital city. Strange as these suggestions seem to us to-day, the choice of the unimproved tract of land upon the Potomac, covered with sparse, marshy growth in some places and with forests in others, in which Mr. Thomas Twining lost his way while journeying to Mr. Law's house, seemed even less promising. So uninviting, indeed, was the prospect that Mr. Andrew Ellicott, the engineer who made the first topographical survey of the district, revealed to his wife, in a sudden burst of conjugal confidence, an opinion as to the relative attractions of the Pennsylvania and national capitals which he would not have her repeat, as "the President is," he says, "so much attached to this country I would not be willing that he should know my real sentiments about it.

* It has so often been said that Philadelphia was not chosen as the seat of the national government in consequence of the frequent and violent outbreaks of yellow fever in the Quaker City that it seems worth while to state that the most severe and prolonged epidemics of yellow fever occurred while Congress was in session in Philadelphia, after the whole question of the residence had been finally settled, and the bill in favor of the banks of the Potomac had passed both Houses.

But with you, my dear, whose love and affection I have constantly experienced almost from our infancy, I am not afraid to make my sentiments known. This country, intended for the permanent residence of Congress, bears no more proportion to the country about Philadelphia and Germantown, for either wealth or fertility, than a crane does to a stall-fed ox."

Although Mr. Ellicott expressed himself with so much caution, it must surely have been an open secret that New York, Philadelphia, and several other towns offered stronger claims for consideration as the permanent seat of government than the embryo city on the banks of the Potomac. For years to come both Senators and Representatives, in common with their respective consorts, bewailed the fate that forced them to relinquish the comforts and social pleasures of New York and Philadelphia for the uncertainties of the new capital. Even that daughter of the Puritans, Mrs. John Adams, according to her own account, found herself in a whirl of gayety in Philadelphia, while her husband, the Vice-President, spoke of theatre-going as one of the relaxations of official life. One night he wrote of accompanying the President's party, which included his nephew, Mr. George S. Washington and his pretty young bride, who was a sister of Mrs. James Madison, to see "The Rage" and "The Spoiled Child." "It rained," said Mr. Adams, "and the house was not full. I thought I perceived a little mortification."

John Adams seems to have been all too ready to ascribe to the President emotions and motives that found a place in his own breast. Some of the most amusing passages in his letters are those in which he falls to wondering whether the President is sincere in his frequently avowed intention to retire at the end of his second term. At the close of one of his letters, Mr. Adams wrote, "I am so fatigued and disgusted with the insipidity of this dull life, that I am half of a mind to vow that if Washington don't resign I will. The old hero looks very grave of late."

In another letter the Vice-President wrote, "Mrs. Washington is very happy at present in a visit from her two granddaughters, N.'s sisters, as I suppose they are. One of them is a fine, blooming, rosy girl, who, I dare say, has had more liberty and exercise than Nelly." The blooming beauty of whom Mr. Adams speaks was doubtless Eliza Custis, who afterwards married Mr. Thomas Law, a nephew of Lord Ellenborough. Mr. Law, who met Miss Custis soon after his arrival in Philadelphia, found favor in her eyes and in those of the General and Mrs. Washington; and the young girl's parents placing no obstacles in the way of his marriage with their daughter, the wedding of Miss Custis and Mr. Law was celebrated at Hope Park, near Fairfax Court-House, the home of the bride's step-father, Dr. Stuart.

Mr. James Greenleaf, of Massachusetts, who was associated with Mr. Law in his speculations in Washington lands, had, like him, interests of a more sentimental nature in Philadelphia. In one of his letters Mr. Law encouraged Mr. Greenleaf with regard to his prospects with Miss Allen by telling him that she had expressed a desire to see him again in Philadelphia.

The young New Englander's family connections and associations were calculated to please the aristocratic Allens, while his manners and conversation are described as dignified and charming. The long descent of the Greenleaf family was celebrated many years after by a worthy member of the ancient Huguenot line, the poet John Greenleaf Whittier, who wrote,—

> "The name the Gallic exile bore,
> St. Malo! from thy ancient mart,
> Became upon our Western shore
> Greenleaf for Feuillevert.
>
> "A name to hear in soft accord
> Of leaves by light winds overrun,
> Or read, upon the greening sward
> Of May, in shade and sun."

One of Mr. Greenleaf's sisters married Noah Webster of dictionary renown. John Trumbull, speaking of this marriage, said, "Webster has returned, and brought with him a very pretty wife. I wish him success; but I doubt, in the present decay of business in our profession, whether his profits will enable him to keep up the style he sets out with. I fear he will breakfast upon Institutes, dine upon Dissertations, and go to bed supperless."

Anne Penn Allen, whom Mr. Greenleaf married in 1800, was a granddaughter of Chief Justice Allen, of Philadelphia, and a niece of another beautiful Ann Allen, whom Mr. John Swanwick described in his verses as "youthful Allen of majestic mien." This Ann Allen became the wife of Governor John Penn, and the niece was evidently named for her. Miss Allen's father, James Allen, died during the Revolution, leaving a beautiful widow of twenty-seven and three daughters. When Mrs. James Allen's days of mourning were over she removed to Philadelphia, where her house is described as one of the most popular in the city. The youngest daughter of the family, Mary Allen, writing of social life in Philadelphia after the Revolution, said, "Crowds of foreigners of the highest rank poured into Philadelphia, and Ministers with their suites from all parts of the world, came to bow to Washington and the Republic;—at this time I was not grown up, but my Mother and her two elder daughters were equally Belles; at length my Mother married a Senator in Congress from New

James Greenleaf
By Gilbert Stuart

York, Mr. Lawrence. She removed there with him, but returned to pass her winters in Philadelphia during the Sessions of Congress. . . . In the Spring we went to Fairy Hill, a beautiful spot on the Schuylkill, which belonged to us, and afterwards to Allentown, where we remained till Autumn."

Mary Allen, in her ingenuous girlish narrative, says that by this time her second sister, Margaret Elizabeth, had become the wife of William Tilghman, afterwards chief justice of Pennsylvania, and that her grandmother and her sister Anne and herself accepted her mother's urgent invitation to spend the winter in New York. It was during this visit that the young chronicler met Henry Walter Livingston, whom she afterwards married, and here Anne Allen probably met Mr. Greenleaf. His name appears in the directory of 1795 as residing at No. 112 Liberty Street, while under the sign "Watson, Greenleaf & Cotton, No. 7 Crane Wharf," an extensive commercial business was transacted.

"Behold us in New York," wrote Mary Allen, "at 37 Broadway, living in splendor, and my young heart intoxicated with pleasure. My beautiful sister (afterwards Mrs. Greenleaf) was a brilliant luminary which seemed to animate everything within its influence, and I was the modest satellite shining with a reflected lustre."

Although Mary Allen speaks so disparagingly of her own attractions, she is described by Dr. Benjamin Rush as one of the most beautiful and charming women of her time. While visiting Linlithgow, Livingston Manor, about 1806, Dr. Rush drew a pen-picture of Mrs. Walter Livingston, which, though written in the stilted and exaggerated style of the day, breathes in every line a sincere admiration and respect for the lovely young châtelaine of Livingston Manor.

Mrs. John Adams's letters from New York and Philadelphia are less full of details about the people whom she met than those of an earlier date, and for the very good reason that her chief correspondent and "dearest friend," the Vice-President, was usually at her side. In a letter to her sister, Mrs. Shaw, she descants upon the attractions of Richmond Hill, which, she says, "for natural beauty may vie with the most delicious spot I ever saw." It is interesting to read Mrs. Adams's description of this place, which is now a part of the city of New York, "with its venerable oaks, and ground covered with wild shrubs, where a lovely variety of birds serenade me every morning and evening, rejoicing in their liberty and security."

If Mrs. Adams's letters are less satisfactory, other chroniclers had arisen whose pens were ready to descant upon the gossip, beauties, and fashions of the day. Miss Mary Binney wrote to her cousin,

Mrs. Simon Jackson, of Newton, Massachusetts, of the extreme gayety of the Quaker City. "I have not," she says, "one minute to spare from French, music, balls, and plays. Oh dear, this dissipation will kill me! for you must know our social tea drinkings of *one or two friends* is an assembly of two or three hundred souls."

Another girl correspondent, writing to Mrs. Jackson about the same time, said, "Now for fashions, and in order to be methodical I will begin at the head, though the dress of that is so varied that I hardly know how to describe it. Small beaver hats are very much worn, not with caps; ribbon through the hair, with a rose on the side, or a half handkerchief put on turban fashion with the corner down behind, the hair cut short at the sides, the curls craped out full, smooth on the forehead."

This arrangement of the hair which the Watertown belle evidently found so attractive appears to be very much like Mrs. Stoddert's description of her own coiffure. "Instead of a wig," she says, "I have a bando, which suits me much better. I had it in contemplation to get a wig, but I have got what I like much better for myself. It is called a bando. I think the former best for those who dress in a different style from myself, but the latter suits me best. I heard the ladies with whom I was in company last night say that the fashionable manner of dressing the hair was more like the Indians—

the hair without powder—and looked sleek and hung down the forehead in strings. Mine will do that to a nicety. I observe powder is scarcely worn, only, I believe, by those who are gray,—too much so to go without powder, I mean. How those ladies in the Indian fashion dress their hair behind I cannot say; but those out of that fashion that I have seen, and who do not wear wigs, have six or eight curls in their neck, and turn up the rest and curl the ends, which I think looks very pretty when well done."

Mrs. Benjamin Stoddert, whose husband was a member of Mr. Adams's cabinet,* wrote from Philadelphia many charming letters to her family, giving them vivid and spicily interpolated descriptions of the gayeties that surrounded her, of the fashion and beauties of the day, of birthnight balls, of levees at Mrs. Adams's and Lady Liston's, and of brilliant, sumptuous entertainments at Mrs. Bingham's. In one of her letters to her niece, Miss Eliza Gantt, of Graden, Mrs. Stoddert, after retailing a piece of current gossip connected with the elopement of Mr. William Bingham's daughter, quotes Mr. Stoddert as saying that "large towns are terrible places for young females," adding "and

* Benjamin Stoddert was in May, 1798, appointed by Mr. Adams Secretary of the recently formed Naval Bureau, and was consequently the first Secretary of the Navy.

I am sure I can find nothing in this to make an old female wish to remain in it one moment longer than necessity obliges."

The social life of the capital, with which Mrs. Stoddert was so ready to find fault, was composed, whatever may have been its shortcomings, of the best elements from Colonial cities, North and South. Here were gathered together representative men from each State of the federation, in days when the best men in the community entered into political life. Even if there was some exaggeration in the Duc de la Rochefoucauld's gallant observation that "in the numerous assemblies of Philadelphia it is impossible to meet with what is called a plain woman," the American women of that day had already proved their ability to bear favorable comparison with those of England and France. In addition to such native beauties as Mrs. William Bingham, Miss Sally McKean, Mrs. Samuel Blodget, and Mrs. Adams's "constellation of beauties," there were Mrs. Ralph Izard, wife of the Senator from South Carolina, and beautiful Mrs. Elbridge Gerry, both New York women; while from a sister State came Mrs. John Jay, who was so wise a woman that her pretty head was not readily turned by compliments, even so great as to have the audience of a French theatre rise *en masse* upon her entrance, mistaking the wife of the American diplomat for their beautiful queen, Marie Antoinette.

Some people and things in Philadelphia Mrs. Stoddert found to her liking, among them the amusing, original conversation of Mrs. Samuel Blodget and the home-like charm of Mrs. Oliver Wolcott, with whom she was on most friendly terms, consulting her about the ailments of her little ones, and exchanging with her what she laughingly called "old women's receipts." Mrs. Bingham's ball the critical lady also found to her taste. This festivity she attended in the good company of Mrs. Harrison, a Maryland woman, and a daughter of General Washington's old friend, Dr. Craik:

"About half-past seven I called for Mrs. Harrison, and we made our appearance at Mrs. Bingham's. But instead of her being in a little room, as you have been told, till all her company arrived, she was seated at the head of the drawing-room, I should call it, or, in other words, on one side of the chimney, with three ladies only. There were some young ladies in another room, where her two daughters were also, who, upon my inquiring after their health, were sent for by their mamma. I should suppose that it was near nine o'clock before the dancing commenced. At the end of the first dance, or near it, punch and lemonade were brought in. That was the first refreshment. Some time after, I think, it was brought in again, and soon after the best ice-cream, as well as the prettiest, that ever I saw was carried around in beautiful china cups and gilt spoons. The latter I had seen there before. Except punch and lemonade, nothing more to eat till supper, which we were summoned to at eleven, when the most superb thing of the kind which I ever saw was presented to our view,—though those who have been

Mrs. John Jay
Copied from a medallion in a bracelet
by Daniel Huntington

there before say that the supper was not as elegant as they had seen there. In the middle was an orange-tree with ripe fruit; and where a common spectator might imagine the root was, it was covered with evergreens, some natural and some artificial flowers. Nothing scarcely appeared on the table without evergreens to decorate it. The girondole, which hangs immediately over the table, was let down just to reach the top of the tree. You can't think how beautiful it looked. I imagine there were thirty at the table, besides a table full in another room, and I believe every soul said, 'How pretty!' as soon as they were seated; all in my hearing, as with one consent, uttered the same thing. . . . At twelve o'clock or a little after Mrs. Harrison and I left the ball. We were among the first to come away. Never did I see such a number of carriages, except on a race-ground."

Of another ball, given before the Stodderts arrived in Philadelphia, which made considerable stir in political as well as in social circles, Mr. Albert Gallatin wrote to his wife: "Do you want to know the fashionable news of the day? The President of the United States has written, in answer to the managers of the ball in honor of George Washington's birthday, that he took the earliest opportunity of informing that he *declined* going. The court is in a prodigious uproar about that important event. The ministers and their wives do not know how to act upon the occasion." Mr. Gallatin added that a most powerful battery had been opened against him to induce him to attend the ball, the arguments in favor of his going being "urged by a fine lady, by Mrs. Law, and when supported by her handsome black eyes they appeared very formidable. Yet I resisted and came off conqueror, although I was as a reward to lead her into the room, to dance with her, etc. Our club has given me great credit for my firmness, and we have agreed that two or three of us who are accustomed to go to these places, Langdon, Brent, etc., will go this time to please the Law family."

Whether Mr. Adams's refusal to attend the birthnight ball was due, as alleged, to conscientious scruples against such celebrations as "anti-republican and dangerous precedents," or to the overmastering and ineradicable jealousy of Washington that marred so much that was fine in the character of John Adams, does not appear. Mr. Morse, in speaking of some changes made in his cabinet by President Adams, says that "He appeared, at this time, in one of his worst moods, mingled of anger, egotism, and that one great foolish jealousy of his life, which consumed his heart whenever he heard the praises of Washington."

Mr. Adams was by no means the only person disposed to find fault with what they considered the dangerously aristocratic tendencies of the republican court under the first President and his lady. Thomas Jefferson is said to have kept the date of his own birth a secret in order to avoid birthday celebrations; while Senator Maclay, who was "nothing if not critical," after donning his best clothes and making his bow at the President's levee, which he characterized as "an idle thing," in the privacy of his chamber gave way to the violence of his emotions in language so intemperate that we wonder he ventured to confide his expressions to the pages of his diary. "If there is treason in the wish," he said, "I retract it, but would to God this same General Washington was in heaven! We would not then have him brought forward as the constant cover to every unconstitutional and un-republican act."

It is a rather significant fact that even his political enemies wished nothing worse for "this same General Washington" than translation to a better world.

Upon another occasion, while near the President's house on Market Street, Mr. Maclay said that he allowed himself to be overpersuaded by Mr. Cyrus Griffin and Mr. Osgood to go into the President's New Year's reception, just as he was, "in top boots and my worst clothes." Although the Pennsylvania Senator's lack of ceremony could not have escaped the discerning Washington, he was, he says, "received with a hearty shake of the hand and asked to partake of punch and cake, which I declined," said Mr. Maclay, "and the diplomatic gentry and foreigners coming in, I embraced the first vacancy to make my bow and wish him good morning." If the coteries of the Lady Presidentess, as one of the New England Senators was wont to call Mrs. Washington's receptions, appeared to provincial eyes and to those of persons who held ultra-republican views to savor of the luxury and ceremony of foreign courts, they seem to us, as we read of them, with their slight refreshment and their early hours, to have been extremely simple, especially when contrasted with the elaborate entertainments of Mrs. Bingham and other leaders of fashion in Philadelphia. Mrs. Adams's receptions, as described in the letters of Mrs. Stoddert and other chroniclers of the day, did not differ materially from those of the first President's wife, except that the hours may have been a trifle later, Mrs. Adams having a much more genuine love for society than her predecessor.

The most agreeable descriptions of the Adams family during their Philadelphia residence are to be found in Mrs. Stoddert's letters. Benjamin Stoddert was a great favorite of the President, and Mrs. Stoddert came in for a share of friendliness from Mrs. Adams, the good lady even carrying her attentions so far as to offer her "some drops" at one of her drawing-rooms, "taking it into her head from my pale looks," said Mrs. Stoddert, "that I was going to faint, which brought a little red to my cheeks."

Elizabeth Stoddert, the "Betsy" of her mother's letters, writing in January, 1800, to Miss Lowndes,

The Children of Benjamin Stoddert

By Charles Willson Peale

gives a pleasant picture of Mrs. Adams ministering to the sweet tooth of the Stoddert family: "I must not omit to tell you that though mamma has not been as yet to wait on Mrs. Adams, that good and handsome old lady called to see her this afternoon, with her daughter, Mrs. Smith, and brought more plum-cake for the children than all of them could eat. You may be sure after this she is a great favorite of the whole family."

"Betsy" Stoddert's pretty face appears in a group painted by Charles Wilson Peale, which includes her brother Benjamin and her baby sister Harriot. The elder sister entered as a very young girl into some of the gayeties of Philadelphia before returning to Georgetown with her parents to enjoy a social life which, if less brilliant, was much preferred by her prudent mamma.

II

A PREDESTINED CAPITAL

IN Boston it is said that the winding streets which so perplex strangers were made to follow the cow-paths of more primitive days. Wandering through the widespread thoroughfares of Washington, losing one's self in a labyrinth of streets and avenues, to awaken in a circle, one might almost believe that these intricate streets and avenues had been laid out upon the circuitous windings of an old Indian trail. This theory, however, falls to the ground before the many documents which prove that the plan of the city of Washington, mysterious and unique as it is beautiful, is the result of a most carefully defined system of streets, avenues, and circles.

Even if we may not trace the footprints of the tribes of the forest in the winding streets of the capital, it is interesting to learn from those who have studied the life and habits of the earlier races upon this continent, that the broad plain and series of terraces which General Washington chose for the site of the federal city was once the favorite gathering-place of the powerful Algonquin federation. Near Capitol Hill, where the laws are now made for the guidance of our nation, was once a central Indian village where sachems met in council and the smoke of signal-fires ascended towards the blue vault that now arches one of the most beautiful of modern capitals.*

General Washington probably knew that "the ten-mile square" had once been the central seat of an Indian nation, says Martin; and although this may have appeared to him an interesting coincidence, his choice of the site of the new city was guided by considerations more practical and less sentimental.

Jefferson and Madison were closely associated with Washington in the choice of a site for the capital; and numerous letters, still preserved in the Department of State, prove how earnestly and conscientiously they all considered this subject.

"In 1800 we are to go to the Indian place with the long name, on the Potomac," wrote Oliver

* "The valley at the foot of the Capitol Hill, washed by the Tiber Creek, the Potomac, and the Eastern Branch, it is stated on the authority of some of the early settlers, was periodically visited by the Indians, who named it their fishing-ground, in contradistinction to their hunting-ground; and that they assembled there in great numbers in the spring months to procure fish. Greenleaf's Point was the principal camp and the residence of the chiefs, where councils were held among the various tribes thus gathered together. The coincidence of the location of the National Legislature so near the site of the council-house of an Indian nation cannot fail to excite interest."—"Gazetteer of Virginia and the District of Columbia," by Joseph Martin.

Wolcott, Secretary of the Treasury. Mr. Wolcott evidently referred to the mouth of the Conococheague, in Washington County, Maryland, as, according to the act of July 16, 1790, "the President was authorized to appoint commissioners to survey, under his own direction, a district of territory, not exceeding ten miles square, at some place on the River Potomac, between the mouths of the Eastern Branch and the Conococheague."

Despite the various disparaging remarks made upon the choice of the V-shaped plateau on the Potomac as the site of the new capital, other persons beside Washington had recognized its possibilities. It is a rather curious coincidence that Thomas Lee, grandson of the founder of the Virginia family, declared long before the Revolution that the Colonies would one day be independent, and that the seat of government would be located near the Falls of the Potomac. All the advantages and disadvantages of the river and its banks were well known to Washington, as he had been familiar with this region from his boyhood. Here he had fished and hunted, and in later years had made an extended exploring tour to the waters of the upper Potomac to ascertain whether it could be navigated above tide-water at Georgetown. Upon this excursion he was accompanied by several gentlemen, among them Governor Johnson, of Maryland. One night, when lodging at the house of a planter whose accommodations were rather scanty, General Washington and two gentlemen of the party were given a room in which were only two beds. Washington, with his habitual courtesy, turned to Governor Johnson and his other companions, and said, with a smile, "Come, gentlemen, who will be my bed-fellow?" Governor Johnson, in relating this incident, added, "Greatly as I should have felt honored by such distinction, yet the awe and reverence which I always felt in the presence of that admirable man prevented me from approaching him *so nearly*."

This same Thomas Johnson was one of the commissioners appointed by the President to attend to all practical details connected with the establishment of the seat of government. The other members of the board were Daniel Carroll—not Carroll of Duddington, as has been so often stated, but a cousin of the same name—and Dr. David Stuart, who was an old and trusted friend of the President. Dr. Stuart was connected with Washington's family by marriage, having become the second husband of pretty Eleanor Custis, the widow of John Parke Custis.

In his diary Washington recorded several meetings with the commissioners during his brief holiday trips to Mount Vernon. On March 28, 1791, he wrote that he found the interests of the landholders about Georgetown and those in Carrollsburgh so much at variance that they might prove injurious to the best interests of the public. Again, however, a dinner and a discussion over a glass of Madeira seem to have been fruitful in good results. The President wrote more cheerfully of the prospects of an adjustment, and soon after sent a proclamation to the Secretary of State, Mr. Jefferson, for his official signature, in which were defined the boundary lines of the territory selected for the permanent seat of government of the United States.

Major Charles Pierre L'Enfant, a French engineer who had served with distinction in the Continental army during the Revolution and performed valuable service for the government in designing fortifications, was commissioned to lay out the new city, while Mr. Ellicott, who, despite his Quaker parentage, had enlisted in the army and had later settled certain important boundary lines in Pennsylvania, was appointed to make a survey of "the ten-mile square."

The principal owners of this tract of land were Daniel Carroll of Duddington, Samuel Davidson, Notley Young, and David Burnes. Thomas Beale, Robert Peter, James Lingan, Benjamin Stoddert, and others also held land within the limits of the new city. Mr. Carroll owned a tract of about two thousand acres, a portion of which was chosen as the site of the Capitol. Some idea of the extent of this holding may be gathered from the fact that the portion marked upon the old map as pasture-land extended from the navy-yard to the mall. The Carroll property failed to appreciate in value, as the city, whose eastern course L'Enfant had outlined and Robert Morris, Samuel Blodget, Thomas Law, and others speculated upon, went the way of all great cities, due west, after that beguiling "Star of Empire" of which Bishop Berkeley was wont to sing. The White House soon becoming the centre of the city, the broad acres of David Burnes, near by, increased in value. The canny Scotchman may have realized that his property would rise in value more rapidly than the eastern lots, and for this reason, or because of a certain native tenacity and obstinacy, he gave President Washington more trouble than any of the other landholders, and frequent visits were made by the President to the little cottage of "Davy" Burnes, which stood for so many years at the foot of Seventeenth Street. By the end of February, 1791, Burnes and all other proprietors had come to terms, and on September 18, 1793, the President took part as a Mason in the ceremonies of laying the corner-stone of the Capitol. Amid discharges of artillery, addresses, and prayers the corner-stone was laid, a plate with an offering of corn, wine, and oil was placed upon it by the President, and an ox of generous proportions was barbecued and partaken of by the company.

By this time Major L'Enfant had had some contentions with the commissioners, and antagonized Mr. Carroll of Duddington by pulling down his house on New Jersey Avenue, which had been begun before the plans for the city were completed. This house stood in the centre of one of L'Enfant's radial avenues, and, thinking more of the beauty of the perfected city than of Mr. Carroll's rights, he, with military directness, ordered the house to be demolished. It should be said, however, in justice to the French engineer, that in writing his report he advised that Mr. Carroll should be "reimbursed" for his outlay, the foundations and first floor of the house having been completed.

The difficulty with Mr. Carroll was finally adjusted by having the new Duddington built upon an adjacent square between First and Second and D and E Streets. This house, so well known as the centre of much generous hospitality during the early years of the federal city, was the home of Mr. Daniel Carroll and his descendants until 1886, when it was destroyed. The Providence Hospital now stands near the site of Duddington Manor.

In consequence of his difficulty with Mr. Carroll, and, as Mr. William Thornton says, of certain differences of opinion "between the commissioners and the ingenuous Major L'Enfant," the work into which he had entered with so much enthusiasm was

Duddington
Built by Daniel Carroll

withdrawn from his hands and placed in those of Mr. Ellicott, who had acted as his assistant.

The question of the justice or injustice of Major L'Enfant's dismissal may never be decided. Whether the fault was his or the commissioners,—and from some expressions in letters of the day it appears that they were at times exasperating, and later gave Mr. Ellicott no small amount of trouble,—it is impossible at this distance of time to determine. It seems, however, safe to believe that the President, who had had much experience in dealing with men of all classes and conditions, and, like all great leaders, possessed the power to read character and put "the right man in the right place," acted with his usual fairness and good judgment in this instance. He summed up the situation in his own terse, forcible style when he said, "Major L'Enfant is as well qualified for the work as any man living, but the knowledge of the fact magnifies his self-esteem." This self-esteem, combined with a certain sensitiveness to criticism and dogged obstinacy, probably precipitated L'Enfant's quarrel with the commissioners. That Major L'Enfant cherished no bitter feeling against the President in consequence of his removal appears from his letters. His punishment, however, seems both summary and severe in view of the work that he had already accomplished for the government in the construction of Fort Mifflin on the Delaware, the renovation of the old City Hall in New York for the use of Congress, and of still more importance, as Dr. James Dudley Morgan points out in his admirable biographical sketch of Charles Pierre L'Enfant, in consequence of his own service in the Continental army in the Corps of Engineers, where he was both wounded and taken prisoner.

Lonely, disappointed, and poor, for L'Enfant had indignantly refused the money offered as compensation for his labors, he was forced to stand aside and see the work that he had planned with high hope carried on by one of his former assistants.

The fact remains that the beautiful and unique plan upon which the capital was laid out—not, as has been said, " for thirteen States and three millions of people, but for a republic of fifty States and five hundred millions; not for a single century, but for a thousand years"—is chiefly due to the genius of L'Enfant. That the value of this work was appreciated to some extent in his own lifetime appears from a testimonial, still extant, signed by James M. Lingan, Benjamin Stoddert, Uriah Forrest, Robert Porter, the Davidsons, and other influential citizens of Washington.

Major L'Enfant evidently possessed the imaginative, creative mind, the seer's vision that could behold a city rise upon this broad plain, while Andrew Ellicott, a Quaker, supplied the practical mathematical ability that was needed to carry out and improve in some respects the design of the brilliant, erratic, headstrong French engineer. Some of L'Enfant's dreams for beautifying the capital were not carried out at the time, probably for good and sufficient reasons. His national church, now much needed for memorial services, which was to stand where the Patent Office was built later, his lofty columns to commemorate the deeds of the army and navy of the republic, and his beautiful cascade from the muddy waters of the Tiber have never seen the light; but the park, or series of parks and gardens, intended by him to connect the White House and the Capitol, are being laid out to-day on much the same lines as those planned by the beauty-loving Frenchman.

The charm and originality of the plan upon which the federal city was laid out has led to many conjectures with regard to its source. Mr. Glenn Brown, who has given much time and thought to this subject in connection with later schemes for the beautifying of the capital, inclines to the belief that the radial avenues and many circles that add so much to the attractiveness of Washington were suggested to Major L'Enfant by an unused plan made by Sir Christopher Wren for the rebuilding of London after the great fire of 1666.

Major L'Enfant had secured through Mr. Jefferson, then Secretary of State, the plans of a number of European cities, "but," says Mr. Brown, "a review of the arrangement of these cities shows few suggestions of which he actually made use. The Champs-Élysées, for the Mall, was the only probable one, for it must be remembered that the radiating streets of Paris were opened by the first and third Napoleons years after the map of L'Enfant was drawn. . . . It is a curious fact that while there was no city with radial streets in Europe at that period, one existed in America at Annapolis. That town was based upon Sir Christopher Wren's plan of London."

General Washington and Major L'Enfant had made a careful study of the site of the new city and together selected the locations for the principal buildings. The French engineer's suggestion that the building where Congress was to hold its sessions—"Congress House," as he called it—should be placed some distance from the other government buildings and from the Executive Mansion appealed so strongly to the General's common sense that he remained firm upon this point, despite John Adams's earnest protest against such an arrangement. In conformity with the idea of separating the legislative and executive offices, the site chosen for the Capitol was the broad plateau upon which it now stands, while the White House and the other official buildings were placed a mile or more west of it. The wisdom of this decision of Washington has recommended itself to all subsequent legislators, while the position of the Capitol is thus spoken of by the English critic, Frederic Harrison:

> "I have no hesitation in saying that the site of the Capitol is the noblest in the world, if we exclude that of the Parthenon in its pristine glory. Neither Rome, nor Constantinople, nor Florence, nor Paris, nor Berlin, nor London possesses any central eminence with broad open spaces on all sides, crowned by a vast pile covering nearly four acres and rising to a height of nearly three hundred feet, which seems to dominate the whole city. Washington is the only capital city which has this colossal centre or crown. And Londoners can imagine the effect if their St. Paul's stood in an open park reaching from the Temple to Finsbury Circus, and the great creation of Wren were dazzling white marble, and soared into an atmosphere of sunny light."

The work withdrawn from L'Enfant's hands in 1792 progressed rapidly in those of Andrew Ellicott, who had made the first topographical survey of "the ten-mile square." Major L'Enfant's plan was, in its main features, carried out, certain modifications and changes being suggested by Ellicott's more practical mind, as we find the plan of 1792, the first engraved map of the city of Washington, marked "L'Enfant's Plan with Ellicott's Additions."

Andrew Ellicott, despite his Quaker ancestry, had, like Charles Pierre L'Enfant, entered the army as a volunteer, and left the service with the rank of major. His mathematical ability was evidently inherited from his father, Joseph Ellicott, a mathematieian and astronomer who, like his contemporary David Rittenhouse, had constructed a clock that was the wonder of all scientific men of his time. Although the younger Ellicott has been spoken of as "a self-educated Pennsylvania Quaker," it appears from his journal upon the survey of the Southern boundary line that he enjoyed the advantage of having Robert Patterson, vice-president of the American Philosophical Society, for his preceptor. A man of acknowledged scientific ability, he was himself a member of the Philosophical Society and the associate of Dr. Franklin, Benjamin Rush, David Rittenhouse, and other learned men of his day. While making a visit to Philadelphia in 1784, Mr. Ellicott wrote to his wife, "Spent the forenoon and dined at the University with the President and Rev. John Ewing, D.D. In the evening returned to my good friend, Mr. Rittenhouse, where I find real satisfaction, his philosophy and agreeable manner, his lady's good sense and uncommon good nature, added to the lively conversation and wise observations of the Daughters, would make even a monkey fond of their Society."

After spending the day in the company of the venerable Dr. Franklin, and expressing surprise that he ventured to shave himself at his advanced age, Mr. Ellicott left this "Nestor of America," as he called him, with one of his clever aphorisms tucked away in his own brain. "I think," said the good

Benjamin Stoddert

Page 34

Andrew Ellicott

Miniature by James Peale

old doctor, "happiness does not consist so much in particular pieces of good fortune that perhaps accidentally fall to a man's lot, as to be able in his old age to do these little things which, was he unable to perform himself, would be done by others with a sparing hand."

In a letter written to his "dear Sally" from a surveyor's camp in Virginia, Mr. Ellicott says that his companion, Major L'Enfant, will pay her a visit the following week, adding, "he is a most worthy French gentleman, and tho' not one of the most handsome men, he is from good breeding and native politeness, a first rate favorite among the ladies." From this and other expressions in Mr. Ellicott's letter there appear to have been no rivalry or ill feeling between Major L'Enfant and himself at this time, even if men and women have later discussed with some asperity the respective claims to distinction of the two engineers who planned and laid out the capital. One faction says that all the honor is due to Major L'Enfant, another feels that a lion's share of the credit belongs to the Quaker engineer who superseded him. The truth probably lies between these two extremes. The qualifications of both of these men seemed to be needed for the important task before them. What the genius of L'Enfant inspired might have been lost to the world without the reasonable, accurate, well-balanced mind of Ellicott; one supplemented the other, and the efforts of both engineers conspired to bring about a result upon which the nation may well congratulate itself.

It is to be regretted that any feeling of rivalry as to posthumous fame exists between the friends and descendants of the two engineers who planned and laid out the city of Washington. American citizens, who are proud of their beautiful capital, may well esteem the man who planned and the man who builded, both perhaps better than they knew, and it seems only fair that Charles Pierre L'Enfant and Andrew Ellicott should be honored by memorial statues in the capital that is to them as enduring a monument as is St. Paul's to Sir Christopher Wren.

Mr. Ellicott and Major L'Enfant were both men of distinct ability in their profession and both were honored by the friendship and appreciation of Washington. From Mr. Ellicott's family letters he appears to have been a man of singularly gentle and confiding nature, while Major L'Enfant, despite his somewhat difficult disposition, evidently possessed the power of attracting people to him and of returning their affection. A warm friendship existed between him and Mr. William Dudley Digges, which the latter showed by offering the hospitality of his home to the French engineer. In a letter written to him from Green Hill in 1824 Mr. Digges says, "I have to inform you that it will give me pleasure if you would come up and take your residence here. I have furnished George with what articles you may stand in need of at present; you will also be able to visit the city house at your ease and as often as you may please in order to attend to your business before Congress. . . . You may rest assured, Dear Sir, that I have considered your situation and know that it has been an unpleasant one; if a hearty welcome to Green Hill will make it more pleasant, I can assure you, you have it from all my family."

Major L'Enfant accepted Mr. Digges's hospitality, so freely extended to him, and spent the remainder of his days at Green Hill. Here he employed his leisure hours in laying out a flower-garden upon the same plan as the city of Washington. Amid the ruins of this deserted garden may still be traced the circles, triangles, and radial walks in which L'Enfant sadly renewed the dreams of his youth, and here lie his remains still unhonored by the nation which he served in war and in peace.

III

HOMES AND HOSTELRIES

MR. THOMAS TWINING, when, in 1796, he rode across a tract of level country resembling an English heath and through a thick wood on his way to Mr. Law's house, found in the rude beginnings of a road some signs of an avenue, and with an imagination equal to his amiability recorded that he had no doubt he was "riding along one of the streets of the metropolitan city."

Faith in things invisible was much needed in the early days of the capital, and for some years to come, when Pennsylvania Avenue was little better than a common country road. "On either side of this avenue," says Mr. Latrobe, "were two rows of Lombardy poplars, between which was a path often filled with stagnant water and with crossing-places at intersecting streets. Outside of the poplars was a narrow footway, on which carriages often intruded to deposit their occupants at the brick pavements on which the few houses scattered along the avenue abutted. In dry weather the avenue was all dust, in wet weather all mud; and along it 'The Royal George,' an old-fashioned, long-bodied four-horse stage, either rattled with members of Congress from Georgetown in a halo of dust, or pitched like a ship in a seaway among the holes and ruts of this national highway. The Capitol itself stood on the brink of a steep declivity clothed with old oaks and seamed with numerous gullies. Between it and the Navy Yard were a few buildings, scattered here and there over an arid common and following the amphitheatre of hills from the southeast around to the heights of Georgetown,—houses few and far between indicated the beginning of the present city.

"The Patent and Post-Offices, in one huge, unornamental, barn-like brick edifice, occupied the place of their marble successors, and at the other end of the avenue 'The White House' had become a conspicuous object, with the adjacent public offices. Still following the amphitheatre around, the eye caught a glimpse of Alexandria and rested upon the broad expanse of water where the Eastern Branch joined the Potomac, with Greenleaf's Point between the two."

Although the machinery of the government and all the persons pertaining thereunto removed to the new city of Washington in the autumn of 1800, it was long before the capital was regarded as an important social centre. The wives and daughters of cabinet officials, Senators, and Representatives from Colonial cities, North and South, looked back with longing to the more elegant and established life of their own homes, some of them even speaking of their residence in the federal city as a species of banishment.

In view of the scattered government buildings and more scattered residences separated by miles of unimproved land, which added to the labors of legislation as well as to those of social life, it is not strange that the Abbé de Serra, who visited Washington several years later in the century, should have dubbed it "a city of magnificent distances," or that a French diplomat should have exclaimed with the characteristic effusion of his nation, "My God! what have I done to reside in such a city?"

To the denizens of Paris, and other capitals of the Old World, Washington presented many discomforts and incongruities. The wheels of the gilded coach of the magnificent Spanish minister rolled over or stuck in depths of yellow clay, while another diplomat thus graphically described the rigors of his journey to a house still standing on Thomas's Circle, which is now in the heart of Washington:

"I went to see Mr. and Mrs. Charles Hill, who live at the extreme end of the city. My carriage sank up to the axletree in the snow and mud; it was necessary to leave the carriage, which had to be dragged out and scraped to remove the mud and slush which stuck to it like glue."

Many fanciful tales with regard to the removal of the government have been repeated until they have gained credence. One story is to the effect that the entire treasure of the United States, and all papers pertaining to the Treasury Department, were brought to Washington in one two-horse wagon, may readily be disproved by the fact that all the government possessions, including books, papers, and moneys, were conveyed in vessels. Christopher Hines, in giving his recollections of this time, says that three vessels landed and discharged their cargoes at Lear's Wharf, and that their contents were carted away to the War and Treasury Offices, the only two government buildings erected at that time. Mr. Hines says that many of the boxes were marked with the name of Joseph Nourse, who was then Register of the Treasury, and that as wagons were scarce in Washington, one cart was employed to remove the contents of the ships. This fact may have given rise to the one-wagon story, as it is not stated how many trips the single cart made from the wharf to the government offices. Another statement that "a single packet-ship" brought all the government furniture and archives to Washington is disproved by Mr. Hines's recollections, in which he speaks of several vessels being used in the transfer. It also appears from the records of the Treasury Department that the expenses of the removal amounted to forty thousand dollars, which was a rather large sum for a moving that could be accommodated in one wagon or one ship.

John Cotton Smith, member of Congress from Connecticut, wrote that the Connecticut officials lodged with a Mr. Peacock, on Jersey Avenue, in company with Senators Chipman and Paine, of Vermont, " all in pairs," except Speaker Sedgwick, who was allowed a room to himself; adding, " to my excellent friend Davenport and myself was allowed a spacious and decently furnished apartment, with separate beds, on the lower floor."

Mr. Abraham Bradley, Assistant Postmaster-General, wrote that he had secured a large three-story house for his own residence and the office of Mr. Habersham, the Postmaster-General, within a few rods of Blodget's Hotel. This inn, named after Mr. Samuel Blodget, who had invested largely in Washington lots, was situated midway between the Capitol and the White House. It was also spoken of as the Great Hotel. Dr. Samuel Busey, who made careful researches into the early life in Washington, located the house engaged by Mr. Bradley for the Postmaster-General's office near the corner of Ninth and E Streets, Northwest. Blodget's Hotel occupied the site of a portion of the Post-Office Department. A house on Sixteenth Street, near what is now Scott Circle, was marked as that of Samuel Blodget in the early plans of Washington; but there is no record of the Blodget family having lived in the new city. Mrs. Blodget, daughter of the Rev. William Smith, first provost

f Pennsylvania, was a noted
ation her portrait by Gilbert
es. An independent, original
t seems to have been, not hesi-
r opinions freely about people
y much amusing a recent ac-
ouncing that her children "all
odget, having small eyes and a
com ne of her daughters she classified
as "a beau a vixen," while another, she said,
was "not pretty, but a sweet creature."

A poetaster of the time, alluding to the Vice-President's opposition to a Southern site for the capital, wrote:

> "And you, Mr. Gerry, be not quite so merry
> About Conogocheague, about Conogocheague;
> For your dull, punning jeers, your mobs and your fears,
> We care not a fig, we care not a fig.
>
> "It is, sir, at Georgetown that you shall be set down,
> In spite of your canting, in spite of your canting."

It is quite evident that Mr. Gerry was not "set down at Georgetown," although his house at the corner of Nineteenth Street and Pennsylvania Avenue was not far from the older town. How much Mrs. Gerry was with her husband in the new city does not appear. Dr. Manasseh Cutler, Senator from Massachusetts, who was chief chronicler of the republican court in these early days, makes no reference to the Gerrys' Washington residence, although he enjoyed visiting them in Philadelphia, and expatiated on the good fortune of Mr. Gerry in winning so beautiful and accomplished a wife. "Few old bachelors," he says, "have been more fortunate in matrimony than Mr. Gerry. I should suppose her not more than seventeen and believe he must have turned fifty."

Mr. Wolcott wrote to his wife that he had been obliged to take lodgings more than half a mile from his office in the Treasury Department, and so situated he finds himself better off than many of his associates. Writing to James McHenry, Secretary of War, under date of July, 1800, Mr. Wolcott says: "General Marshall has been gone a fortnight, but will soon return. The law character (meaning Attorney-General Lee) has gone to Norfolk with his lady, and Mr. Stoddert, Mr. Dexter, and myself govern this great nation; but how wisely is not for me to determine."

Mr. John Cotton Smith said that the only really comfortable houses within the city limits were those of Daniel Carroll, Esq., and Notley Young. These were surrounded by gardens. Sir Augustus Foster, secretary of the British minister, spoke of "three houses of consequence in Washington, those of Mr. Brent, Mr. Taylor, and Mr. Carroll." The house of Mr. Carroll, which Mr. Cotton Smith and Sir Augustus Foster mentioned, was evidently

Mrs. Isaac Coles
By John Ramage
Page 140

Mrs. Elbridge Gerry
By John Ramage

Mr. Daniel Carroll's mansion Duddington, about whose location he had some contention with Major L'Enfant, which was finally built between D and E Streets. Mr. Carroll, the owner of the property, always known as Daniel Carroll of Duddington, a son of Charles Carroll, Jr., was born in 1764, at the house of his father upon the Carrollsburg estate, which is now part of Washington city.

Another old country-house, still standing, is Brentwood, near Q Street, Northeast, and Florida Avenue, which was formerly Boundary Street. The Brentwood Road ran northeast of the Capitol. This property belonged to the Youngsborough estate, and came into the Brent family through Mary Young, who married Robert Brent, first mayor of Washington. Near Brentwood was Eckington, which belonged to Joseph Gales, Jr., who assisted Samuel Harrison Smith in editing the *National Intelligencer*, and afterwards became its sole editor and proprietor. The Brent house of which Sir Augustus spoke was probably a mansion at the corner of Twelfth Street and Maryland Avenue. Mayor Robert Brent built another house adjoining his own for his son, Robert Young Brent, at the time of his marriage. The "Mr. Taylor" alluded to by Sir Augustus was evidently Colonel John Tayloe, who owned Mount Airy, one of the finest country-seats in Virginia, and in 1800 built the famous

Octagon, which still stands at the intersection of New York Avenue and Eighteenth Street.

Mr. Thomas Peter and Mr. Thomas Law, who had married granddaughters of Mrs. Washington, lived in the federal city in the last century, and General Washington frequently recorded in his diary that he had dined with Mr. T. Law or lodged at Mr. T. Peter's. Mr. Peter's house is said to have been one of six built by Mr. Robert Peter for his six sons on a tract of land between Twenty-fifth and Twenty-seventh Streets, which was called "Mexico" on the original plan of the District.

Mr. Law's estate was large, as he was one of those who speculated heavily in Washington lots. His own spacious residence commanded a fine view of the Potomac. In an entry in his diary as late as November, 1799, General Washington recorded: "Viewed my building in the Fed'l City—Dined at Mr. Laws—and lodged at Mr. Thos. Peter's."

Mr. Thomas Law's mansion, which Mr. Twining described as "only a few yards from the steep bank of the Potomac, and commanding a fine view across the river, here half a mile wide," although located at the southeast corner of Sixth and N Streets, had all the appearance of a country residence. Mr. Twining approached the house through a dense growth of forest-trees, and no other dwellings were in sight until Robert Morris and John Nicholson began to build a row of small houses on what was later known as Union Street. It was probably of a house on New Jersey Avenue to which the Laws removed, afterwards the Varnum Hotel, that Mr. Wolcott referred to when he spoke of the Laws as living in great splendor. Here they extended hospitality to such foreign guests as Louis Philippe' and his two brothers; to Monsieur Volney, the free-thinking and free-speaking French author; the Polish Niemcewicz, statesman and poet, who visited America with Kosciusko in 1796; the practical gentleman farmer Richard Parkinson, and many distinguished Americans.

When Mrs. Law arrived in her chariot, the like of which had not been seen in America, Mr. Albert Gallatin felt quite rejoiced that "there should be some female in our circle in order to soften our manners." Softness of manners did not prove to be a distinguishing characteristic of the Law household, as the married happiness of the pair whose dawn General Washington considered bright and propitious was not destined to last until noon. The high-spirited beauty of nineteen probably had little patience with the eccentric Englishman who was nearly twice her age; which is not to be wondered at, in view of the nature of some of Mr. Law's eccentricities. Eliza, the only child of this union who survived infancy, inherited much of her mother's beauty. She married Mr. Lloyd N. Rogers, of Druid Hill, near Baltimore.

Mr. Law had three Indian sons, or "Asiatic sons," as it pleased some Washingtonians to call them. John and Edmund Law were much esteemed and beloved in Washington, and entered considerably into the social life of the capital. Mrs. William Seaton described these young men as unexceptional as regards manners, principles, and acquirements, and wrote of dancing cotillions with John Law, who, she says, "ranks high in William's estimation." John Law married Miss Frances Ann Carter, and Edmund married Mary Robinson.

Mr. Thomas Law, a man of considerable importance in his day, is remembered now as an odd, eccentric figure in the life of old Washington. Mr. Christopher Lowndes recalled him as a grave, sweet old man, whom he and his father met at an oyster-house, who read a poem of his own composing, which served as a dessert after their oysters. Was this Mr. Law's poem upon his wife and children, all of whom had preceded him to the land of shades and left him to mourn their loss in numbers? or was it "A Family Picture," whose opening verse so aptly epitomized the disappointments of his life?

> "Look not in public places for a wife;
> Be not deluded by the charms of sight.
> Retirement only gives the friend for life
> Who shares your grief and doubles your delight."

Something infinitely pathetic there must have been about the frail, keen-eyed old man who had known the life of three continents, and held positions of trust in England and India, who with all his ability and wealth had failed to please the woman of his choice, and lived to mourn his loneliness at seventy-seven, while still hoping and planning for the future greatness of the city in which he had cast his lot and wrecked a large share of his fortune.

James Greenleaf, John Nicholson, and Robert Morris, who formed the North American Land Company and owned so much real estate in Washington, did not live there in the early years of the century. William Cranch, who had married a favorite sister of Mr. Greenleaf, was sent to Washington in 1795 to represent the interests of the company, at a salary of one thousand dollars a year, which was probably considered munificent in those days. Mr. Cranch, afterwards Judge Cranch, was a nephew of Mrs. John Adams, the son of her sister Mary, and the "brother Cranch" of whom Mr. Adams spoke so affectionately in his letters. When this young man removed to Washington with his bride, Mr. Adams gave him a letter of introduction to Mr. Charles Carroll of Carrollton, in which he speaks of William Cranch as a nephew of his and very much like one of his own sons.

Mr. and Mrs. Cranch lived for a time in a house

on N Street, Southwest, which they leased from Mr. Greenleaf, and afterwards in Georgetown and Alexandria. When Mr. Greenleaf made Washington his permanent residence, about 1831, he built himself a house at First and C Streets, near the home of Judge Cranch. Here, says Mr. Clark, "Mr. Greenleaf daily exchanged greetings and confidences with his beloved sister Nancy and the dear judge, who were just around the corner."

Mrs. Greenleaf accompanied her husband for an occasional visit, and Mr. Clark says that their daughters were belles in Washington society "in the reign of Adams the second;" but the aristocratic lady never made the new city a permanent residence. She evidently preferred the dignified seclusion of her Allentown home, where Mrs. Greenleaf's father had built a handsome house, surrounded by an extensive park.

Of the death of Mr. Greenleaf and his favorite sister Mr. Clark tells the following touching story: "Mrs. Cranch had been seriously ill; Mr. Greenleaf moderately ill. Perhaps in him it was sympathy of soul. Who can say? Mr. Greenleaf called his youthful assistant, and laying gently his hand upon his shoulder, said, 'Bushrod, go to the judge's and see how sister is.' The lad went to the back door. The judge himself appeared, and answered, 'Tell James she is dead.' The messenger returned. Mr. Greenleaf drew closer the garments, and sank upon the couch. The shock was too severe; the vital current ceased to surge." *

As Mr. Greenleaf was buried in the Congressional Cemetery, it is to be hoped that his prejudices with regard to this place of sepulture were not equal to those of John Randolph. In speaking of this cemetery, which is now one of the interesting landmarks of old Washington, Mr. Randolph said, at the time of Senator Gaillard's death, "Gaillard was our oldest Senator, and is greatly to be pitied,—to be pitied, not because he died, but because he died in this place. I have been ill here and have feared death; feared it because I would not die in Washington, be eulogized by men I despise, and buried in the Congressional Burying-ground. The idea of lying by the side of —— ——. Ah, that adds a new horror to death."

When President Adams arrived at the capital he evidently lodged in Georgetown, as his letters are dated from the Union Tavern. This was in June, 1800, when the President went to Washington for a short stay, after making a circuitous journey by way of Lancaster, Pennsylvania, and Fredericktown, Maryland, which détour afforded many opportunities for entertainment en route.

The Georgetown *Centinel of Liberty* of June 6

* "Greenleaf and Law in the Federal City," by Allen C. Clark.

quaintly announced the coming of Mr. Adams: "The President of the United States arrived in this place on Tuesday last. At the boundary-line of the District of Columbia he was met by a large crowd of respectable citizens on horseback and escorted into town, where he was received with pleasure and veneration. The military of the city of Washington and the marines stationed there manifested their respect by sixteen discharges of musketry and artillery."

The following November, when Congress met in the federal city for the first time, the White House was still in an unfinished condition, and accommodations for Congressmen were quite insufficient. The Indian Queen had not yet hung out its sign of the Princess Pocahontas, nor had the sun of the famous Gadsby's, dear to the Congressional soul, yet arisen. The cost of living in the federal city in these early days was not great. The rate at the Indian Queen, kept by one Jesse Brown, was one dollar and a half per day, brandy and whiskey being free,—all too free, it sometimes appeared, especially on holidays, when the landlord dispensed liberal potations of egg-nog from a huge punch-bowl that had been used at Mount Vernon. A few boarding-houses there were at this time; but the large army of impecunious ladies who made Washington a city of boarding-houses rather than a city of homes had not yet arrived. A little later we read of Mrs. Matchin's on Capitol Hill, where Mr. Varnum, from Massachusetts, Speaker of the House, resided, and of Mrs. Wilson's, also on Capitol Hill, where Mr. Clinton lived during his term as Vice-President, in company with five Senators and fifteen Representatives, composing what was familiarly spoken of as "The Washington Mess."

Those officials who could not find lodgings at the "swinging sign of the Black Horse," kept by Mr. Betz on F Street near Fourteenth, at Tunnecliffe's on Capitol Hill, or in one of the houses of the two blocks on Pennsylvania Avenue between Nineteenth and Twenty-Second Streets, long known as the "Six and Seven Buildings," were obliged to establish themselves in Georgetown. This old town, despite its separation from the Capitol by three miles of bad road, which necessitated a daily ride in the "Royal George" through the mud of winter and the dust of summer, proved to many sojourners a pleasant and congenial place of residence and was long looked upon as the court end of Washington.

If, as a witty French visitor remarked, "Washington was a city without houses and Georgetown a city without streets," houses were more important than streets for the needs of daily life, and for some years the old borough, with its substantial houses and more comfortable hostelries, proved a formidable rival to the federal city. Indeed, it is currently reported that there are persons now living in Georgetown who still regard Washington as a suburb of the older town.

Mr. Twining, when he visited Georgetown in 1796, offered up thanks for a feather bed and a bountiful supper at the Fountain Inn after his long stage-journey from Philadelphia. Here also were Suter's Inn, and a tavern kept by Joseph Semmes, at both of which places General Washington frequently stopped. At the Union Tavern, a fashionable inn, he often recorded that he met the Potomac Company and afterwards dined. At this old-time hostelry were entertained such guests from abroad as Louis Philippe, Talleyrand, the eccentric French traveller Volney, Lafayette, Jerome Bonaparte, and Baron Von Humboldt. Of this learned German nobleman Mrs. Madison wrote in 1804, "He is the most polite, modest, well-informed, and interesting traveller we have ever met, and is much pleased with America. I hope one day you will become acquainted with our Baron Humboldt. . . . He had with him a train of philosophers who though clever and entertaining did not compare to the Baron."

Into the life of the new capital, with its crudities, its inconveniences, and its strangely assorted social elements, there entered as central figures a man and woman no longer young, who had seen much of official life at home and abroad. A thoroughly domestic pair were the Adamses, who would have enjoyed their fireside at Braintree, Massachusetts, far more than the excitements and exactions of the capital, had it not been for the fires of an overmastering ambition that burned in their breasts, which even the disappointment of the last closely-contested Presidential election had failed to extinguish. Abigail Adams's buoyant spirits, which had heretofore enabled her to meet with cheerfulness the various trials and discomforts of her life, seem to have almost deserted her upon her arrival in Washington. The straggling houses of the unfinished city and its miles of muddy roads evidently weighed heavily upon her spirits. The White House, with its bare, uninhabitable rooms and its "principal stairs not up," added the final touch to the serio-comic appearance of a city planned upon generous lines, with its Capitol standing like the sun, from which radiated majestic beams of streets and avenues of enormous breadth, all halting and limping in the execution. The Executive Mansion, modelled after the design of an Irish nobleman's palace, failed to afford the ordinary comforts of living to the modest family of the President. Mrs. Adams might well have exclaimed, with Gouverneur Morris, that this city offered great advantages "as a *future* residence."

It has often been said, and with an undertone of disapproval, that Mrs. John Adams used the East

Room for drying clothes. A wiser use was this, surely, although the clothes must have dried but slowly in the moist atmosphere, than to have given the President and his Cabinet officers rheumatism by requiring them to sit in the penetrating dampness of the East Room to transact business of state, as some thrifty housewives of that time would have done.

The ladies of Georgetown and Alexandria, being of a social nature, promptly called upon the President's lady, and were received in a hastily-improvised parlor at a safe distance from the drying clothes. It soon appeared that these visiting dames required some gayety in the White House. Mrs. Adams yielded with a good grace, although, as appears from her letters to her daughter, she was in anything but a festive mood. The first drawing-room was held on New Year's Day, 1801, Mrs. Adams receiving her guests in the oval room on the second floor, which was afterwards used as a library.

If, upon her arrival at Bush Hill, Philadelphia, Mrs. Adams had exclaimed, in disappointment at the inconveniences of her suburban residence, "This, alas! is not Richmond Hill," she must have more than once confided to the sympathetic ears of Mrs. Albert Gallatin and such of the Congressional ladies as had been sufficiently courageous to accompany their husbands to Washington, "This, alas! is not Philadelphia."

With all the inconveniences incident to life in the new capital, it is not strange that the Adams administration was unmarked by much gayety in social life. Mrs. Benjamin Stoddert wrote to her niece of dining at the President's and of having a dozen or fourteen to dine with her. Although Mrs. Stoddert seems to have entertained numerous guests herself, which necessitated constant recourse to the pages of "Mrs. Glasse," she says that there was not half the gayety she expected too see follow the advent of Congress.

Mr. Adams's four years of official life ended in March, 1801, and the elderly couple, who had spent only a few months in the White House, returned to their Lares and Penates at Braintree, Massachusetts, reflecting, and with some justice perhaps, upon the ingratitude of republics.

IV

COUNTY FAMILIES

AN interesting and varied life was that of Washington and the older towns surrounding it in the early years of the last century. Upon the heavy dirt road that stretched between the White House and the Capitol was often to be seen the spare, slight figure of the Democratic President, well mounted, not very well dressed, frequently unattended, and not seldom bespattered with mud, while nearby the elegant gilded coach of the French or Spanish minister made its way with difficulty through the tenacious clay.

Familiar figures upon the streets of Washington in those days were Judge Story, his friend the great Chief Justice John Marshall, and John Randolph of Roanoke, the latter a picturesque personage, as described by more than one visitor to the capital, in blue riding-coat, buckskin breeches, and top-boots, on his way to the Senate, attended by his black servant, both master and man well mounted.

The coach of the charming woman who was the first lady in the land through two long administrations was often to be seen on the Georgetown or Bladensburg roads, for Mrs. Madison greatly enjoyed a dish of tea and a gossip with Mrs. Forrest in Cherry Alley, Georgetown, or with one of her Bladensburg friends.

Even if Washington was a city existing chiefly upon paper when the government was removed thither in 1800, it was fortunate in being near several old towns. Georgetown, Alexandria, and Bladensburg were places of considerable influence in the trade of the Colonies, and all boasted a social life of more or less distinction, according to the value placed upon education, refinement, and the graces of life. The established residents of these boroughs and those of the neighboring counties furnished a stable and respectable background for the floating society which the government brought to Washington. Presidents might come and go, but the old families remained, living in their stately homes as their fathers had lived, extending a generous hospitality to strangers, and mingling more or less with the official life of the capital, in proportion to their approval or disapproval of the manner in which social affairs were conducted in the White House.

Sir Augustus Foster, who entered freely into the social life of Georgetown and of the counties surrounding the capital, found much to admire in the style of living and the possessions of these landed proprietors. " In the district nearest Washington alone, of which Montgomery County forms part, I was assured," he wrote, "there were five hundred persons possessing estates which returned to them an income of £1000." Among these magnates were Mr. Ringgold, Mr. Charles Carroll, Colonel John Tayloe, and Governor Lloyd. Of this latter gentleman, he adds, with amusing minuteness of detail, that he "possessed a net revenue of between £6000 and £7000, with which he had only to buy clothes for himself and family, wines, equipages, furniture, and other luxuries."

As we wander through the streets of Georgetown to-day, which with their many charming doorways and high-terraced gardens give us the impression of a life that has been lived and a history that is finished, it is difficult to realize that this sleepy old town was once an important commercial centre.

The original tract of land upon which Georgetown is situated was owned by two Georges, George Beall and George Gordon. Whether the town, which was laid out in 1751, was named after these two gentlemen, or after his British majesty, does not appear. The early date of the founding of the borough proves conclusively that it could not have been named in honor of the much greater George, whose surname was given to the capital.

In consequence of its commercial prosperity a number of substantial and spacious houses were built in Georgetown before the Revolution. Some of these fine old mansions are still standing on Prospect Street and on Georgetown Heights. Among them is the Mackall house, which stands on an eminence overlooking the city of Washington. It was built by Benjamin Mackall upon Beall property, which was part of the marriage portion of his bride, Christiana Beall. Another Benjamin Mackall lived in a house on Prospect Street which was given to his wife by her father, William Whann, of White Hall, Maryland. Mr. Martineau, minister from the Netherlands, afterwards occupied the Mackall house, on Prospect Street.

Although several beautiful mansions were built on the Heights, Miss Mackall says that in early days the fashionable part of Georgetown was below Bridge Street. "Cherry Alley," she says, "with its narrow, winding streets, was the court end of the town. The quaint two-story houses were built of brick brought from England, and had sloping roofs and queer-shaped gables, with rows of dormer windows, where the housekeeper delighted in sunning her preserves and pickles, of which the boys in the neighborhood, uninvited, would enjoy a sample every now and then. Many a taste did Francis Scott Key have of these same preserves." In Cherry Alley lived the Whanns, Peters, Keys, Masons, Smiths, Foxalls, Bronaughs, Balchs, Bealls, and Forrests.

Dr. Cutler wrote to his wife, in 1803, of a dinner at the Balch's, in the company of many members of Congress. Miss Anna King was one of the guests, which revived delightful recollections of the previous winter spent in her father's house in Washington, where the company was very agreeable. "I very much miss," he says, "the amusement Miss Anna King used to afford us, with her forte-piano and excellent voice. She is the most intimate friend and companion of Miss Harriet Balch. They attend together the boarding-school, dancing-school, and assembly."

Other visitors besides Dr. Cutler recorded pleasant memories of hospitable Georgetown homes, such as the country-seat of the Linthicums, which was up near the reservoir; the house of Brooke Williams, still standing on U street; and Tudor Place. This charming house, which architecturally combines the best characteristics of the earlier and later Georgian schools, was built by Mr. Thomas Peter in 1814, and stands to-day seemingly untouched by the hand of time. Beautiful without and within, crowning the heights with its substantial but graceful architecture and surrounded by its old-fashioned, box-bordered gardens, the spacious halls and stately rooms of Tudor Place are replete with associations and relics of the past. Here are unfolded pages of the history of the eighteenth and of the early years of the nineteenth century that may be read nowhere else. This house, which is the home of Mr. Thomas Peter's daughter, Mrs. Beverly Kennon, the great-granddaughter of Martha Washington, is the repository of many cherished possessions linked with the daily life of the Washingtons in New York, in Philadelphia, and at Mount Vernon.

West of Tudor Place is Sydney, the home of Mr. S. Harrison Smith, founder, first editor, and proprietor of the *National Intelligencer*. This house, which was the gathering-place for distinguished men from near and far and the scene of many animated political and legislative discussions, is still standing within the grounds of the Catholic University. Georgetown was an early stronghold of Catholicism in America, and the college founded there by Bishop John Carroll in 1789 was the first Roman Catholic educational institution of any size established in the United States. John Carroll was a son of Daniel Carroll, of Upper Marlboro, and a cousin of Charles Carroll of Carrollton. Like other members of his family, Dr. Carroll was an ardent patriot as well as a devoted member of the Jesuit order, with which religious body he identified himself in early youth. Having enjoyed the advantages of an education in Continental schools and having held chairs at St. Omer's and Liege, John Carroll returned to America to found the University at Georgetown and the Cathedral at Baltimore, both of which are monuments to his zeal and devotion. Upon Bishop Carroll's representations Pius VII. erected Baltimore into an archiepiscopal see in 1808, of which he was appointed the first archbishop.

Archbishop Carroll was aided in many of his religious and philanthropic undertakings by Dominick Lynch, who was authorized to receive the New York subscriptions for the projected "Academy at Georgetown." This gentleman, a direct descendant of the doughty mayors of Galway, after many successful commercial ventures in Galway and at Bruges, in Flanders, entered into partnership with Thomas Stoughton and emigrated to New York with his wife and family. Mr. Lynch, who brought to the land of his adoption the zeal and patriotism of his race, entered with enthusiasm into the political, religious, and social life of the new republic. He does not seem to have lived in either Georgetown or Washington, although a house and some lots owned by him appear upon the old plan of the capital. When in 1790 it was deemed expedient that the Roman Catholics of America should address to General Washington a letter of congratulation upon the occasion of his unanimous election as first President of the United States, through the five most distinguished Catholic citizens of the country, Dominick Lynch was one of those selected to sign this document, the other signers being Archbishop

Archbishop John Carroll
By Gilbert Stuart

Carroll, Charles Carroll of Carrollton, Daniel Carroll and Thomas Fitzsimons of Philadelphia.

The buildings of the Convent of the Visitation and the Young Ladies' Academy, where so many of the belles and beauties of Georgetown, Baltimore, and Annapolis were educated, adjoin the college grounds. This convent, one of the oldest in the United States, was founded by some French nuns of the order of the Poor Clares. The buildings were erected upon part of the property of Mr. John Threlkeld. The home of John Cox, sometime mayor of Georgetown, was built upon a part of this estate, which was given to his wife, Jane Threlkeld, at the time of her marriage.

Georgetown College owes much of its picturesque beauty to the steep bluff above the Potomac on which it is situated, for it gives to its river-side exposure a garden terrace where one may readily fancy Italian monks of the sixteenth century sunning themselves in ecclesiastical leisure and content among the vines and blossoms of this bit of Italy in the New World. Upon a part of this same high bluff the Honorable Benjamin Stoddert built a house which is still standing, a typical Georgetown residence of the old time, with its high terraces in front and large garden at the back overlooking the Potomac. Family tradition relates that a lover of one of the beautiful daughters of this house threatened, when his addresses were rejected, to throw himself into the river, whereupon the damsel, innocent as she was obdurate, ran into the garden to see whether her despairing Romeo would carry out his threat.

Imagination as well as sentiment played an important part in the love-making of that earlier time. Do lovers ever threaten self-destruction in these more prosaic days? and if they should venture upon such flights of fancy, would Juliet take the matter *au sérieux* and follow Romeo into the garden to witness the fatal leap?

We have it upon the authority of Sir Augustus Foster that Georgetown was a famous "marriage market," the balls being attended by the families of members and others who came for the season. Despite the excess of small talk, the "small amount of literature and improving conversation," the predilection of the fair ones for the uncertainties of "loo" and the beguilements of rouge and powder, Sir Augustus frankly avows that he has "never seen prettier, more lively, or better tempered girls anywhere—mostly from Virginia and Maryland. . . . Much dancing," he adds, "much singing of popular and sentimental ditties. The favorite song, 'Just Like Love in Yonder Rose.' No matter how this was sung, the words alone were the men traps." One may read between the lines that the secretary to the British Legation was young and unmarried, and had probably been warned by prudent parents in

Mrs. Edward Lloyd   Mrs. John Mason
By Bouchét

words of like intent to those used by the *pater patriæ*, to "beware of entangling foreign alliances."

Among Mr. and Mrs. Benjamin Stoddert's neighbors in Georgetown were Dr. Charles and Nicholas Worthington, who lived near the Aqueduct Bridge, and General and Mrs. Mason, who, in addition to their Georgetown residence, had a home on Analostan Island, in the Potomac, which is described as a veritable elysium, rich in native and cultivated plants, flowers, and fruits. Mrs. Stoddert, in writing of Mrs. Mason in 1796, said, "She is a charming woman—not so much in her face, as in her whole deportment—her face tho' quite pretty enough for she has charming eyes and fine teeth—and plays delightfully and sings really sweetly—her face as I before began to say is not as pretty as I expected, but she has sufficient reason to be satisfied with it. I know I should if I had such a one—her sister I imagine is more a beauty to please the Ladies than Mrs. Mason is, for Miss Murray looks all *amiability*, very pretty too." The Miss Murray whom Mrs. Stoddert found so charming was probably Sally Scott Murray, who soon after married Governor Edward Lloyd, of Wye House, Maryland, and thus became the sister-in-law of Francis Scott Key, whose wife was Mary Tayloe Lloyd. Another of the Murray sisters, Catherine, married the Honorable Richard Rush, of Philadelphia.

Mr. Stoddert and the Bealls owned a large tract of land north of Georgetown, called Pretty Prospect. General Uriah Forrest's home, Rosedale, was included in this tract and Major Stoddert and General Forrest are among the signers of the original agreement made between the land-owners and President Washington in March, 1791.

Rosedale, a tract of one thousand acres, belonged to General Forrest, and the house with its "thicket of roses three feet deep" was the home to which he brought his bride, a beautiful daughter of Governor Plater.

A portion of the Rosedale tract was bought from General Forrest by Philip Barton Key, and called Woodley, while another brother-in-law, William Plater, purchased from him the Greenwood estate, which was afterwards owned by Dr. Snyder.

General Forrest, the owner of Rosedale, was a friend of Washington. The house in which the President dined with General Forrest and the Commissioners is still standing upon the Tennleytown Road. It is occupied by the descendants of General Forrest, who take pleasure in showing the broad piazza where the President and the Commissioners sat discussing preliminaries, while in imagination they beheld the well wooded and watered plain before them transformed into the beautiful city of their dreams.

A short distance from Rosedale is the pict-

The Highlands
Built by Charles J. Nourse

uresque Highlands, built by Charles J. Nourse, from stone quarried in the neighborhood. No house in the vicinity of Washington is more replete with associations of the past than The Highlands, where the Madisons, Thomas Jefferson, Timothy Pickering, and other distinguished people of the day were wont to congregate. The Rev. Manassah Cutler describes more than one dinner with "Mr. Nourse at his country-seat, back of Georgetown in company with Mr. Van Ness and lady, Mr. Lawrie and lady, Mr. J. Q. Adams and lady," or with "Messrs. Pickering, Hillhouse, Boyle, McCrary, and Rhea." Members of the Nourse family living in the old house still cherish some shrubbery planted on the grounds by Thomas Jefferson, or point out the corner of the parlor from which the charming face of Mrs. Madison smiled upon the bride at a sister's wedding. Opposite the Highlands is an extensive and attractive country-seat with the alluring title Friendship. One may readily fancy the growth of friendship among the lovely walks and groves of this charming place, as at Strawberry Hill or Moor Park. This house was built by Mr. George French, whose wife, a romantic lady and a reader of novels, named the place Eden Bower, after a country-seat in a popular novel of the day. The name was afterwards changed to The Retreat and The Villa, as the old place passed into the hands of successive owners. General Jesup and Colonel Richard Pyle, the latter an Englishman from the Barbadoes, owned this property in turn, until it was finally bought by Mr. John R. McLean, when it was called Friendship, the name which once belonged to the whole undivided tract of land.

Woodley, the home of Philip Barton Key, and afterwards of President Van Buren, is one of the beautiful old places on the Tennleytown Road. The home of his cousin, Francis Scott Key, was in Georgetown, although he owned another house on Capitol Hill. It is a curious coincidence that this old town should hold associations with two Americans, each one of whom was the author of a single song that made him famous the world over. The house of the author of "The Star-Spangled Banner," near the Aqueduct Bridge, is still pointed out to the Georgetown visitor, while the mortal remains of the roving poet who sang in touching strains of the joys of "Home, Sweet Home" lie in Oak Hill Cemetery.

Nine miles south of Georgetown, on the Potomac, is Alexandria, first known as Hunting Creek Warehouse and afterwards as Bellhaven. It is difficult now to believe that the quiet streets of this old town, whose names, King, Princess, Duke, and Royal attest to their English origin and seem to belong to a past even more remote than that of

Georgetown, were once the scene of active business life. Yet the trade of Alexandria formerly rivalled that of Baltimore. Bishop Meade wrote, "So promising was it at the close of the war, that its claims were weighed in the balance with those of Washington as the seat of the National Government. It is thought but for the unwillingness of Washington to seem partial to Virginia, Alexandria would have been the chosen spot, and that on the first range of hills overlooking the town the public buildings would have been erected."

In addition to its commercial prominence, Alexandria was the centre of a charming social life and of religious interest as well. Christ Church, in Fairfax Parish, was resorted to by the planters and their families from the neighboring countryside, and here General Washington and several of his friends were vestrymen. Near Christ Church, at the corner of Cameron and Royal Streets, still stands the famous inn where many distinguished guests were lodged, among them the beautiful and mysterious "Unknown," whose death in the inn and whose nameless grave in Christ Church burying-ground lend a touch of romance to the old town.

In the Alexandria inn many balls were given in Colonial days and later, as the old town boasted its dancing assembly. The long hall, now divided into several rooms, is shown where Washington and Lafayette entered into the gayeties of the hour. To the balls in Alexandria, as to those in Annapolis, which was a much gayer little town, the county belles rode upon their ponies, with protecting skirts over their brave attire. These young damsels jogged over the rough roads, followed by negro servants on horseback, "with their hoops," says an old writer, "arrayed fore and aft, like lateen sails; and after dancing all night, they would ride home in the morning."

The master and mistress of Mount Vernon were in the habit of attending the dancing assemblies of Alexandria, taking with them any young people who were their guests. From an entry in his diary it appears that the General and his family attended the celebration of his birthday in Alexandria, in February, 1798, when a fine ball was given in his honor. In reply to an invitation from the managers of the dancing assembly, sent to him the following winter, he wrote a courteous note "to the Gentlemen of Alexandria," expressing his own and Mrs. Washington's thanks and their regrets that they would be unable to attend, adding, "Alas! our dancing days are no more. We wish however, for all those who have a relish for so innocent and agreeable an amusement all the pleasure the season will afford them."

Many associations with Washington the Virginia gentleman and planter cluster around Alexandria. Here he cast his first vote in 1754 and his last in 1799, here stands the Masonic Lodge of which he was a member, and in this old town resided some of his life-long friends. Tradition relates that it was at Belvoir, in Alexandria, at the home of Mrs. George William Fairfax, that Washington first met Mary Cary, for whom he entertained an affection so deep and lasting. The Washington coach was often seen on the old road between Mount Vernon and Alexandria, on its way to Christ Church on Sundays, and on week-days to the homes of the Masons, Fitzhughs, Hunters, Herberts, Piercys, Dades, Fairfaxes, Dulanys, Craiks, and other friends who lived in or near Alexandria. Mount Eagle, the country-seat of the Reverend Bryan Fairfax, rector of Christ Church, Alexandria, was on this road, and from the General's diary it appears that he and Mrs. Washington often stopped at this hospitable Virginia home. Sometimes there was a dinner or a hunt at Mount Eagle, or the General and Mrs. Washington were called upon to stand sponsors for one of the children. Among the last entries in the General's diary is one which records that he "rode to Mount Eagle to visit Mr., now Lord, Fairfax, who has just got home from a trip to England."

Other near neighbors and friends of General Washington were George Mason, of Gunston Hall, author of the famous Bill of Rights, and

George A. Digges, who lived at his country-seat, Warburton, on the Maryland side of the Potomac, near the present site of Fort Washington.

The Diggeses of Maryland belonged to the Virginia family of that name, whose ancestors, Edward and Dudley Digges, had served for many years as members of "His Majesty's Council for Virginia." Of the Councillor, Dudley Digges, who died in 1744, the following quaint epitaph was written:

> "Digges, ever to extremes untaught to bend;
> Enjoying life, yet mindful of his end.
> In thee the world a happy meeting saw
> Of sprightly humor and religious awe.
> Cheerful, not wild; facetious, yet not mad;
> Though grave, not sour, though serious, never sad."

There was evidently much sociable visiting between the Washingtons and the families at Warburton, Gunston Hall, Belvoir, and other neighboring country-seats. In addition to the hospitality extended by the planters on the Potomac during the hunting season, Mr. Irving speaks of "water-parties upon the Potomac in those palmy days, when Mr. Digges would receive his guests in a barge rowed by six negroes arrayed in a uniform whose distinguishing features were check shirts and black velvet caps." As Mr. Irving's "palmy days" were before the Revolution, the "Mr. Digges" referred to was evidently Mr. George A. Digges, who lived at Warburton until his death in 1792. At this time Warburton passed into the hands of a bachelor brother, Thomas. As was customary with the sons of the Virginia planter, Thomas Digges had spent his youth in London, where he was known in his circle of friends as the handsome American,—to which epithet his right is proved by his portrait by Sir Joshua Reynolds. Although young Digges lived the life of a youth of fashion among the "Macaroni" of his day, when his services were needed by his country he proved himself to be a man of resolute character and ardently patriotic. The Continental Congress required a secret and confidential agent near the Court of St. James, and Thomas Digges was, through the influence of General Washington, selected for this hazardous and important mission. While in London, if Mr. Digges heard discouraging news of the defeats and sufferings of the Continental army he also had the satisfaction of hearing of the surrender of Burgoyne, the victories in the Jerseys, and the final triumph at Yorktown. When sitting to Sir Joshua Reynolds for his portrait he doubtless heard expressions in favor of the American cause from such friends of freedom and justice as Lord Chatham and Charles James Fox, or he may have been present when Dr. Johnson, who was a warm friend of Sir Joshua, growled forth in his gruff, direct fashion his famous diatribe, "How is it we hear the loudest yelps for liberty from the drivers of slaves?"

It appears from a letter of Mr. William Dudley Digges, of Green Hill, that Major L'Enfant was staying at Warburton before he accepted that gentleman's hospitable invitation to make his home at his own country-seat. At this time Mr. William Dudley Digges and his wife, a daughter of Daniel Carroll of Duddington, were living at Green Hill, near Bladensburg, which country-seat was a portion of the Digges estate known as the Chilham Castle Manor, lying between Rock Creek Church and Bladensburg. Chilham Manor remained in possession of the family until 1863, when it became a part of the Riggs estate. Another Digges seat was Melwood, the home of Dr. Ignatius Digges. Mrs. Digges, a sister of Daniel Carroll of Duddington, was living at Melwood at the time of the battle of Bladensburg. A party of British officers stopped at Melwood and ordered a dinner. When the table was spread the officers sent for Mrs. Digges and asked her to preside over the meal. She appeared as desired, but declined to avail herself of the hospitality of her self-constituted entertainers, saying that she could not eat or drink with the enemies of her country. As Mrs.

Digges left the room, the British officers filled their glasses and drank to the health of the valiant and patriotic lady.

Northeast of Washington, on the Eastern Branch of the Potomac and across the District line, is Bladensburg, chiefly remembered to-day as the scene of the disastrous and ignominious battle fought there in 1814. This straggling hamlet of scattered frame houses was a flourishing portage town long before the federal city was dreamed of. Some of the buildings once used for the storage of tobacco, large quantities of which were exported, are still standing. In and near the town are some fine old mansions. Among these, Bostock House, with its buttresses, so seldom seen in domestic architecture, is a fine example of a spacious, substantial, old-time residence. This house was built in 1756 by Christopher Lowndes. His daughter, Mrs. Benjamin Stoddert, in her letters from Philadelphia, often speaks of Bostock House and its lovely garden, as well as of that of Graden, which was another family mansion in the neighborhood of Bladensburg. No flowers seemed to this loyal lover of her old home as sweet as those that graced the gardens of her childhood, and in one of her letters to her cousin, Miss Gantt, of Graden, she says that she often dreams of these gardens, adding, almost pathetically, " I very often put myself in mind of the Prodigal son, and think how glad I should be of the fruit that is left at your table when the family are done with it."

Not far from Bostock House is the Bladensburg battle-ground, and another equally famous field, that upon which gentlemen of the old régime were wont to vindicate the honor which, according to the prevailing fashion of the day, could only be maintained by a sword-thrust. The Bladensburg duelling-grounds, the scene of many historic encounters, are situated in a shaded ravine, beside a running stream, one mile beyond the village of the same name, in Prince George's County, Maryland, and half a mile from the District line.

A short distance north of the village of Bladensburg was Mr. George Calvert's country-seat, Riversdale, once an estate of many hundreds of acres. Wealth, taste, education, and an extensive acquaintance combined to enhance the charm of the entertainments given at this hospitable home. Mr. Calvert's mansion was built much later than Bostock House, and between the large drawing-rooms are some columns which were originally made for the Capitol. George Calvert was a brother of beautiful Eleanor Calvert, who won the heart of John Parke Custis when she was a girl of fifteen and married him before she was seventeen. Arthur Lee met Mrs. Custis during her widowhood, and spoke of her as a "most tempting widow independent of the jointure lands." Mrs. Custis afterwards married Dr. Stuart, of Hope Park and Ossian Hall.

John Parke Custis owned a tract of over a thousand acres on the Potomac, which was named Arlington, as was the country-seat of old Colonel John Custis on the Eastern Shore of Virginia. This property, which had been a part of the Alexander estate, John Custis bought on account of its nearness to Mount Vernon, and on his death in 1781 it passed into the hands of his only son, George Washington Parke Custis, who was always known in Washington life as Mr. Custis of Arlington.

Young Custis and his sister Eleanor were the adopted children of General Washington, and lived at Mount Vernon during his lifetime and that of their grandmother, Mrs. Washington. It was not until after his grandmother's death, in 1802, that Mr. Custis built the Arlington mansion, which is still standing in grounds used to-day as the burial-place of the soldiers of the nation.*

* When General Robert E. Lee left Arlington to take command of the Virginia troops, some Federal troops took possession and converted the mansion into a head-quarters and the grounds into a camp. A hospital was established there, and as the war continued, the level plateaus and grassy slopes of Arlington were by order of Quartermaster-General Meigs devoted to the purpose

This handsome house, with its lofty portico, whose roof is supported by Doric columns said to be modelled after those of the Temple of Theseus at Athens, stands on a bluff two hundred feet above the Potomac and is surrounded by fine trees. To this home Mr. Custis brought his bride, Mary Lee Fitzhugh, a daughter of William Fitzhugh, of Chatham, Virginia. Bishop Meade and other writers of the time have spoken of the loveliness and charm of Mrs. Custis, who entered with her husband into the social life of Washington and the country neighborhood surrounding it, as much as the cares of her own little family and those of a large family of slaves permitted. Bishop Meade testifies to Mrs. Custis's unfailing kindness and conscientious performance of her duty towards every slave on the plantation.

Many guests of the nation came to Arlington in the early years of the century, as this was a home of generous hospitality, among them friends

of a military cemetery. By a strange coincidence, the first grave prepared was that of a Confederate prisoner who had died in the hospital. In the year 1864 the property was sold for delinquent taxes, and the government bought it, paying twenty-six thousand one hundred dollars. In 1877 George Washington Custis Lee, heir under the Custis will, established his legal title to the property, and the claim was adjusted by the payment to him by the United States of the sum of one hundred and fifty thousand dollars.

of General Washington who delighted to visit the adopted son of their old comrade in arms. The Marquis de Lafayette and his son visited Mr. and Mrs. Custis in 1824, and pronounced the view from the heights one of the most beautiful they had ever seen. In one of the large rooms on the ground floor, once the drawing-room of Mrs. Custis, lovely Mary Custis was married upon a June day, in 1831, to Robert E. Lee, the great general of the Southern Confederacy. In April, 1861, General, then Colonel, Lee left Arlington with his family, never more to return to this beautiful and peaceful home.

V

JEFFERSONIAN SIMPLICITY

DR. MANASSEH CUTLER, who spent many evenings at the house of the Secretary of State and delighted in the gracious manners and spirited conversation of Mrs. Madison, said that upon one occasion this usually amiable woman expressed herself quite forcibly upon the dishonesty of Democrats. Dr. Cutler remarked, inquiringly, "You do not believe all the Democrats are dishonest?" "Yes," she said, "I do; every one of them!" This unequivocal rejoinder provoked a merry laugh, in which the grave little Secretary of State joined heartily.

When Mrs. Madison gave expression to her sweeping strictures upon Democrats, she must surely have made a mental reservation in favor of Mr. Jefferson, with whom she was a great favorite and for whom she entertained a sincere regard. Indeed, it was in consequence of Mr. Jefferson's having given the precedence to Mrs. Madison at a state dinner that he aroused the animosity of the British minister, Anthony Merry. White House etiquette does not seem to have occupied Mr. Jefferson's thoughts very considerably at this time, and either from carelessness or because of his defiant red-republicanism, he quite seriously offended a number of persons.

Sir Augustus Foster, writing of the difference between the etiquette of the Executive Mansion during an earlier administration and that of Mr. Jefferson, gave utterance to his dissatisfaction in no measured terms. "Mr. Jefferson," he said, "knew too well what he was about—he had lived in too good society at Paris, where he was employed as Minister from the United States previously to the French revolution, and where he had been admitted to the coteries of Madame du Deffaud, not to set a value on the decencies and proprieties of life, but he was playing a game for retaining the highest office in a State where manners are not a prevailing feature in the great mass of the society, being, except in the large towns, rather despised as a mark of effeminacy by the majority, who seem to glory in being only thought men of bold, strong minds and good sound judgment."

Although Sir Augustus was often extreme in expression with regard to the existing administration and the hardships of life in Washington, which he compared very unfavorably with that of Philadelphia, he probably reflected the mental attitude of the majority of the diplomats in the capital at the time. The Spanish envoy, the Marquis de Casa Yrujo, who had been upon friendly terms with

Mr. Jefferson while in Philadelphia, opposed himself to the President, and was recalled, doubtless for good and sufficient reasons, while Anthony Merry, who was the most conventional of mortals, found his path in Washington so thorny that he must have been thankful when his summons came to return to his native Britain.

It was upon the occasion of one of Mr. Jefferson's state dinners, given at rare intervals, that he committed the "unpardonable sin," in the eyes of the punctilious, of taking in the lady who stood next to him—Mrs. Madison—and requesting his guests to do the same. Mr. Merry happened to be beside his wife, and as no other lady appeared to be disengaged, he walked into dinner with his "tall, fair, fat dame" upon his arm, "breathing out threatenings and slaughter" against the Democratic President. Sir Augustus, who warmly resented what he chose to consider indignities to his chief, said that "Mr. Merry never met his Excellency any more at table since the President, unlike our social monarchs of the north, keeps his State—neither he nor his family accepting of invitations." The young secretary proved that he was not deficient in humor by relating in this connection, and with evident satisfaction, the story of an eccentric member from the South, a printer and publisher, who wrote in answer to an invitation from the President, "I won't dine with you, because you won't dine with me."

A New England Congressman wrote to his daughter that he and his colleagues were invited to dine at the White House "by billets sent into the Hall." Some of these "billets," still preserved in Washington families, are interesting, not only on account of their extreme simplicity, but because of their generous inclusiveness. An invitation sent to Mr. and Mrs. S. Harrison Smith reads as follows:

"Th. Jefferson requests the favor of Mr. and Mrs. Smith to dine with him on Tuesday next (26th) at half after three, and any friends who may be with them.

"April 25: 1803.

"The favor of an answer is asked."

A marked difference is to be observed between this wording and that of a dinner-invitation of the first President and his wife, which is almost identical with one of to-day, proving that after a hundred years of experience in official etiquette no more appropriate form has been found than the one used by this courteous and dignified couple. One of Mr. Jefferson's invitations to Mr. Joseph Nourse was worded with far more regard to affairs of state than to the excellence of the dinner or the temper of the cook. This particular invitation was a request to Mr. Nourse to dine with Mr. Jefferson "whenever the House shall rise."

Mr. Joseph Nourse, who was Register of the Treasury, retained his position through several administrations in days when the term "civil service" was unknown in its present significance; his son, Charles J. Nourse, was chief clerk in the War Department, while other members of the family were in office, which circumstance gave point to the clever *mot* attributed to General Jackson, who said that when he became President he would "soon clear out the *Noursery*."

However Mr. Jefferson might choose to scant the measure of form and ceremony at the White House, there was no limit to his hospitality. Edmund Bacon, the steward from Monticello, in his recollections, said of the President's dinners, that the table was "chock full" every one of the sixteen days he was visiting him. The dinner was at half-past three or four o'clock; and although there was no more form and ceremony observed than at a family dinner, Mr. Bacon said that the guests usually sat and talked until night, and he, finding it tiresome, would "quit when he got through eating." He adds that Lemaire, who was the purveyor for the household, told him he often spent fifty dollars upon one day's marketing. Whether or not this last statement is to be relied upon, all guests who were entertained at the

White House during Mr. Jefferson's administration testify to the generous hospitality of their host. If Petit, the steward who followed Mr. Jefferson from Paris, carried out his intention *de rester toujours*, and was still a member of the household, this extravagant American living must have greatly vexed his frugal French soul.

Dr. Cutler recorded many dinners at "his Democratic Majesty's," at which the bill of fare, jotted down for the amusement of his daughter, proved that the entertainment was generous, if somewhat incongruous,—fried eggs and fried beef being given place upon a board that was graced by the more distinguished company of turkeys, ducks, and rounds of beef, "the new foreign dish macaroni," ices, and various fancy dishes, among them "a new kind of pudding, very porous and light, inside white as milk or curd, covered with cream sauce." This last delicacy seems to have appealed strongly to the gastronomic sensibilities of the Reverend Manasseh.

At another White House dinner, given soon after Mr. Jefferson's inauguration, Dr. Cutler, like the traditional busy bee, "improved the shining hour" by presenting the President with "a specimen of wadding for Ladies cloaks and of bedticks from the Beverly Factory."

The Arcadian simplicity of a dinner at which such important staples as wadding and bed-ticks were handed around among the guests and discussed was calculated to please a farmer President, who, with his large share of ideality, was eminently practical and was ever ready to turn from grave questions of statesmanship and international policy to enter with enthusiasm into the consideration of agricultural experiments at Monticello or the introduction of new manufactures into the Northern States.

At the numerous dinners described by Dr. Cutler and other members of Congress, when Democrats were invited at one time and Federalists at another, it is evident that affairs of state were discussed by the President and his guests in the long afternoons and evenings when they lingered around the board. Mr. Parton says that while in France Mr. Jefferson formed "the habit of mitigating business with dinner," which custom he seems to have observed during his official life in Washington.

Although this was an administration when Senators and Representatives were hospitably wined and dined, little amusement seems to have been provided for their wives and daughters. The weekly levee was abolished by Mr. Jefferson, and no receptions were held except on New Year's Day and the Fourth of July. Whatever visions of gayety in the White House may have been cherished by the maids and matrons of the capital, they were doomed to disappointment. Mr. Parton tells of an effort made by some persistent dames to cajole Mr. Jefferson into resuming the customary levees; but, with his habitual courtesy and gallantry of address in the presence of women, he was the last man in the republic to yield to cajolery or flattery when he had decided upon any given course of conduct. Consequently, when a number of ladies donned their bravest attire and appeared at the White House to do honor to the new President, the reception accorded them, although quite within the bounds of civility, was so wanting in cordiality as to prevent a repetition of the experiment. The lack of gayety in the Executive Mansion was due not only to the simplicity of Mr. Jefferson's tastes and his conscientious scruples against anything approaching the formality of a court, but also to the fact that no woman presided over the President's household during this administration.

The President's daughters were with him very little during his eight years residence at the White House, although his sons-in-law, Mr. Randolph and Mr. Eppes, were both in Congress. Mrs. Randolph's large family naturally claimed her presence at home and Mrs. Eppes's health became extremely delicate soon after her marriage. Maria Jefferson, who was much more beautiful than her sister, was so shy and reticent that she failed to make friends readily, while Mrs. Randolph always produced a pleasing impression in every circle that she entered by the charm of her manners and conversation. In her own home Maria, or Polly, as her father usually called her, was most engaging. The Duc de la Rochefoucauld, who visited Monticello in 1796, when Mr. Jefferson's youngest daughter was his inseparable companion, shrewdly remarked, "Miss Maria constantly resides with her father; but as she is seventeen years old, and is remarkably handsome, she will doubtless soon find that there are duties which it is sweeter to perform than those of a daughter."

It was John Wayles Eppes, the "Cousin Jacky" whom Maria had known and loved all her life, who claimed the shy beauty; and so cheerfully did Mr. Jefferson face the fulfilment of the French nobleman's prophecy, that we find him writing to a friend at the time of his daughter's engagement that he would have chosen Jacky Eppes for his little Polly if he had had the whole world to choose from.

Dr. Cutler wrote in 1802 of the President's daughters being present at a large dinner, adding, "They appeared well-accomplished women, very delicate and tolerably handsome." This was during the one visit which Mrs. Randolph and Mrs. Eppes made to the White House together, when they entered considerably into the social life of the capital. We find Mrs. Randolph preparing for her Washington campaign by writing to her friend Mrs. Madison to ask her to attend to some commissions, among them the ordering of two wigs, one for herself and one for her sister, which she wishes to be of the most fashionable shapes and to reach Washington before she does. "They are universally worn," she added, "and will relieve us as to the necessity of dressing our own hair, a business in which neither of us are adepts." That Mrs. Randolph, who was a woman of superior intellect, should so far conform to the dictates of fashion as to disfigure her own head and that of her beautiful young sister with a wig, entirely regardless of the fact that Mrs. Eppes's masses of auburn hair were her crowning glory, is a revelation of the greater tyranny of fashion in those days than in our own. Although Mrs. Randolph wrote to her father of the ordering of wigs as part of her own and her sister's trousseau, the announcement appears to have elicited no remonstrance from him, which is surprising, in view of the fact that Mr. Jefferson found no detail of his daughters' lives too trifling to occupy his thoughts, and had been wont to turn from his arduous official duties to write to them upon every subject that appertained to the appearance, mind, and manners of a well-conducted young woman. In one of his letters, written when Mrs. Randolph was a child, Mr.

Jefferson expressed his desire to have her dance three days in the week from eleven until one, while in another letter he begs her to be tidy in appearance, in the morning as well as in the evening, and never to allow herself to be seen carelessly attired by any one, especially by gentlemen, adding the powerful argument that his sex despised slovenliness.

A little over a year after Mrs. Eppes's visit to her father in Washington she died at Monticello. Of this sorrow Mr. Jefferson wrote to his old friend, Governor John Page, the same to whom he had once confided his youthful troubles about "Belinda," "My loss is great indeed. Others may lose of their abundance; but I, of my want, have lost even the half of all I had."

Mr. Jefferson's friends said that he never recovered from the shock and grief of his daughter's death. It is difficult to believe that the man who viewed with apparent stoicism the sufferings of the royal family and *noblesse* of France, which drew tears from the eyes of Edmund Burke and Gouverneur Morris, was the same Thomas Jefferson who in his domestic relations and in his friendships manifested the most extreme sensibility.

In order to help her father to bear the grief and loneliness occasioned by the death of his youngest daughter, Mrs. Randolph spent the winter of

1805–06 in Washington. It was during this winter that her second son, James Madison Randolph, was born, the first child of the White House. All of Mrs. Randolph's children were with her this winter, and her daughter Anne, an exceedingly beautiful girl, entered into some of the youthful gayeties of the capital. Anne Randolph was always a prime favorite of her grandfather, who, like Victor Hugo, had been apt in learning "*l'art d'être grandpère.*" In one of his letters, written during her babyhood, he exclaimed "dear little Anne, with whom even Socrates might ride on a stick without being ridiculous!" Mrs. William Seaton, in one of her letters from the capital, spoke of another and later occasion when the admiring grandfather had reason to feel that homage to Anne Randolph would not have been unworthy of the Greek philosopher; this was when she translated from the Spanish an important paper that had puzzled some of the wise heads at the Department of State.

Mrs. Randolph was the mother of twelve children. Of her seven daughters, Septemia, who married Dr. Meikleham, was the youngest. One little girl died in childhood. The Abbé Correa da Serra, who was a warm friend of the family, once said to Mrs. Randolph, when at Monticello, that her daughters were "like the Pleiades, there were seven of them but only six were visible."

During one of Mrs. Randolph's visits to Washington Mrs. Merry attempted to revenge herself for the indignities that she considered had been heaped upon her by the President. The British matron, in all probability instigated by her husband, wrote to Mrs. Randolph asking her whether she were visiting the White House as the President's daughter or as the wife of a Virginia gentleman; as in the former case she would make the first call, but in the latter she would expect to receive it. Mrs. Randolph promptly replied with the clever checkmate that she was in Washington as the wife of a Virginia gentleman, and as such should expect the first call from the wife of the British minister, as, according to the code of etiquette drawn up by Mr. Jefferson, all strangers in the capital should be called upon by the residents. From this and other anecdotes it appears that Mr. Jefferson, despite his democratic notions, had no idea of allowing himself or his family to be treated with any lack of respect. Poor Mr. Merry had borne several severe shocks in consequence of the informality and simplicity of this administration, and after receiving some salutary lessons in etiquette from the Father of Democracy was succeeded by David Montague Erskine, afterwards Lord Erskine. Mrs. Randolph and Mrs. Madison, who were warm friends, doubtless had many a hearty laugh over the Merrys and their grievances,

The Marchioness de Casa Yrujo
By Gilbert Stuart

The Marquis de Casa Yrujo
By Gilbert Stuart

and rejoiced when the English minister's "resignation," which appears never to have been sent, was accepted by his government with alacrity.

Philadelphia beauty and grace were well represented in Washington during Mr. Jefferson's administration by the wives of the British and Spanish ministers. Mrs. Erskine, a daughter of General John Cadwalader, was greatly admired at home and abroad, while the dark, dreamy eyes of the Marchioness Yrujo, which look forth from her portrait by Stuart, seem to proclaim her more truly a child of the South than the blue eyes and blond coloring of her Spanish husband. This young woman, as Sally McKean, had been an intimate friend of Mrs. Madison and her sister Anna Payne, and later in the diplomatic circle of the capital they renewed their acquaintance.

Whatever social joys may have been lacking in the Executive Mansion there was a house on F Street whose mistress "daily sacrificed to the graces." At the hospitable home of the Secretary of State there was always a warm welcome, and usually a circle of charming women and clever men gathered around the hostess. It was during the early years of her official life that Mrs. Madison began a social reign in Washington that, with some interruptions, during her sojourns at Montpelier, lasted for over forty years. Into the life of the new capital, which Mrs. Adams had found uncomfortable and arduous, Mrs. Madison entered with enthusiasm, bringing to her task a natural taste for social life, tact, charm, an inexhaustible fund of good humor, and a heart that could never grow old. The most self-forgetful, the least self-seeking of mortals was Mrs. Madison; her happiness seemed always to be bound up in that of others, yet to her all good things came as if by natural attraction.

Dr. Mitchill, who was in turn Representative and Senator from New York, has left a pen-picture of Mrs. Madison as she appeared at the time. This description is introduced by a bit of the gossip which learned men in that day, even as in our own time, seem to have relished.

"While Congress sat in New York," wrote Dr. Mitchill, "it was reported that he [Mr. Madison] was fascinated by the celebrated Mrs. Colden, of our city, she who was so noted for her masculine understanding and activity, as well as for feminine graces and accomplishments. But Mr. Madison was reserved for another widow, who some years after became connected to him by the nuptial tie. This lady was Mrs. Todd."

From the irrefragable testimony of a letter of the time, it appears that the affections of Mr. Madison had been engaged by still another fair one before Aaron Burr introduced him to the vivacious Widow Todd. This earlier charmer was Catherine Floyd, who when she jilted the "great little Madison" sealed her letter with a bit of rye dough. Whatever symbolism was connected with rye dough seems to be unknown to the mischievous flirt of to-day, but of the import of the missive which it sealed there seems to have been no question. These unrequiting ladies, damsel and widow, were doubtless quite forgotten in the great happiness that came to James Madison in his marriage with a woman who thoroughly appreciated and loved him, of whom the admiring Dr. Mitchill said, in 1802, when Mrs. Madison was about thirty-five years of age:

"She has a fine person and a most engaging countenance, which pleases, not so such from mere symmetry or complexion, as from expression. Her smile, her conversation, and her manners are so engaging, that it is no wonder that such a young widow, with her fine blue eyes and large share of animation, should be, indeed, a QUEEN OF HEARTS."

In another letter Dr. Mitchill wrote to his wife of New Year's Day, 1802, which he spoke of as a time of great parade in the city of Washington. This was evidently one of the occasions upon which the President set aside his personal inclinations and prejudices for the sake of the pleasure of the many. Dr. Mitchill wrote that the Secretaries of the Navy, State, Treasury, and other departments, and the foreign ministers, with their wives, were in attendance to pay their homage to the Executive.

"Arriving late," he recorded, "I met a whole troop of ladies and their attendant gallants coming down the outside stairs and going to their carriages. On passing the great hall and entering the north drawing-room, I found still a large party there. The President was standing near the middle of the room to salute and converse with visitors. The male part of them walked about or made groups for conversation, while the ladies received the bows and adorations of the gentlemen. Among the ladies were the President's two daughters, Mrs. Randolph and Mrs. Eppes, to whom I paid my obeisance; then to Mrs. Madison and her sister Miss Payne; then to Miss Gallatin and Miss Nicholson, besides a number of others. Beaux growing scarce or inattentive towards the last, I had to officiate myself, and to escort several of the fair creatures in succession to their carriages. Several belles from Virginia and elsewhere were brought out on this gala day, and it was allowed on all hands that the company made a brilliant appearance."

This New York gentleman, who so gallantly accepted the rôle of squire of dames, was one of the most learned men in Congress. So varied and accurate was Dr. Mitchill's knowledge, that Mr. Jefferson was wont to call him "the Congressional

Dictionary," while his associates dubbed him "the Stalking Library." On one occasion Dr. Mitchill was put upon a certain committee with several other gentlemen, among whom was Dr. Dana, of Connecticut, also distinguished for learning. Wishing to confer with Dr. Mitchill personally on the business of the committee, Dr. Dana was looking for him at the door of the House, when he met Mr. Randolph. "I am looking," said Dr. Dana, "for our 'Stalking Library.'" "Are you?" said Mr. Randolph; "I just heard him inquiring for his 'Index.'"

It is pleasant to read of these grave and reverend legislators indulging in quips and quirks and jests, after the fashion of lesser mortals. An amusing instance of the relaxing of judicial dignity is to be found in Josiah Quincy's reminiscences of Judge Story. When Mr. Quincy was about to accompany the judge to Washington, he explained that he could do little for his young friend socially, as he and his colleagues took no part in the society of the capital.

"We dine once a year with the President," he said, "and that is all. On other days we take our dinner together, and discuss at table the questions which are argued before us. We are great ascetics, and even deny ourselves wine, except in wet weather." Here the judge paused, as if thinking that the act of mortification he had mentioned placed too severe a tax upon human credulity, and presently added: "What I say about the wine, sir, gives you our rule, but it does sometimes happen that the Chief Justice will say to me, when the cloth is removed, 'Brother Story, step to the window and see if it does not look like rain.' And if I tell him that the sun is shining brightly, Judge Marshall will sometimes reply, 'All the better; for our jurisdiction extends over so large a territory, that the doctrine of chances makes it certain that it must be raining somewhere.' You know that the Chief was brought up upon Federalism and Madeira, and he is not the man to outgrow his early prejudices."

From various letters of the time, it is evident that Mr. Madison's learned associates were in the habit of dropping in at his house on F Street in the evening for a sociable hour with Mrs. Madison and her friends. Dr. Mitchill wrote of dining at the Secretary's, in a large company, and of spending an evening with Mrs. Madison soon after. It was at Mr. Gallatin's that the New York Senator met the author of "Common Sense" and "The Age of Reason;" but he doubtless found a welcome in Mrs. Madison's drawing-room, for, objectionable as Tom Paine's views might be to this good lady, the rites of hospitality were, in her opinion, scarcely second to those of religion. Here, also, was to be met the poet and philosopher Joel Barlow, who returned to America in 1805, and built his mansion, Kalorama, on a natural terrace above Rock Creek, not far from Twenty-first Street. Mr. Barlow welcomed his literary and ingenious friends to his beautiful home, among them John Howard Payne and Robert Fulton, who is said to have launched "his prophetic kettle" on Rock Creek.

Mrs. Madison was upon intimate terms with the Barlows. "Our girls," wrote Mr. Barlow from Paris, "will write you all about courts and fashion and finery," and, truth to tell, such subjects occupied many pages, until Mrs. Madison was forced to turn her eyes from beholding vanity in the form of Parisian gowns, laces, and gewgaws, as she confided to Mrs. Barlow that the enchanting order she had just filled for her had cost two thousand dollars in duties.

Mrs. Madison's presence in Washington seems to have been quite as important in Mr. Jefferson's administration as in that of her husband, and numerous letters are still to be seen in which the President requested her and her sister to help him "to take care of his female friends," as he expressed it. These notes were written in the third person, not with any attempt at formality, but probably because by so doing Mr. Jefferson avoided the use of a capital for the first person singular, which he very much objected to. In a letter addressed to Mayor Cox, of Georgetown, he entered into a long dissertation upon the extreme egotism of the use of a capital for the first person singular, while in addressing another person the *you* or *your* employed was spelled with a small letter. In the President's most informal notes, he thus adroitly avoided the use of the objectionable and consequential I:

"Thomas Jefferson was much disappointed at breakfast this morning, not having until then known of the departure of Mr. and Mrs. Madison and Miss Payne; he hopes they will come and dine to-day with the Miss Butters, who were assured they would meet them here, and to-morrow with Mrs. Gallatin and Mrs. Mason. Affectionate salutations."

The years when Mr. Madison was Secretary of State were full of happiness to his wife; more so perhaps, than her later life in the White House, which brought with it more care and responsibility. Mrs. Madison's younger sister, Anna, was with her during her early residence in Washington, bringing to her house the charm and variety of a young girl's pleasures and interests, including a bevy of friends with their attendant cavaliers. Among the many girls who were to be met at Mrs. Madison's were Harriot Stoddert, Anne Randolph, and lovely Marcia Burnes, the daughter of old Davey Burnes, whose cottage stood until recent years on Seventeenth Street near E.

After the death of her father, Marcia Burnes had been received into the home of Luther Martin, in Baltimore, and there educated and trained with his two daughters. Returning to Washington a beauty and an heiress, she soon captivated the affections of a young Congressman from New York, John P. Van Ness, whom she married in 1802. Two years later Anna Payne married Richard D. Cutts, and Mrs. Madison had the satisfaction of a brilliant wedding, dear to her pleasure-loving soul, and the pain of seeing this beloved sister depart for the District of Maine with her husband.

During the early years of Mr. Madison's administration, there occurred that fatal encounter on the banks of the Hudson which deprived the nation of one of its ablest and most devoted sons. Whatever may have been the failings of Alexander Hamilton, his most severe critic has never been able to find a flaw in his devotion to a country which owed so much to his astute statesmanship and financial skill. Mr. Jefferson, who was opposed to Mr. Hamilton in politics, had a warm admiration for his ability, and upon more than one occasion made use of his popularity to bring about measures of public importance, knowing that Hamilton was a man who was ready to set aside political preferences and opportunities of personal advancement for the good of his country. That this great man, who of all the statesmen of his time was the closest friend of Washington, should have engaged in a duel with an adversary as devoid of patriotism as he was of principle, incapable of any high or noble sentiment, is one of the saddest travesties upon the so-called code of honor existing among gentlemen at that period. The death of Alexander Hamilton cast a gloom over the social and political life of the capital, for men and women realized that the republic had lost a friend whose place would not soon be filled, in addition to which Hamilton possessed many personal traits of the most endearing nature. No more fascinating character is to be found in the public life of the day, with the exception of his great political opponent Thomas Jefferson, than the large-brained, versatile statesman who fell mortally wounded by Aaron Burr on a July day in 1804.

A few months later there occurred a trial in Washington that was of so much general interest and was attended by so many ladies that it partook of the nature of a social event,—the impeachment of Judge Chase, of Maryland. This trial involved a question of no less importance than whether the judicial department of the government could be controlled and manipulated at the pleasure of the other departments. Upon this occasion the Senate was presided over by the Vice-President, Aaron Burr, with a grace and fairness that won universal recognition, or, as an opposition newspaper reported, "with the dignity and impartiality of an angel, but with the rigor of a devil."

"With the love of dramatic effect which characterized the man," said Mr. Goddard, "the Vice-President had the Senate Chamber fitted up as a court, in which the Senators were arranged in a semicircle about himself as centre, with the accused, his counsel, the managers of the impeachment, and the House all effectively placed, while extra galleries, draped in green cloth, were provided for spectators, with handsome boxes for ladies, for the Diplomatic Corps, and members of the government. The Senators' seats were draped in crimson, those for the managers and counsel in blue.

"Among the Senators sitting in judgment on the case was the future President, John Quincy Adams, who steadily voted in favor of the accused, and many other wearers of historic names, such as Bayard of Delaware, Breckenridge of Kentucky, Dayton of New Jersey, Giles of Virginia, Tracey of Connecticut, Pickering of Massachusetts, and Sumter of South Carolina. The chief manager of the impeachment on the part of the House was John Randolph of Roanoke, then but thirty-one years of age, and already the leader of the House, yet more feared than loved for his sarcastic eloquence. Of his five associates, Cæsar Rodney of Delaware was the most notable. Around Judge Chase, who was fully able to plead his own cause yet shrewd enough to draw about him the ablest advocates of his day, there gathered as counsel his life-long friend Martin, Charles Lee, late Attorney-General of the United States, and Robert Goodloe Harper, who had just ceased to be the Federal leader in the House, and who has passed into history as one of Maryland's greatest advocates."

After a trial which lasted four weeks, Judge Chase was acquitted, chiefly, it is said, through the indefatigable energy and great ability of his counsel, Luther Martin, whom Henry Adams describes as "the rolicking, witty, audacious Attorney-General of Maryland; boon companion of Chase and the whole bar; drunken, generous, slovenly, grand; Bull-dog of Federalism, as Mr. Jefferson called him; shouting with a schoolboy's fun at the idea of tearing Randolph's indictment to pieces, and teaching the Virginia Democrats some law,—the notorious reprobate genius Luther Martin." The Maryland lawyer's success in this affair, and his acknowledged ability, led Aaron Burr to retain his services in an even more dramatic trial that took place at Richmond two years later.

The intricacies of Aaron Burr's alleged conspiracy which have baffled later historians, evidently vexed the legal souls of his contemporaries. Burr's acquittal was due to Judge Marshall's

Maria Martin

Luther Martin

ruling on technical grounds, even more than to Luther Martin's marvellous pleading. The dramatic, impassioned presentation by William Wirt of the cruel treachery of Burr, and the desolation of the peaceful home on Blennerhassett Island, with its opening interrogatory, "Who is Blennerhassett?" could not avail against the vehement harangues of Martin and the technical ruling of the great Chief Justice, who decided that "the assembling and enlisting of men on Blennerhasset's Island showed no overt act; that even if it did, Burr's agency did not appear, and that the overt act must be established before testimony as to Burr's conduct or declarations could be admissible."

Aaron Burr was declared innocent in the eyes of the law, although he left the court covered with the opprobrium which still clings to his name. Those who read to-day the touching story of the Blennerhassetts are constrained to believe that Harman Blennerhassett was the too credulous tool of an unscrupulous intriguer.

True to his better nature, Luther Martin was faithful to his clients, and at the price of his popularity received Burr and Blennerhassett into his own home in Baltimore as guests. This created great indignation in the city, and handbills were posted about, stating that "effigies of Chief Justice Marshall, of Burr, and Lawyer Brandy-Bottle" would be hanged on Gallows Hill that evening,—a plan which was carried out, the police only preventing a public riot.

In the recollections of John Barney, quoted by Parton in his life of Burr, Mr. Barney stated that he was present at a dinner given in Burr's honor by Martin at this time. During the dinner Burr rose from the table and went to the window to bow to a passing band, which he supposed had come to serenade him, but when he discovered that the tune was "The Rogue's March," the windows were quickly closed.

The trial of Aaron Burr was the exciting event of the year 1807, to be followed soon by another excitement, the question who should be the next candidate for the Presidency. James Madison and James Monroe, the latter having recently returned from France, were the strongest Federalist candidates. In spite of considerable opposition and strenuous efforts made by John Randolph and other men of influence, who indulged in bitter invective and innuendo against what they were pleased to call a "Yazoo President," when the electoral votes were counted in Congress, in February, 1809, it appeared that Dr. Mitchill's prophecy was to be fulfilled, and that Mrs. Madison would be "mistress of the sumptuous mansion on Palatine Hill for four years."

At no time were the charming personal traits of

Jefferson more conspicuous than when he was about to leave the high position which he had held for eight years. Unlike his predecessor, who left Washington abruptly, as if to avoid the discomfiture of witnessing the inauguration of another President, Mr. Jefferson seemed determined to do all in his power to show his friendliness to the new administration. Never had he appeared more genial and witty or lighter of heart, than at Mrs. Madison's first reception. Full of jest and repartee, he spread about him an atmosphere of gaiety and good fellowship. As the ladies pressed near him, a friend whispered, jestingly, "You see, they will follow you." "That is as it should be," answered Jefferson, "since I am too old to follow them. I remember," he added, "when Dr. Franklin's friends were taking leave of him in France, the ladies almost smothered him with embraces. On his introducing me to them as his successor, I told them that among the rest of his privileges, I wished he would transfer this one to me. But he answered, 'No, no; you are too young a man.'" When the ex-President had finished, a young lady who stood near him suggested that that invidious bar no longer existed. What response he made is not recorded; but when some one commented on the contrast which his gaiety presented to the exhausted and careworn aspect of the newly-installed President, Jefferson responded, "Can you wonder at it? My shoulders have just been freed from a heavy burden, his just laden with it." With good wishes for his successor, whose sincerity none could doubt, and a jest upon his lips, this great statesman disappeared from the political life of the capital. Although, as Augustus Foster and even less friendly writers have stated, Mr. Jefferson would certainly have been elected a third time to the Presidential office had he chosen to allow himself to be nominated, he cheerfully turned his face towards the peaceful shades of Monticello and the companionship of his daughter and her family, which were far dearer to him than any honors that were to be gained in political life.

VI

A QUEEN OF HEARTS

THE inauguration of the fourth President of the United States was celebrated with great rejoicings. Salutes of cannon from the Navy Yard and Fort Warburton ushered in the day, and troops of militia, which gathered early at Georgetown and Alexandria, marched to Washington to escort Mr. Madison to the Capitol. In the Hall of Representatives, where were gathered members of Congress, judges of the Supreme Court, foreign ministers, and a large concourse of ladies, the oath of office was administered to the new President by Chief Justice Marshall. "Mr. Madison appeared to great advantage," wrote an eye-witness of the scene, "the excitement of the occasion lending color to his pale, student face, and dignity to his slender figure."

At a ball which was given at Davis's Hotel in the evening—the first inaugural ball in Washington of which there is any record—it is said that "upwards of four hundred persons graced the scene, which was not a little enlivened by the handsome display of female fashion and beauty."

The "Lady Presidentess," who was the centre of all eyes, was resplendent in a gown of yellow velvet, her neck and arms hung with pearls, and her head surmounted by a Parisian turban, from which nodded a bird-of-paradise plume.

From the incontrovertible testimony of a bill presented to Congress in May, 1809, it appears that the White House was refurnished at this time, "splendidly," says one account, which statement is to be accepted with reservations, as the sum appropriated for the work was the modest one of five thousand dollars. An additional thousand was granted Mr. Latrobe for the curtains, chairs, and sofas of the drawing-room, which was upholstered in yellow satin damask, the sofas being stiff and the chairs high-backed. In this room, whose walls were hung with mirrors and whose fireplace was ornamented with a gorgeous "rising sun" in yellow damask, Mrs. Madison received her own friends, her husband's, and those of her country, men and women of all sorts and conditions, with a delightful impartiality of manner that was the wonder of her day and the envy of her successors.

A distinguished group of statesmen surrounded Mr. and Mrs. Madison at this time. In addition to the President's official family, which included the Vice-President, George Clinton of New York, William Eustis of Massachusetts, Paul Hamilton of South Carolina, William Pinkney, Gideon Granger, Albert Gallatin, and James Monroe,

Mrs. James Madison

Miniature by James Peale

Mrs. James Monroe

Miniature by Sené, Paris, 1794

there was the great Chief Justice John Marshall, with his tall figure and marvellous deep-set eyes, and Henry Clay from Mrs. Madison's own Hanover County, his low, resonant voice in strong contrast with that of John Randoph, which was high pitched and sometimes shrill. Here also were Daniel Webster and John C. Calhoun, already showing some measure of the ability that was to make them great leaders in later days.

Several of the members of Mr. Madison's Cabinet had served in that of his predecessor, as the Postmaster-General, Gideon Granger of Connecticut, and the Secretary of the Treasury, Albert Gallatin, who proved that to be born in Switzerland was no obstacle to being a good American.

Edward Coles, who had been private secretary to Mr. Jefferson, retained his position under his successor until he was sent by Mr. Madison as special ambassador to Russia. Mr. Coles, one of Mrs. Madison's numerous Virginia cousins, was a man of much more than ordinary ability and breadth of view. After his return from Russia, being conscientiously opposed to slavery, Mr. Coles removed to Illinois and there freed the large number of slaves that he had inherited from his father, giving each head of a family one hundred and sixty acres of land. He was afterwards elected governor of Illinois and thus prevented the pro-slavery faction in that State from gaining control. Edward

Coles passed the last years of his life in Philadelphia, where he helped to found the Republican party.

Mr. Monroe had recently returned from abroad, where, in conjunction with Robert R. Livingston, he had successfully negotiated the purchase of Louisiana. This vast acquisition of territory, which is one of the glories of Mr. Jefferson's administration, cost the United States sixty millions of francs and some additional millions in the satisfying of claims.* It is said that Bonaparte was so well satisfied with the transaction that he gave his agent, M. Marbois, one hundred and ninety-two thousand francs of the proceeds, with the remark that sixty millions was a pretty good price for a province of which he had not taken possession, and might not be able to retain twenty-four hours, adding, "This accession of territory strengthens forever the power of the United States, and I have just given England a maritime rival that will sooner or later humble her pride."

Under Mr. Madison's administration, Mr. Monroe occupied the responsible position of Secretary

* The French spoliation claims were estimated, at the time of the purchase, to amount to three million seven hundred and fifty thousand dollars, which made the whole cost of this vast tract of land, including the shores of the Mississippi and many of the Northern and Western States, amount to about fifteen million dollars.

of State. He is described as tall of figure and dressed in the old style, with small-clothes, silk hose, knee-buckles, and pumps; indeed, Mr. Monroe adhered to this costume so long as to earn for himself the *sobriquet* of "the last cocked hat." His face, which was not strikingly handsome, was illumined by eyes so clear and straightforward that they seemed to justify Mr. Jefferson's remark that Monroe was so honest that if you turned his soul inside out there would not be a spot or speck found on it.

Mrs. Monroe, who, as Elizabeth Kortright, had been a belle and beauty in her own city, New York, is spoken of as graceful and distinguished as well as beautiful. She and her daughters, having lately returned from abroad, were regarded with great interest by Washington women, as exponents of the latest fancies of the fickle, arbitrary Parisian world. Nor did the women of the period alone occupy themselves with the prevailing modes. Mr. Robert Goodloe Harper is said to have appeared in great splendor at the inauguration ball, his clothes cut after the latest fashion, "perfumed like a milliner, with a large knot of black ribbon on each shoe." A distinguished Virginia jurist who visited the Monroes soon after their arrival in Washington was so captivated by the costume of little Maria Monroe that he thus recommended it to his daughter:

". . . Your mama has refer'd you to me for an account of little Maria Monroe, who is I believe a few months older than our darling Fancilea. She was dress'd in a short frock, that reach'd about half way between her knees and ancles—under which she display'd a pair of loose pantaloons, wide enough for the foot to pass through with ease, frill'd round with the same stuff as her frock and pantaloons. I was so pleased with it, and so persuaded you would immediately adopt it for Fancilea and Lisba that I took more than ordinary notice of it. The little monkey did not fail to evince the advantages of her dress. She had a small Spaniel dog with whom she was continually engaged in a trial of skill—and the general opinion seemed to be that she turned and twisted about more than the Spaniel. . . . I must recommend her dress for my dear Brats."*

With Mr. Madison's administration there was a marked restoration of form and ceremony in the Executive Mansion, a return to the dignity and propriety of the days of Washington and Adams, yet what most impressed those who were received in the White House by Mrs. Madison was not the stateliness of the ceremony, but the easy grace and warm-hearted Virginia hospitality that characterized her drawing-rooms and dinners.

Visitors to the capital then, as in our own day, were expected to leave their cards at the White House. In one of her letters to a friend in another

* Extract from a letter written by Judge St. George Tucker, of Williamsburg, Virginia, to his daughter, Anne Frances Bland, wife of Judge Coalter, of the High Court of Appeals of Virginia, dated Williamsburg, Virginia, December 18, 1807.

city Mrs. Madison expressed lively regret that some of her Philadelphia acquaintances had not left their cards, as she wished to invite them to dinner, and had no idea where they were stopping, having sent to several of the "principal taverns" to try to find them.

No friend or acquaintance of Mrs. Madison's who came to Washington was neglected. Old and young, gentle and simple, Quaker and worldling, were bidden to the White House, and made welcome there. This hospitable lady's great-nieces take pleasure in telling how a Friend from Philadelphia, who was dining with the President, paid back the raillery of the gay hostess in her own coin. As Mrs. Madison, looking very handsome in an evening gown that displayed her plump shoulders to great advantage, took her seat at table, she raised her wineglass to her lips, and bowing to her guest, said, gayly, "Here's to thy absent broadbrim, Friend Hallowell," to which the Quaker, nothing daunted, said, returning the bow of his hostess, "And here's to thy absent kerchief, Friend Dorothy!" How Mrs. Madison and her sisters must have laughed over this clever rejoinder!—those "Merry Wives of Windsor," as Washington Irving was wont to call them.

Numerous stories are told of Mrs. Madison's quick-wittedness and ready tact, which smoothed the path of many a shy or awkward stranger, unaccustomed to the social ways of cities or the usages of diplomatic circles. One of the most amusing of these is the tale of a country lad at a White House reception, who was surprised in the midst of his enjoyment of a cup of coffee by the approach of his hostess. In his confusion, it is said that the poor boy dropped his saucer and thrust the cup into his pocket. Mistress Dolly, who, though her eyes were keen and searching, never saw anything that she was not intended to see, chatted away so pleasantly of the weather, the crowd, and, finally, of the young man's mother, whom she had known or heard of, that he recovered from his embarrassment, and was soon at ease and ready to accept the fresh cup of coffee that his hostess ordered, despite a certain curious and unexplained bulge in his pocket.

Mr. William C. Preston recorded in his journal a somewhat similar experience when he went to the White House as a young man to pay his respects to the President and Mrs. Madison. When he entered the drawing-room, which was brilliant with uniforms and gay toilettes, overwhelmed with embarrassment, he would gladly have retreated from the unaccustomed scene, but Mrs. Madison had observed him, and advanced towards him, magnificent in high turban and stiff brocade, her snuff-box in one hand, the other extended cordially towards her young guest, with the question, "Are you William

Campbell Preston, the son of my old friend and most beloved kinswoman, Sally Campbell? Sit down, my son, for you are my son, and I am the first person who ever saw you in this world." Turning then with a graciousness which charmed the young man, she introduced him to the circle of young girls about her, giving some special clue to each, and ending with "your kinswoman, Sally Coles."

The tales that have come down from that dim past are simple and homely, only worthy to be recorded because they prove once more that whatever may have been this woman's beauty or grace, the secret of her success was to be found in the quickness of her perceptions and the warmth of her heart. These qualities, with a certain enthusiasm that she brought to her social duties, created an atmosphere of homelike comfort and enjoyment wherever she appeared.

The Sally Coles to whom Mrs. Madison presented young Preston was the daughter of Colonel John Coles of Enniscorthy, one of her near relatives. It is related of Colonel Coles, who was a genial, horse-loving, hospitable Virginia gentleman of the old school, that in recounting his blessings he would speak with pride of the ability of his sons, adding, like the French poet Martial, that he was glad his daughters were not too learned. Colonel Coles's felicitations are rather amusing, in view of the fact that these daughters, whether learned or not according to the code of their day, proved themselves capable of filling with grace and distinction prominent positions in social and diplomatic circles.

Eliza Coles married Colonel Richard Singleton, of South Carolina, Emily married Governor Rutherford, of Virginia, while Sally, Mrs. Madison's favorite, became the wife of Andrew Stevenson, who was afterwards Speaker of the House of Representatives and minister to England under President Van Buren.

Another of Mrs. Madison's numerous Virginia cousins was Colonel Isaac Coles, of Halifax County. Colonel Coles was elected a delegate to the First Congress, and again represented his State from 1793 to 1797.

While in New York, attending the sessions of Congress, Colonel Coles met Miss Catherine Thompson, a daughter of Mr. James Thompson and a sister of Mrs. Elbridge Gerry. Bishop Meade recorded that Colonel Coles and Miss Thompson were married by Bishop Provoost in 1790. When his services in Congress were concluded, Colonel Coles took his young wife to his large estates in Halifax and Pittsylvania counties. He held no official position in the new capital, but it is to be hoped that Colonel and Mrs. Coles sometimes visited their Cousin Dolly in the White

House, as both were well-fitted to enjoy social life. Colonel Coles has been described as a man of agreeable, courtly manners and a delightful *raconteur*. Mrs. Coles, who had been a belle and a beauty, accustomed to a large and gay circle of friends in New York and to the society of the most cultivated and refined men and women of the day during her residence in Philadelphia, must have found her life in a sparsely-settled district in strange contrast with her previous surroundings. To these new conditions this young woman adapted herself with spirit and enthusiasm. In addition to the cares of her large family and the duties which in those days devolved upon the mistress of a plantation, Mrs. Coles assisted Bishop Meade to establish an Episcopal Church, the first in Halifax County. The services were, said the bishop, often held in Mrs. Coles's house.

It is evident that Sally Coles was a frequent visitor at the White House, as there are many references to her in Mrs. Madison's letters. In one of these the hospitable lady speaks of a prospective visit from another Virginia belle, Miss Maria Mayo, of Richmond, whom Mrs. Madison considers even more beautiful than Miss Caton from Baltimore, although the latter exceeds her in grace. The races and drawing-room will, she hopes, afford amusement for her young guest, in addition to which she says that "the French

Minister is paving his road and intends to *frolick continnually*, and Miss Hay is to be in the city soon, as well as Madame Bonaparte and a multitude of Beauties."

The White House seemed always to have been full to overflowing. Mrs. Madison's sister Lucy, the widow of George Steptoe Washington, was living with her, and Mrs. Richard D. Cutts, whose husband represented Maine in the House, was often in Washington, in addition to which there were cousins and friends innumerable, and of political adherents an ample contingent.

During Mrs. Madison's residence in Philadelphia, before and after her marriage, and during some weeks spent in the Quaker City in 1805, for the purpose of being under the professional care of the distinguished Dr. Physick, she made many life-long friends, among whom were Mr. and Mrs. Anthony Morris. Some of Mrs. Madison's most charming letters were written to Phœbe Morris, the daughter of these old friends, and abound in expressions of affection for her and her family.

In one of her letters to Phœbe Morris, the lady of the White House, then just over forty and in the full possession of charms that were destined to win many hearts, wrote thus modestly of her appearance: "You will accept, my beloved Phœbe, the inclosed resemblance of your 'Parent's friend,' that tender friend who loves and

Mrs. Richard D. Cutts

By Gilbert Stuart

admires you!—I should have sent you a Picture long 'ere this, but those in my possession were too young, and I waited to procure my *present self.*"

It does not appear from Mrs. Madison's letter what portrait of herself she sent to Phœbe Morris. It was probably a replica of a miniature, with roses in the turban, which James Peale is said to have painted in the White House. Another miniature of a sweet, girlish face, surmounted by a demure cap, was painted in Philadelphia by James Peale when Mrs. Madison was Mistress Todd.

Gilbert Stuart was in Georgetown while Mr. Madison was Secretary of State, and at this time painted a portrait of Mrs. Madison and a companion picture of her husband. Among numerous other portraits executed by Stuart were those of Colonel and Mrs. John Tayloe of the Octagon, and of Mr. and Mrs. Richard D. Cutts. In the background of this latter portrait, for which Mrs. Cutts sat a short time before her marriage, is to be found an exaggerated outline of the artist's own features. The story runs, that while Anna Payne's portrait was being painted that lively young woman entered into an animated discussion with the artist as to which feature of the face is the most expressive. Mr. Stuart gave his verdict in favor of the nose, while Miss Payne contended for the superior claims of the eyes and mouth. Stuart, who greatly relished a joke, even at his own expense, presented to his sitter the next morning a canvas upon which *his own* profile, the long nose somewhat exaggerated, occupied the place of the usual drapery in the background, inquiring, with a triumphant smile, whether he had not proved to her satisfaction that the nose was the most expressive feature of the face. Although the laugh was against her, Miss Payne was so much pleased to have secured a profile of her old friend, that she insisted that the very odd background should remain a part of the portrait.

Early in the year of 1812, a year destined to be an eventful one to the citizens of Washington, as well as to the whole country, Phœbe Morris and her brother visited Mrs. Madison. To her sister Rebecca, in Philadelphia, the young guest wrote:

"The President and Mrs. Madison expected me before the first of January, and were extremely sorry that we did not arrive by that time, as it was a great day there. The House was crowded with company from *top to bottom*, the chambers and every room was occupied with Ladies and Gentlemen and all descriptions of persons. I have a dear little room with an alcove Bed which adjoins Mrs. Washington's. The chamber I occupied last year was too large and too cold for me, Mrs. Madison said, but she has given it to Brother. He seems very well contented and went with me yesterday to see Mrs. Gallatin. To-day he has set off with Mr. Payne on horseback to ride over the city and visit the Patent Office. Yesterday we had a crowd of morning visitors, Miss Caton, Mrs. Van Ness, the Miss Worthingtons and a number of others whose names I cannot recollect. Maria Ringgold is here, but I have not seen her, she is in deep mourning and scarcely goes out at all."

The Maria Ringgold of whom Miss Morris wrote was a daughter of Maria Cadwalader, of Philadelphia, who married Mr. Samuel Ringgold, of Fountain Rock, Maryland, and consequently a niece of Mrs. Erskine, wife of the British minister. Maryland women of that day, as of a later time, were celebrated for their beauty and charm, and as Baltimore and the country-seats surrounding it were within two days' staging distance of Washington, many of the belles of the gay little city spent the winter months in the capital.

In the famous constellation of beauties of which Elizabeth Patterson, who married Jerome Bonaparte, was the "bright particular star," were her lovely sisters-in-law, Mary Ann Caton, Charlotte Nicols, and Anne Gittings, the last named a daughter of Mr. James Gittings, whose good farming had excited the admiration of Richard Parkinson. Another charming woman who belonged to this family connection was Polly Sterett, a daughter of John Sterett and Deborah Ridgely, of Hampton. Miss Polly, a belle and a beauty in her own city, extended her conquests to Philadelphia, where she visited her uncle Samuel Sterett, who was a delegate to Congress during the Washington administration. Here she had the pleasure of meeting the President, who was a friend of her uncle, and the honor of being led out to dance by him at one of the Philadelphia balls. From the scene of her joys and triumphs, of which traditions have floated down to her Baltimore descendants of to-day, Miss Sterett returned home to marry Mr. Richard Gittings and to live with him at Berry Hill, which was his portion of the extensive Long Green estate in Baltimore County. Mrs. Gittings doubtless visited Washington after her marriage and enjoyed its social attractions, but the scene of her youthful triumphs was the older capital on the banks of the Delaware.

In one of her letters little Miss Morris speaks of another Baltimore beauty, Miss Hay, as sharing the honors of belledom with Miss Caton and Madame Bonaparte. These three are, she hears, the greatest belles in Washington. At this time Phœbe Morris says that she has not yet seen Madame Bonaparte, as she was suffering from an attack of rheumatism brought on, Mrs. Washington said, by an imprudent display of her beautiful shoulders, the expression of the good dame's opinion being given in much more vigorous Saxon than would be considered polite in our day.

In a letter dated February 17, 1812, Miss Morris gave her impressions of the famous Baltimore beauty who had captured the unstable affections of Jerome Bonaparte:

Mrs. Samuel Ringgold
(Maria Cadwalader)

Mrs. Moses Poor
By Edward Greene Malbone
Page 230

"How I wish you could see Madame Bonaparte in all the splendor of dress, and all the attractions of beauty. I think I never beheld a human form so faultless. To the utmost symmetry of features is added so much vivacity, such captivating sweetness! and her sylphic form 'thinly veiled' displays all the graces of a Venus de Medicis. She appears particularly lovely in a fine crepe robe of a beautiful azure colour interwoven with silver, in this attire she is truly celestial, and it is impossible to look on any one else when she is present."

It is not strange that this Quaker girl, who had seen little of the gay world, should have been dazzled by the charms of this woman, who excited admiration wherever she appeared and drew from Madame Récamier the compliment "*Vous êtes la plus belle femme au monde, plus belle même que la parfaite Pauline Borghese.*"

"*Mais ça est bien, impossible,*" was the clever reply, "*vue que ma belle sœur est parfaitement belle.*"

Witty, wise, and diplomatic, as well as beautiful, was this young woman, whom the Emperor Napoleon refused to meet, perhaps because he feared that his resolution might yield to the influence of a charm that few could resist. Some grim amusement he may have extracted from the *mot* attributed to Madame Bonaparte, who, when asked by Emil de Girardin for her true estimate of Jerome Bonaparte, replied, with generous appreciation of the Emperor and withering scorn for her faithless spouse, "*C'est un liard qui s'est glisse par hazard entre deux Napoléons.*"

It was this brilliant and spirited woman that the Emperor proposed to dispose of, after King Jerome's alliance with the Princess of Wurtemburg, by marrying her to General Turreau. Turreau was afterwards imprisoned, and being released by his jailor's daughter, married her. If lively, his gratitude was of short duration, as he treated his wife so brutally while living in Georgetown as French minister that his atrocities and the poor woman's cries were the scandal of the neighborhood.

Only less beautiful than Madame Bonaparte was Mary Ann Caton, who married her brother, Robert Patterson, and when a widow in 1825 became the wife of the Marquess of Wellesley, then Viceroy of Ireland.

Richard Lalor Shiel waxed eloquent over the mature charms of the American beauty as she appeared at a tabinet ball in Dublin, in a gown of white tabinet crossed with a garland of flowers. After likening Lady Wellesley in turn to Pomona and to Byron's "Lady Adeline Amundeville," he added, with admirable condescension: "Nobody would have suspected that she had not originally belonged to the proud aristocracy to which she had been recently annexed. She had nothing of *la bourgeoise parvenue*. She executed her courtesies with a remarkable gracefulness, and her stateliness sat as naturally upon her as though she inherited it by royal descent."

Mr. Benjamin Ogle Tayloe, while abroad with the Honorable Richard Rush on a diplomatic mission in 1818, says that, as an American, he was gratified by the admiration excited by the three Caton sisters at a ball given by the allied sovereigns of Europe at Aix-la-Chapelle. This entertainment, which was held at the close of a congress convened after the final defeat of Napoleon to deliberate upon the withdrawal of the army of occupation from France, was attended by the Emperor of Russia, the King of Prussia, and other great sovereigns, with their families. Here were Wellington and other generals of the army of the allies, and such masters of diplomacy as Metternich, Nesselrode, Hardenberg, Bernstorff, Castlereagh, Richelieu, and Capo d'Istria. In this brilliant and distinguished company, and "amid the extraordinary constellation of European beauty there assembled," Mr. Tayloe noticed, with pride, that his "beautiful countrywomen, Mrs. Patterson, Lady Hervey, and Miss Caton of Maryland, attracted universal admiration and received marked attention from the Emperor Alexander."

The Miss Caton who called upon Miss Morris at the White House was probably Louisa Caton, who married Colonel Sir Felton Hervey, and after his death became the wife of the Marquess of Caermarthen, afterwards Duke of Leeds.

Miss Morris's letters are all filled with clever

descriptions of the persons whom she met and the entertainments she attended. Among the latter were dinners at the houses of Dr. Charles Worthington, General Van Ness, and other hospitable Washingtonians.

The handsome mansion which General Van Ness built soon after his marriage with Marcia Burnes is still standing southwest of the White House, near the Potomac flats which Tom Moore so bitterly anathematized. This house, for which Mr. Latrobe drew the plans and which cost over sixty thousand dollars, was for many years considered the finest dwelling in Washington, with the exception of the Octagon. The glories of the White House, even with its new furniture, mirrors, and "rising suns," paled before those of the Van Ness mansion, with its Italian marble mantels, handsome carvings, spacious drawing-rooms, and numerous guest-chambers.

Men and women of the older generation still recall the grandeur and elegance of this house in which Phœbe Morris dined in company with the President and Mrs. Madison, and describe the liveries of the fine coach-and-four in which the General and Mrs. Van Ness were wont to drive through Washington and Georgetown. With drawing-rooms and dinners at the White House, and dancing assemblies, balls, and visits elsewhere, Miss Morris says that her head is almost turned.

The Van Ness Mansion

Washington, D. C.

This statement is, however, entirely disproved upon another page of her sprightly letter by the writer's discriminating remarks upon Captain Chauncey and Dr. Bullus, "two gentlemen of the navy," the Misses Mason, and other men and women whom she met. Miss Morris was under the protection of the Honorable Richard Rush on her journey from Baltimore to Washington, whom she characterized as one of the "most charming, polite, agreeable men she had ever met," while Mr. Augustus Foster, Secretary to the British Legation, who called upon her at the White House, she considered "rather an agreeable than a handsome man, of very pleasing conversation and great politeness."

Little Miss Morris was not the only person who was influenced by the charm and elegance of Mr. Rush's manners and appearance. Mr. Benjamin Ogle Tayloe related that upon his presentation as American minister at the Court of St. James, "the Prince Regent exclaimed with astonishment, upon learning that this was Mr. Rush's first visit to England, 'Never before in Europe!' as much as to say, where did he get his good manners?"

In one of her letters Phœbe Morris gave a description of John Randolph, which accounts for the youthful charm of the Stuart portrait, painted when Randolph was over thirty, and also for the expression, "the young, old face of Randolph," so often used in describing him. "His appearance is eccentric in the extreme," wrote Miss Morris to her father. "At a distance you would almost suppose him to be a youth of not more than sixteen, though I am told at a nearer view he appears quite old. His hair is long and simply confined by a ribbon, not in the style of a queue, but as you wear yours sometimes of a morning when you first get up—only it looked so droll on him. When he began to speak, what a silence reigned throughout the House! every one appeared to wait in anxious, almost breathless, expectation, as if to catch the first sound of his voice, and what a voice!—clear, melodious, and penetrating, it fascinates and arrests the attention which had before slumbered over the humdrum of the preceding speakers. You forget for a moment in listening that he is an enemy to our revered and excellent President. I heard but a few words, yet those few impressed me with an admiration which I was afterwards angry with myself for having felt."

Miss Phœbe would have been still more disposed to take herself to task for her admiration of the great Virginia orator had she heard him pause, at the conclusion of a vehement, impassioned period, to express himself with regard to the faint foreshadowings of "the new woman" that already appeared in the Washington life of his day. Upon this occasion, when Mr. Randolph allowed his prejudices

John Randolph
By Gilbert Stuart

to overpower his gallantry, the floor and gallery of the House were crowded by eager listeners among the fair sex. Randolph stood silent, and while all eyes were fastened on his weird figure, he pointed his long, skeleton index-finger towards the ladies in the gallery, and in his peculiar, shrill, squeaking voice said, " Mr. Speaker, what, pray, are all these women doing here, so out of place in this arena? Sir, they had much better be at home attending to their knitting!"

It is quite evident that Mrs. Madison required no admonition from Mr. Randolph about keeping away from the political arena, as in describing the doings of the gay world during the debates upon the war she wrote:

"The mornings are devoted to Congress, where *all* delight to listen to the violence of evil spirits. I stay quietly at home (as quietly as one can be who has so much to feel at the *expression for and against their conduct*)."

Mrs. Madison's "their" is doubtless intended to refer to her husband and his advisers, as her own "conduct" could not have been questioned. Indeed, although Mr. Blaine spoke of Mrs. Madison as a "political force," her influence was simply that which a good and gracious woman always exerts upon the life about her. No general discussion of political questions was encouraged in her drawing-room, and the letters of the President's wife, with the exception of expressions of uneasiness at the prospect of war, are confined to social and family matters. In writing to Phœbe Morris, Mrs. Madison frequently retailed the latest social event or a bit of gossip about the young girl's many friends and admirers in Washington. In a letter written in 1813 she says:

"You remember the Judges; they have been some time amongst us, and are as agreable as ever. They talk of you continually, particularly Story—all but Judge Todd who has remained with my dear Lucy to nurse their young daughter of whom they are very proud. It is called Madisonia Dolley. The last name I am determin'd shall be left out when they come to me next summer."

This baby, whose complex name Mrs. Madison proposed to simplify, was the child of her sister, Mrs. Washington, who, in March, 1812, was married at the White House to Justice Todd, of Kentucky. The honor of having owned the first bride of the White House, which has been claimed by several families, unquestionably belonged to that of Mrs. Madison, as is proved by a note, written by the sister-in-law of the bride-elect, acknowledging the invitation of the President and his wife.

In another clever, gossiping letter written by the President's lady to Phœbe Morris, in Philadelphia, she sends messages to her dear Mary Morris and Becky Waddell, and expresses her pleasure in the announcement that "John Pemberton has succeeded with Miss Clifford." Being addicted to match-making, like most happy wives, Mrs. Madison sometimes rallied Miss Morris upon her Washington conquests, telling her how sad and disconsolate her lovers are during her long absences. It is not strange that Mrs. Madison was fondly attached to this charming girl, whom she often called her "dear child," and her "precious daughter." That the good lady wished to claim Phœbe Morris for her daughter in very truth is evident from more than one expression in her letters, and from the frequency with which she coupled the young girl's name with that of her n'er-do-well son, Payne Todd. No evidence of the slightest attachment between the young people is to be found in the letters of Phœbe Morris, although it would be interesting to know what answer she made to the following sally from the fond mother, who, in quoting from a letter of her sister, Mrs. Todd, says: "She tells me to say she loves you sincerely and hopes you'll take a Kentucky Beau she has in reserve for you—what then will become of Payne? I will send him to bring me your sweet Rebecca—I will so! . . . We have had several marriages," continues this voluble lady. "Mr. Todd, Mr. Cutts, and Mr. Campbell, your old lover, found consolation in the smiles of Miss

Stodard, whom you have often seen here with her sister Ewell. Lucy wrote me from the town in which Campbell lives and desired me to describe his House and the preparations he was making to receive you; but as he has sealed his destiny, I will withold her long string of remarks."

The "Miss Stodard" of Mrs. Madison's letter was Harriot Stoddert, a daughter of the Honorable Benjamin Stoddert, one of the bright belles of the capital. Family tradition relates that when Harriot Stoddert made her début at the Turkish Legation, under the chaperonage of Mrs. Madison's sister, Mrs. Richard Cutts, in all the bravery of a ravishing costume of orange-colored Canton crape, her charms so wrought upon the susceptible heart of her Oriental host that he followed her from room to room, and finally, to her great dismay, asked her to be one of his wives. The Turkish minister's appreciation of American beauty was much greater than that of his predecessor, who, upon the occasion of a grand ball given in his honor, proved quite insensible to the charms of the pale-faced beauties around him. Suddenly spying a portly negress on her way from the kitchen to the supper-room, Méley Méley rushed to her side, and throwing his arms around her, declared that she reminded him of his "favorite and most costly wife."

Miss Stoddert's engagement, which was sufficiently romantic to satisfy girl readers of "Evelina" or "Sir Charles Grandison," was the result of a quarrel and a duel.

Mr. George W. Campbell, Senator from Tennessee, had a dispute with Mr. Gardenhire, of New York, upon some political subject. In the natural course of events a duel at Bladensburg ensued, in which Mr. Gardenhire fell seriously wounded. He was carried to Bostock House nearby, where he was hospitably entertained and tenderly nursed back to health by the ladies of the family. During Mr. Gardenhire's illness and convalescence Mr. Campbell rode out every day from Washington to inquire after his fallen foe. Here, at her grandfather's house, he met Miss Stoddert, and, like the Turkish minister, soon succumbed to her charms. Mr. Campbell was more fortunate than the Oriental gentleman in having his affection returned, and Harriot Stoddert became his wife in the winter of 1812.

In the midst of weddings, assemblies, and drawing-rooms, brilliant entertainments at the Russian minister's, where the recently introduced waltz was danced, and balls at the Navy Yard, where the gay folk frolicked until daybreak, the war-cloud that had been hanging over the country for months drew nearer and nearer to the capital. Mrs. William Seaton, whose letters are as charming in their way as those of Mrs. John Adams, described a ball given in November, 1812, in honor of Captains Hull, Morris, and Stewart, whose signal victory over the British on the sea cast a gleam of light across the lowering sky. "The assembly was," Mrs. Seaton says, "crowded with a more than usual proportion of the youth and beauty of the city, and was the scene of an unprecedented event,—two British flags unfurled and hung as trophies, in an American assembly, by American sailors. *Io triumphe!* Before we started our house had been illuminated, in token of our cheerful accordance with the general joy which pervaded the city, manifested by nearly every window being more or less lighted."

In another letter Mrs. Seaton speaks of Lieutenant Hamilton, son of the Secretary of the Navy, presenting the captured flags to Mrs. Madison. Mrs. Seaton had been discussing the prevalence of rouge and "pearl" among the belles of Washington, which is spoken of, she says, "with as much *sang froid* as putting on their bonnets," adding, "Mrs. Madison is said to rouge, but not evident to my eyes, and I do not think it true, as I am well assured I saw her color come and go at the naval ball, when the Macedonian flag was presented to her by young Hamilton."

Reading of the gay life of the capital during the months preceding the entrance of the British, it seemed as if Washingtonians, like the French *noblesse* in the days before the Revolution, danced and amused themselves without regard to the threatening storm until it finally broke over their heads. Much of the gayety was on the surface and in official circles was more than usually perfunctory. It seemed indeed as if Washington, by presenting a smiling face, sought to conceal her insecurity. The New Year's reception of January, 1814, was quite as brilliant as any that had preceded it. Mrs. Madison's face was wreathed in smiles and her ostrich feather nodded as gaily as in happier days; but at this time her letters contained many references to her own anxieties and those of her "dear Husband." In one of these she wrote:

"It is a sorrowful fact that there appears nothing better in our perspective than disgrace, or war. . . . My Husband has done all he could for the honor and good of his country, and further responsibility must rest on Congress."

Mrs. William Seaton, whose husband, in conjunction with his brother-in-law, Mr. Gales, and Mr. S. Harrison Smith, was editing the *National Intelligencer* up to the morning of that fateful August day in 1814, wrote to her mother some months before the capture of Washington, with a clear understanding of the situation of affairs:

"When our removal to Washington was in contemplation, you expressed apprehension lest we should be exposed to British invasion and consequent cruelty. You will see by the *Federal*

Republican, that the plan might be carried into execution without a miracle, of seizing the President and Secretaries with fifty or a hundred men, and rendering this nation a laughing-stock to every other in the world. I did not think much of these possibilities until hearing them discussed by General Van Ness and others, who, far from wishing a parade of guards or ridiculous apprehensions to be entertained, were yet anxious that the city should not be unprepared for a contingency the danger of which did certainly exist."

VII

THE BLADENSBURG RACES

A NEW ENGLAND girl who reached Washington in May, 1814, has left for the entertainment of her family her impressions of the capital and an account of her adventures in escaping from the city.

After explaining that she was making a visit at the house of Mr. Benjamin Homans, Chief Clerk in the Department of State, Miss Brown wrote:

"I explored in company with some young friends the intricacies of the Capitol, often pausing to admire its many architectural beauties. A flight of stairs commencing in the centre of a rotunda and branching off to reach a gallery that surrounded this room excited my admiration. While gazing on these and other beauties, among them the full-length portraits of Louis XVI. and his Queen, Marie Antoinette, in their royal robes, I then little dreamed of the devouring flames that were soon so ruthlessly to feed upon them. . . . There were the two magnificent wings of the Capitol connected by a long, unpainted wooden shed. Passing over a mile of rough road, bordered here and there by Congress boarding-houses, with veritable swamps between, you came to the President's house—beautiful with architecture, upholstery, gilding and paintings, set down in the midst of rough, unornamented grounds. Then another stretch of comparative wilderness till you came to Georgetown. Almost every one of any distinction drove four horses, and these fine equipages on these wretched roads, with their elegant occupants, formed no trifling part of the contrasts."

Miss Brown's notes are valuable, as they give some idea of the capital as it appeared just before the entrance of the British,—an interesting time of which few records remain. Mrs. William Seaton, to whose ready pen we are indebted for many descriptions of persons and events, left Washington some time in July, with her brother, Mr. Joseph Gales, who accompanied his sister and his young wife to a place of safety. When Mr. Gales returned to his office in the building occupied by the *National Intelligencer*, he found it sacked by the enemy and much of its valuable contents destroyed.

In the anxious days of the summer of 1814, when Admiral Cockburn and his fleet were in the Chesapeake, with prospects of considerable reinforcement from Bermuda, there were still men at the head of affairs who contended that Washington was not the objective point of the British.

General Van Ness, General Wilkinson, and other officers of experience, seem to have fully appreciated the danger of the situation and the necessity of protecting the capital; but to all their warnings the over-confident Secretary of War replied, "They will strike somewhere, but they will not come here. No, no; Baltimore is the place, sir; that is of so much more consequence."

Miss Brown described a reception which took place at the White House as late as July 4, when Mrs. Madison appeared as gracious and hospitable as ever.

"I can see her now," wrote the young visitor. "As we entered she was crossing the crowded vestibule, conducted by two fair girls, one on each side. Where they were conducting her I do not know, but she had evidently surrendered herself to their sprightly guidance with her usual benignant sweetness. She stopped to receive our greetings, and that gave me time to admire the tasteful simplicity of her dress. White—but of what material I forget. Her hair hung in ringlets on each side of her face, surmounted by the snowy folds of her unvarying turban, ornamented on one side by a few heads of green wheat. She may have worn jewels, but if she did they were so eclipsed by her inherent charms as to be unnoticed.

"These festival times did not last long. The news soon came that the British had landed at Benedict, the scene of former ravages, about thirty miles below us on the river. Then we hear of fifty-one British ships in Chesapeake Bay. The military are ordered out, those of Pennsylvania, Maryland, and Virginia, by order of General Armstrong, Secretary of War, commanded to be in readiness in case an attack should be made. The publick officials began packing up their valuable papers to be removed to places of safety. Now all is hurry and panic, armies gathering, troops moving in all directions, the citizens trying to secure such things as were most valuable and most easily transported, and flying from their homes to the country, Mr. Homans, in whose family I was a visitor, among the number.

"What became of the Secretary of State I do not remember, but much of his household furniture, together with the books and papers of the Department, were put on board of sundry flour boats and committed to the guardianship of Mr. Homans, who sent them up the Potomac. Himself and family, including myself, retreated to the residence of Mr. Obed Rich on the Georgetown Heights. There in that lovely retreat it was decided to tarry and watch the further development of affairs, while the boats rested at the entrance of the canal round the Little Falls of the Potomac, ready at any alarm to push up the river to a more remote place.

"My mother and sister had been invited to sojourn with some English friends in Georgetown and were enabled to visit us while we remained at the house of Mr. Rich. My brother had been entrusted with the books and papers of the Post Office with which he was connected.* He was a youth of about nineteen years, this circumstance affords fine illustration of the panic which overwhelmed the minds of public men. After he had seen his important charge safely deposited in the cellar of a farmhouse far from all suspicion of the enemy he with the ardor of youth made frequent visits to the city to see for himself what was going on.

"Mr. Madison was with the army and Mrs. Madison, with such assistance as in the confusion could be obtained, was bravely endeavoring to secure what she could in the White House."

An unheroic figure was that of the little President, as he appeared at this time, when promptness and decision in action were more needed than sagacious and prudent statesmanship. Nor is it

* According to traditions of the Jones family of Clean Drinking, the Postmaster-General, Return J. Meigs, and his wife took refuge in this famous old house, and kept the post-office open there until the British left the city. Clean Drinking, which still stands on Jones's Mill Road, off Connecticut Avenue, was built by Charles Jones in 1750, and is the oldest and one of the most interesting houses in the neighborhood of Washington.

strange that men for the time forgot the nation's early and heavy debt to Madison in the framing of the Constitution, in view of the exigencies that threatened to deprive them of the blessings promised by that document. A timid and inefficient commander-in-chief Madison appeared in these August days, when he hurried from the capital to the camp, giving orders about warlike movements of which he knew little, pencilling notes to his wife, confusing General Winder with his counsel, and then, in the face of Congreve rockets sent up by the enemy, hastily turning his horse's head towards Washington. As the President quitted the field, it is said that he called out to the members of his Cabinet who had accompanied him to Bladensburg, "Come with me and leave the defence with the military authorities, where it belongs."

The withdrawal upon the eve of battle of a commander-in-chief of the army and navy of the United States who knew nothing about war, was doubtless a wise measure; but it failed to appeal to the enthusiasm of a people with whom a military hero has ever been the chosen ideal. Nor is it strange that, with the keen appreciation of the humor of even the gravest situation inherent in the mind of the American, caricaturists and poetasters of the time should have seized upon this inglorious retreat of the President as a fit subject for the sharpening of their wits. One verse-maker parodied Scott's "Marmion," while another, finding a curious coincidence in the fact that the "flights of Mahomet, of John Gilpin, and the flight from Bladensburg all occurred on the 24th of August," proceeded to put forth a number of verses in which the President appears as acting the rôle of the "citizen of courage and renown." In these lines, which have attained a distinction quite out of proportion to their merit, Mr. Madison is represented as saying to the Secretary of War and the Attorney-General:

> "*Armstrong* and *Rush*, stay here in camp,
> I'm sure you're not afraid; —
> Ourself will now return; and you,
> *Monroe*, shall be our Aid.
>
> "And, *Winder*, do not fire your guns,
> Nor let your trumpets play,
> 'Till we are out of sight—forsooth,
> My horse will run away."

Whatever may have been the President's shortcomings, it seems, as we look back upon this period of storm and stress, that it was an unkind fate that placed the peace-loving statesman and scholar James Madison at the head of an administration which had inherited international complications that were predestined to lead to war.

More fortunate than her husband, Mrs. Madison, even in those perilous days, commanded the situation with her wonted grace and dignity. The most valiant soul in the White House, she remained at her post, guarding its treasures, as the President had admonished her to do when he set forth for Bladensburg. Unintimidated by the sight of friends and acquaintances making their escape from the city, of the officials of the State and Treasury Departments withdrawing with valuable papers, or even by the sound of guns at Bladensburg, Mrs. Madison calmly awaited the return of her husband. Cool and collected in the midst of confusion and dismay, she made ready for flight should it become necessary. In a letter written to her sister on August 23, when the British fleet had sailed up the Patuxent and landed their troops at Benedict, Maryland, about thirty miles southeast of Washington, Mrs. Madison said that the President had gone to join General Winder, and that she had received two dispatches from him desiring her to be ready, at a moment's warning, to enter her carriage and leave the city.

"I am acccordingly ready," she wrote. "I have pressed as many Cabinet papers into trunks as to fill one carriage. Our private property must be sacrificed, as it is impossible to procure wagons for its transportation. I am determined not to go myself until I see Mr. Madison safe and he can accompany me. My friends and acquaintances are all gone, even Colonel C—— with the hundred men, who were stationed as a guard in this enclosure. French John [a faithful servant] offers to spike the cannon at the gate, and lay a train of powder which will blow up the British should they enter the house. To this proposition I positively object, without being able, however, to make him understand why all advantages in war may not be taken."

Mr. and Mrs. Richard Cutts and their children were evidently with Mrs. Madison at this time, although she makes no mention of them in her letter to Mrs. Todd. They are all grouped together humorously in "The Bladensburg Races," in which Mrs. Madison is described as counselling flight, which she in reality delayed until she was in danger of being captured by the enemy.

"'Tomorrow then,' quoth she, 'we'll fly
As fast as we can pour
Northward, into Montgomery,
All in our coach and four.

"'My sister *Cutts*, and *Cutts*, and I,
And Cutts's children three,
Will fill the coach;—So you must ride
On horseback after we.'"

Among the friends who stopped at the White House to warn its mistress of her danger were Charles Carroll of Bellevue and Mrs. George W. Campbell. Mr. Campbell, then Secretary of the Treasury, was with the President, but his wife, having been told by an official of the War Department that the British would be in Washington in two hours, put on her bonnet and shawl and hastened to urge Mrs. Madison to leave the city. Two messengers also came from Mr. Madison urging flight. After these and other warnings Mrs. Madison consented to set forth without her husband, but not before she had secured the large picture of General Washington by Stuart, which was hanging in the dining-room, although she says that her kind friend Mr. Carroll was in a very bad humor with her on account of this delay.

So many tales have been told about the rescue of this picture, of its being cut out of the frame with a carving-knife by Mrs. Madison, or with a penknife by Mr. Carroll, and then conveyed to Arlington by Mr. Custis, that it may be of interest to read Mrs. Madison's own account of the affair and that of Mr. Jacob Barker, who was one of the gentlemen in whose hands she placed the portrait.*

* Mr. Jacob Barker was in Washington frequently before and after the war, as he was engaged in negotiating a ten-million-dollar loan for the government. His great financial ability and the confidence which his name inspired in business circles appears in his correspondence with Mr. George W. Campbell, Secretary of the Treasury, with his successor the Honorable Alexander J. Dallas, Charles J. Ingersoll, and other prominent men of the day. Mr. Ingersoll, writing to Mr. Barker, in May, 1814, after taking him to task for neglecting to visit him when he passed through Philadelphia, complimented him in high terms upon his services to the government by saying that he considered Mr. Barker's aid to the Treasury during the late crisis quite as important as that of Mr. Morris during the former struggle.

Of the unscrewing of the picture from the wall she wrote,—

"This process was found too tedious for these perilous moments. I have ordered the frame to be broken and the canvas taken out. It is done and the precious portrait placed in the hands of two gentlemen of New York for safe keeping. And now, dear sister, I must leave this house, or the retreating army will make me a prisoner in it by filling up the road which I am directed to take. When I shall again write to you or where I shall be to-morrow I cannot tell."

Mr. Barker's own account of the saving of this portrait entirely agrees with that of Mrs. Madison.* Writing to the son of Mr. Charles Carroll of Bellevue, the kind friend who had urged Mrs. Madison to leave the White House, Mr. Barker said,—

"As soon as our troops broke and retreated the President sent his servant express to warn his good lady of her danger, with directions to leave immediately. This messenger must have reached the White House by two o'clock, and Mrs. Madison, Mr. and Mrs. Cutts and servants left immediately thereafter. . . .

"Whether I found your father there [at the White House] or whether he came in subsequently, I do not know; but I do know that he assisted in taking down the portrait of Washington and left the house with the President, leaving the portrait on the floor of the room in which it had been suspended to take care of itself, where it remained until the remnant of our army, reduced to about four thousand, passed by, taking the direction of George-

* In a letter written by Mrs. Madison to Mr. Robert G. L. Depeyster, in 1848, she again corroborated Mr. Barker's statement with regard to the picture.

town, when the portrait was taken by Mr. [Robert G. L.] Depeyster and myself, assisted by two colored boys, from the said room; and with it we fell into the trail of the army and continued with it some miles.

"Overtaken by night and greatly fatigued, we sought shelter in a farm house. No other persons assisted in removing or preserving the picture."

In relating his experiences with this portrait, Mr. Barker was wont to speak of the interest shown by the inmates of the farm-house when they saw it,—one colored servant exclaiming, as she beheld the familiar features of the great General, that the city wouldn't have been taken if he'd been about.

After a lapse of a month or two, Mr. Barker returned to the farm-house where the painting had been left, and caused it to be taken back to Washington and delivered to Mrs. Madison. That good lady had the portrait reinstated in the White House as soon as it was rebuilt, encircled by an appropriate frame.

Miss Brown wrote that her mother and sister saw "Mrs. Madison in her carriage flying full speed through Georgetown, accompanied by an officer carrying a drawn sword. Where the poor fugitive found a refuge I did not learn."

From various reliable authorities it appears that Mrs. Madison's place of retreat was Rokeby, the country-seat of Mr. Richard H. Love, a mile or two beyond what is now known as the chain bridge.* Here the weary traveller found much-needed rest and refreshment, to which she was welcomed by the mistress of the house, although, probably for the first time in her life, she was grudgingly served by the domestics. When Mrs. Love told the old colored cook to hurry and make a cup of coffee for Mrs. Madison, who was suffering from the excitement and fatigue of the day, the cook replied, "I make a cup of coffee for you, Mis' Matilda, but I'm not gwine to hurry for Mis' Madison, for I done heerd Mr. Madison and Mr. Armstrong done sold the country to the British." This ignorant woman's words were evidently a reflection of the expressions that she heard on all sides with regard to the President and the Secretary of War, against whom popular feeling was very bitter at this time.

While Mrs. Madison was anxiously awaiting the arrival of her husband at Mr. Love's, Miss Brown describes herself and her friends as undergoing various trying experiences "by field and flood." This party, consisting of the Homans family, Mr. and Mrs. Obed Rich, Colonel and Mrs. Gardiner, and several children, spent the first night

* Rokeby, now a dairy-farm, is one of the interesting old places near Washington. Mr. Love, whose wife was Elizabeth Matilda Lee, named his country-seat after Sir Walter Scott's poem, "Rokeby," recently published, whose heroine, Matilda, bore the same name as his wife.

of their exile on the shores of the Potomac, where boats, fitted up with beds and such other comforts as could be hastily gathered together, were ready for flight on the ensuing day. While Mrs. Homan's maid prepared a scanty repast of ground rice and coffee, which was all the larder afforded, Miss Brown said that "the gentlemen of the party stood around a fire of blazing logs discussing the situation of affairs with General Van Ness, who had made his way up to our anchorage, while all gazed, from time to time, upon a large portion of the horizon illuminated by the burning Capitol and other public buildings."

As a proof that small matters will often occupy the mind in the midst of events of great importance, Miss Brown recalled, many years after, her keen regret at the loss of certain articles of dress in the course of this rapid flight, especially the destruction of a cherished pink and white bonnet.

"On leaving the city," she wrote, "I wore a bonnet that was considered just the style for a young lady of fifteen beginning to think her personal adornment of some importance; it was of white satin, gaily trimmed with pink; also, as was the fashion, a large shell comb. Being pretty tired, and having no place to make a proper night *toilette*, I tumbled down regardless of costume. After a refreshing nap, I waked finding myself still adorned by my white and pink satin night-cap, while a shower of rain was gently falling on my face. I suppose provisions were afterwards procured from the neighboring country, but the coffee and ground rice were our only supply for about thirty hours."

The next day, while being pulled up the Potomac by sturdy boatmen, a great storm overtook the little party, which necessitated their landing and sheltering themselves under the trees of the forest.

"The government papers and other valuables," says Miss Brown, "were covered with tarpaulins. Into the corners under these we crept, but failed to find entire protection from the deluges of rain. The boats were lashed together and to the trees on shore, which we were afterwards told bent over us like hoops, while the clouds seemed to pause over our devoted heads and pour down one continuous stream of electricity. How long this lasted I know not, I only have an abiding sense of my forlorn condition, wet and comfortless without a change of clothing. When the storm abated we again *put to sea*, in no condition to pass the night. As we were being pushed up stream, anxiously scanning the shore for some house where we might find shelter, we were so happy as to descry a log cabin known to the boatmen as the Hominy House."

The Hominy House, which stood near Cabin John, seems to have well deserved its name, as at this primitive inn "hog and hominy" was the *pièce de résistance* of each and every meal. Here the travellers were forced to content themselves for several days, with no amusement save that afforded them by their own good spirits and by Colonel Gardiner's amiable habit of sitting on a barrel and singing "Through all the changing scenes of life," when the dulness of the hours and the monotony of their fare became well nigh intolerable. It is pleasant to learn that this young girl, who bore so cheerfully the trials and hardships of her enforced journey, suffered no greater ill from exposure to the elements than the destruction of her cherished pink bonnet, and lived to relate to her children and to her children's children the incidents of her flight from the British.

The great storm on the afternoon of the 25th of August, which added so much to the discomfort of Miss Brown and her friends, caused the British to stop in their ruthless destruction of public offices, but not before the Capitol, the White House, the Treasury, and other buildings were sacked and burned. The Secretary of the Navy, Mr. Jones, had, before leaving the city, ordered the Navy Yard and some ships of war in the river to be set on fire, and the devastation thus begun was soon completed by the enemy.

Admiral Cockburn, after encouraging his men in their destruction of the Capitol, partaking of whatever good cheer was to be found in the White House and then applying the torch to its furniture, turned his attention to the office of the *National Intelligencer*, which journal had denounced Cockburn's practices on the coast. The rooms were sacked, the types thrown out of the window, and the books and papers piled up on the banks of the canal and burned. The building was spared, at the intercession of some women in the neighborhood, who guarded the premises in the absence of the men. By a strange coincidence some of the types were saved by a member of this feminine patrol, an Englishwoman who in her childhood had known Samuel Johnson, having lived in the same village, and perhaps for that reason had acquired a respect for letters.

Impeded in their work by the cyclone, which was almost as destructive in its way as the torch of the invader, and alarmed by a rumor which spread through the camp of the advance of American troops in large numbers, the British beat a hasty retreat from the city, leaving their dead unburied and their wounded uncared for.

It is only just to state that the vandalism of General Ross and Admiral Cockburn was bitterly denounced by the leading English journals of the day, while in Parliament the burning of the American Capitol was spoken of as a measure that exasperated the people without in the least weakening the government.

When the President and Mrs. Madison returned to Washington, after an absence of forty-eight hours, they found their home a black and still smoking ruin. For some months the Madisons occupied the home of Mr. and Mrs. Richard Cutts on F Street, from whence they removed to the Octagon, which was placed at their disposal through the generous hospitality of its owner, Colonel John Tayloe.

Colonel John Tayloe
By Gilbert Stuart

Mrs. John Tayloe
By Gilbert Stuart

Situated at the point where Eighteenth Street and New York Avenue meet, the rounded façade "set on the bias," like so many attractive buildings in Washington, the charming doorway offering its hospitality to both streets, the Octagon stands to-day lightly touched by the hand of time.

This house, which was begun in 1798 and completed in 1800, was designed by Dr. William Thornton, the architect of many buildings in Washington. Through the beautiful circular vestibule the most distinguished men of the first half of the century passed,—such soldiers and sailors as Jackson, Brown, Scott, Barney, Bainbridge, Porter, and Decatur; while Randolph, Clay, Webster, and Calhoun were familiar figures in the drawing-room, whether it was presided over by Mrs. Tayloe or Mrs. Madison. In the circular room over the entrance-hall, whose long windows once commanded an uninterrupted view of the Potomac, a notable group of statesmen assembled in February, 1815, when the Treaty of Ghent was signed.*

There was in 1814 considerable opposition to the reconstruction of the Capitol, and numerous arguments against it were brought forward by those in favor of the removal of the seat of government to another locality. The question of the

* The circular room of the Octagon is now used as the office of the American Institute of Architects, into whose guardianship the fine old house has passed.

rebuilding of both Capitol and White House upon the same sites was, however, settled at a special session of Congress, held in September, 1814, in the Great Hotel, once known as Blodget's Hotel. The work of restoring and refurnishing the White House was intrusted to James Hoban, its original architect, while Mr. Benjamin H. Latrobe was called from Pittsburg to draw plans for the reconstruction of the Capitol. In 1817 Mr. Latrobe resigned, and was succeeded by Mr. Charles Bulfinch, a Boston architect, who designed a dome much higher than the one proposed by Mr. Latrobe.

It was doubtless the unwelcome suggestion of the removal of the seat of government that stirred old Thomas Law's muse to a flight of fancy in which Columbia was represented as sitting grief-stricken and dismayed before the blackened ruins of the Capitol, while "smiling Liberty, with heavenly grace," urged her to raise her drooping head and hear and see, as she did with prophetic smile,

> "A peal of victory rung
> And a new edifice in splendor sprung,
> Like Phœnix from its ashes, while a sound
> Of triumph and rejoicing rose around."

VIII

PEACE AND PLENTY

AMID general rejoicings the season of 1815, "the peace winter," opened. The Madisons were established in the Octagon, which, having formed the habit of opening wide its doors during the residence of its hospitable owners, now as the home of the President and his wife closed them to none. Especially wide were these portals swung to admit the messengers of peace, whose good tidings, if not published upon the mountains, were noisily heralded across the plain by a coach-and-four that thundered along Pennsylvania Avenue one afternoon in February. Cheers greeted the carriage as it sped on its way to the Octagon, where a warm welcome awaited those who brought with them the Treaty of Ghent.

In the hours of rejoicing that followed the arrival of the peace commissioners, hospitality reigned in the house, which was crowded with visitors until midnight. Mrs. Madison received in the large parlor to the right of the entrance hall, while in the dining-room to the left good cheer was dispensed with a liberal hand. Tradition relates that the household servants were not overlooked in the general merry-making, as Miss Sally

Coles flew to the basement stairs, crying, "Peace, peace," while the distribution of meats and drinks in their quarters was so bountiful and the good cheer was partaken of so joyously that French John was incapacitated for service for some days.

While the President and his Cabinet officers were engaged with the commissioners, Mrs. Madison flitted from room to room and from guest to guest, her face reflecting the happiness that warmed every heart. Whatever mistakes the President may have made were forgotten in the gladness of the hour, and more than one writer has said that Mrs. Madison was at that time the most popular person in the United States. Friends old and new gathered around her to offer their congratulations, the soldiers marching home stopped before the house to cheer her, and the special ambassador from Great Britain, Sir Charles Bagot, declared that the wife of the republican President looked every inch a queen.

The rejoicings over the signing of the Treaty of Ghent had scarcely subsided when news of General Jackson's victory over the British at New Orleans reached the capital and called for renewed festivities.* Washington was so gay during the

* The fact that the battle of New Orleans was fought while the peace commissioners were on their way to America affords a notable illustration of the slow communication of news between the different States of the Union.

winter of 1815 that it would have been difficult to believe it had so recently known war and devastation had it not been for those silent witnesses, the ruined Capitol and White House, whose charred remains were blots upon the smiling plain.

Mr. Benjamin H. Latrobe was at work upon plans for the new and improved Capitol, while, as Mrs. Seaton wrote some months later,

> "About fifty members have arrived and marked their seats in the new building on Capitol Hill, erected for their accommodation by old Mr. Law, Carroll, and others, who wished to enhance the value of their property."

This building, near the eastern grounds of the Capitol, whether erected from motives of public spirit or of private gain, was used by the government for several years, and was long after known as the "Old Capitol."

Popular enthusiasm reached fever-heat the following autumn, when General Jackson visited Washington. Balls, receptions, dinners, and plays were given in honor of the hero of New Orleans.

One chronicler of the time has spoken of Mrs. Jackson as being in Washington with her husband in 1815. There is no proof of this, however, and everything connected with the General's visit points to her not having accompanied him. Indeed, the fact that General Jackson made the long journey to the capital on horseback seems to preclude the idea that his wife was with him.

One of the interesting social events of the last year of Mr. Madison's administration was a ball given at Annapolis in honor of the President and his wife, when they went to the Maryland capital to visit the "seventy-four" which was to carry Mr. William Pinkney on his mission to Russia.* Mrs. Seaton, who went to Annapolis with her husband, and, like the Madisons, stopped *en route* at the home of Judge Duvall, where they were enter tained with "every luxury in and out of season," described this Annapolis ball as a brilliant affair. "Every one was there," wrote the vivacious lady, "Governor and Mrs. Ridgely, General Scott, Rogers, Porter, Mrs. Rush, Mrs. Loundes, Captain Chauncey and his wife, who all fraternized very cordially."

Mrs. Seaton attempted no description of this vessel, then considered a wonder of the seas, whose inspection was the ostensible cause of the jaunt to Annapolis, as she said that to give any idea of the interior of such a magnificent man-of-war tran-

---

* William Pinkney, of Maryland, a statesman of great ability, who was one of the commissioners sent to England under John Jay in 1796. Mr. Pinkney was minister to England in 1806, and was in 1816 appointed to represent his country at the court of St. Petersburg.

scended her power. During the visit to the ship this amiable chronicler noticed that "the little President was as gay as a lark, and jested very humorously on the incidents of their journey; the cares of state thrown off his shoulders completely metamorphosed him and relaxed his frigidity amazingly."

A few months later the cares of state were finally relinquished by Mr. Madison, he and his wife turned their faces towards Montpelier, and James Monroe, his friend, reigned in his stead. To this important position Mr. Monroe seemed to be the natural successor, the Presidency having come to him at fifty-nine, after forty years spent in the service of his country. As a lad of nineteen he had commanded a company of Virginia volunteers during the Revolution, and in the years that followed he had represented his State in the Senate, acted as its chief executive, and at the most important formative period of the government had represented his country as minister to France, England, and Spain.

The ceremonies attending the inauguration of the fifth President of the United States were held in the open air, as had been those of the first President. This change, which is said to have been made to prevent any wrangling about seats on the part of the members of the Senate and House, was favored by the heavens, which beamed benignly upon the new Executive. March being of a capricious temper, and her smiles not to be counted upon, Mr. Monroe was fortunate in being able to deliver his inaugural address from the unfinished portico of the Capitol amid balmy breezes. Inauguration day four years later, was, however, ushered in by a storm of rain and snow.

One of the journals of the day recorded that the ceremonies attending the inauguration of James Monroe were "simple but grand, animating and impressive. The President and lady received at their dwelling the visits of their friends and of the heads of the departments. The evening concluded by a ball at Davis's, which was attended by the President and his family."

Mrs. Monroe, who had in her girlhood entered into the social life of New York and had seen much of the gay world of London and Paris, was admirably fitted to do the honors of the White House with grace and dignity. Some writers of the time have spoken of the President's wife as having been too great an invalid to enter into the gayeties of the capital. Whether ill or well, Mrs. Monroe had seen enough of the social life of the last administration to realize that, with the increase of the Congressional and Senatorial representation and the influx of visitors from other cities, the social duties of the White House were becoming too arduous to be conducted upon the generous lines established by Mrs. Madison. Mrs. Seaton wrote in 1818:

"It is said that the dinner-parties of Mrs. Monroe will be very select. Mrs. Hay, daughter of Mrs. Monroe, returned the visits paid to her mother, making assurances, in the most pointedly polite manner, that Mrs. Monroe will be happy to see her friends morning or evening, but that her health is totally inadequate to visiting at present! Mrs. Hay is understood to be her proxy."

Such proportions did the subject of visiting in official circles assume, that Mr. Adams, the Secretary of State, was called upon to draw up a code of social etiquette. This code, which was in its main features similar to that of President Washington, has, with a few modifications, regulated the official life of the capital from that time until our own. It was again decreed, as in the days of Washington, Adams, and Jefferson, that the President and his wife should not be expected to make or return visits.

Indeed, it seemed as if the mistress of the White House fulfilled her duty to the public when she received one evening in each week the miscellaneous assemblage that gathered around her. Here, according to one of the leading papers,

"in addition to the secretaries, senators, foreign Ministers, consuls, auditors, accountants, officers of the Army and Navy of every grade, were farmers, merchants, parsons, priests, lawyers, judges, auctioneers and nothingarians, all with their wives, and some with their gawky offspring ; some in shoes, most in boots, and many in spurs; some snuffing, others chewing and many longing for their cigars and whiskey punch at home."

Some offence Mrs. Monroe undoubtedly gave by what certain persons were pleased to call her exclusiveness, especially, says Dr. Busey, "among the 'old Washington families,' just then beginning to lay claim to antiquity." Her limitations, however, being dictated by a good sense and good taste, must have been gratefully appreciated by her successors in the White House.

Mrs. George Hay, Mrs. Monroe's elder daughter, assisted her in her social duties. In March, 1820, Maria Monroe married her cousin, Mr. Samuel L. Gouverneur, of New York, who was acting as Mr. Monroe's private secretary. This wedding, according to Mrs. Seaton and other chroniclers, was conducted in the New York style, which seems to have been distinctly exclusive, as only the relatives, the attendant bridesmaids and groomsmen, and a few old friends of the family witnessed the ceremony, which was solemnized in the East Room of the newly rebuilt and refurnished White House.

Miss Ann Albertina Van Ness wrote to her friend Miss Ann Chew, in Philadelphia, telling her that Maria Monroe's wedding was the absorbing topic of conversation in the capital at that time. Miss Mason, she says, had been to see her to hold a consultation, as they were both to be Maria Monroe's bridesmaids. Miss Van Ness, who thought it so amusing that her old schoolmate "little Rias" should so soon be Mrs. Gouverneur, was herself destined before long to become the bride of Arthur Middleton, son of Governor Middleton, of South Carolina. The other bridesmaid to whom Miss Van Ness referred as Miss Mason was a sister of James Murray Mason, Senator from Virginia, who had recently married Miss Chew of Philadelphia.

A drawing-room was held at the White House a few days after Miss Monroe's wedding, when the Washington world was afforded an opportunity to pay its respects to the bride. This reception inaugurated a series of festivities. Commodore and Mrs. Decatur gave a grand ball in honor of Mr. and Mrs. Gouverneur, invitations were out for an entertainment at the home of Albertina Van Ness and at other houses, when the wedding gayeties were suddenly interrupted by the sad termination of the duel between Barron and Decatur. This encounter took place at Bladensburg, both combatants fell wounded at the first shot, and Commodore Decatur was taken to his home on Lafayette Square, where he died in a few hours. The house, which had been the scene of gayety and happiness a few days before, was now shrouded in gloom.

No more significant or pathetic page is to be found in the whole history of duelling than that which represents these two good sailors and patriots lying wounded upon the field of Bladensburg, exchanging all too late the few words of explanation that would have entirely cleared up the misunderstanding that led to their unfortunate encounter.

Mrs. Seaton's letters reflect the prevalent feeling with regard to the duel. She speaks of

> "the *murder* of Decatur which will prevent any further attentions to the President's family. . . . The explanation which took place *after* the encounter, and before they were removed from the ground, would have prevented it. So *many* friends were privy to this intended duel, that it appears most extraordinary it should not have reached the ears of the President, who alone could have averted it. Mr. Wirt, Bomford, Rogers, Porter, Bainbridge, General Harper, his father-in-law, Mr. Wheeler, all, all kept secret, though they did everything else to prevent it."

Public sentiment was strong against Commodore Barron at this time. He recovered, contrary to all expectations, and outlived the prejudice against him, as it was generally admitted that he had been placed by Decatur in a most unfortunate position.

The widow of Commodore Decatur soon after his death removed from the house at the corner of H Street, facing Lafayette Square, which is still spoken of as the Decatur house, and established herself at Kalorama. After a period of seclusion she laid aside her mourning, and her home was soon known as the most hospitable in the capital.

Mrs. Edward Livingston, who came to Washington two years later when her husband represented Louisiana in the Senate, evidently found much at Kalorama to compensate her for the social delights of New Orleans.

> "There are," she wrote, "elements here to form very good society, but dispersed on so large a space that people are seldom brought together, except in immensely crowded assemblies, where it matters little whether a man is a fool or not, provided he can fight his way through. There is, however, one exception to this ; it is at Mrs. Decatur's ; she has small evening parties, where you meet by turn every person of distinction in Washington—foreign ministers, chargés d'affaires, etc., etc. To be admitted into her set is a favor granted to comparatively few, and of course desired by all. We are among the highly favored, having been invited three times in one week. . . .
>
> "Mrs. Monroe is certainly the Ninon of the day, and looks more beautiful than any woman of her age I ever saw. . . . She did the honors of the White House with perfect simplicity, nothing disturbed the composure of her manner. Around her were grouped Mrs. Adams, Mrs. Crawford, Mrs. Rush, and Mrs. Hays, the daughter of Mr. Monroe, who had been intimate at the school of Madame Campan with Hortense Beauharnais after whom she named her daughter Hortensia."

The friendship between Mrs. George Hay and the daughter of Josephine lasted during their lives.

In a letter written to Mrs. Hay in 1823 Queen Hortense speaks of sending her portrait to her god-daughter. This portrait is still carefully preserved in the family, many of whom speak of the strong resemblance that existed between Hortensia Monroe Hay and her royal god-mother. Hortensia Hay became the second wife of Mr. Lloyd Nicholas Rogers, of Baltimore, whose first wife was Eliza Law.

Mrs. Livingston, whom Edward Livingston had married in New Orleans when she was a widow of nineteen, was still in the perfection of her matronly beauty when she came to Washington. In addition to her personal attractions, she was intelligent, a charming *raconteuse*, and possessed the power of gathering around her the most interesting men and women of her time. The salon of Mrs. Livingston soon became famous in the capital of the nation, as it had been in the chief city of Louisiana. Here were to be met the great Chief Justice John Marshall, the Associate Justices Joseph Story and Bushrod Washington, and the members of that unrivalled group of politicians who, whatever might be their differences in public, were too closely allied by mental affinities not to enjoy together the pleasures of social intercourse. Clay, Calhoun, Webster, Wirt, and Randolph were frequently the guests of Mrs. Livingston, often after a sharp debate in the House or Senate had placed them on opposite sides of the lists. After listening to the conversation of these able men, the hostess would sometimes confide to a friend that, brilliant and eloquent as they were, she had never talked to any one who could compare with her brother-in-law, Chancellor Livingston. It is quite evident that the critical and sometimes querulous John Randolph yielded unwavering allegiance to the charms of the Southern matron, as, in writing to Mr. Livingston in 1833, when he had been offered the position of minister to France, Mr. Randolph said,—

> "Let me conjure you to accept the mission to France, for which you are better qualified than any man in the United States. In Mrs. Livingston, to whom present my warmest respects, you have a most able coadjutor. *Dowdies*, dowdies won't do for European courts, Paris especially. There and at London the character of the minister's wife is almost as important as his own. It is the very place for her. There she would dazzle and charm, and surely the salons of Paris must have far greater attractions for her than the yahoos of Washington."

Among Mrs. Livingston's chosen associates were Mrs. Adams, whose intellectual tastes made a close bond between these women, although their husbands differed so widely upon political subjects; Mrs. Van Rensselaer, the wife of the Patroon; and Mrs. Andrew Stevenson, the Sally Coles of earlier days.

Other attractive women in Washington at this time were Mrs. Crawford and Mrs. Calhoun, whose husbands were destined to be the rivals of Mr. Adams and General Jackson in the curious, several-sided contest for the Presidency in 1824. Mrs. Crawford, wife of the Secretary of War, although cultivated, charming, and fitted to shine in society, was so simple in her tastes that she deplored her husband's entrance into political life, as it would compel them to relinquish to a considerable extent their domestic habits. Mr. Crawford, who was once so close to the Presidency, is described as a man of high integrity and great social charm, as well as of superior mental endowments.

Mrs. Calhoun, the wife of another member of the Presidential quintette of 1824, a South Carolina girl and a cousin of her husband, was often in Washington during the Madison and Monroe administrations. Of this charming young matron Mrs. Seaton wrote,—

"I have mentioned the very agreeable accession to our neighborhood in the Calhouns. You could not fail to love and appreciate, as I do, her charming qualities; a devoted mother, tender wife, industrious, cheerful, intelligent, with the most perfectly equable temper. Mr. Calhoun is a profound statesman and elegant scholar, you know the public report; but his manners in a private circle are endearing, as well as captivating; and it is as much impossible not to love him at home as it would be to refuse your admiration of his oratorical powers in the Hall of Representatives."

Judge Campbell, who had been appointed minister to Russia by Mr. Monroe, returned to America before the Presidential campaign of 1824. Mrs. Campbell, once charming Harriot Stoddert, wrote many interesting letters from St. Petersburg, and during her travels on the continent met the brilliant and erratic Madame Krüdener. This high-priestess of mysticism, who exerted so powerful an influence over the Emperor Alexander that he submitted to her his draft of the Holy Alliance, Mrs. Campbell described as a delicate blonde who was always dressed in blue.

While at St. Petersburg Mr. and Mrs. Campbell met with a severe affliction in the loss of their three young children, who had died about the time the Emperor Alexander lost his only surviving child. In consequence of their common sorrow the Emperor and Empress showed Mrs. Campbell great kindness and consideration, sending her messages of sympathy and insisting that their own physician should attend her and her child in an illness that followed the death of her little ones.

When Mrs. Campbell had sufficiently recovered her health to bear the fatigue of a drive to the palace, notice was sent her that the Empress would receive her on a certain day. Mrs. Campbell wrote to a member of her family, that although her great sorrow had deprived her of all inclination to go anywhere, she was told that it was still considered expedient that she should be presented to the reigning Empress, having already been presented to the Empress dowager, who received her during the illness of her daughter-in-law.

"After the usual forms, I went last Sunday," wrote Mrs. Campbell, "it being always the day presentations take place, and was received in so kind a manner that it is a gratification to me that I went. I was made to sit down on the same canopy with the Empress, he (the Emperor) sat close by; they showed a great deal of feeling and commiseration for our dreadful loss and dispensed with many of the usual formalities; such as being entirely alone, having no maids of Honor as is usual: making me sit down, offering me her cheek both when I went in, and when I came away. The Emperor put my shawl on and accompanied me through two or three rooms."

Mrs. Campbell in other letters spoke of the delicate kindness and simplicity of manner of this royal pair. Alexander I., the handsomest man in Europe, and his lovely young Empress impressed her more as sorrowing parents than as great sovereigns. A daughter was born to Mr. and Mrs. Campbell while in Russia. To this child they gave the charming name of the young Empress, Lizinka.

In the early part of December, 1824, before the result of the recent election had been officially

Mrs. George W. Campbell
By George Dawe, R.A.

announced, General Jackson and his wife reached the capital. His presence there is explained by the fact that he was United States Senator from Tennessee; but those who knew him best felt that he was confident of his election to the Presidency. It later appeared, from the report of that mysterious body known as the Electoral College, that although General Jackson had received a plurality of votes no President had been elected. The country having failed in its duty, it devolved upon the House of Representatives to elect a President from the three candidates who had received the highest number of votes, Jackson, Adams, and Crawford. This has always been spoken of as the time when Henry Clay elected a President. His own electoral vote being too small to entitle him to enter into the competition, he for some reason threw his great influence in the House of Representatives in favor of Mr. Adams.

Many and various were the descriptions given of General Jackson as he appeared then and later. Mrs. Seaton spoke of him as "not striking in appearance; his features are hard favored (as our Carolinians say) his complexion sallow, and his person *small*." This last was evidently a mistake, as the General was undoubtedly tall; and a curious mistake to be made by an observing woman and one who frequently met him during his stay in Washington. Colonel Robert J. Chester, who had served under General Jackson at New Orleans, recalling his impressions of his old commander, related with great pride that he had worn a suit of the General's clothes after being overtaken by a storm on his way to the Hermitage. The old gentleman, who was of tall and commanding figure, drew himself to his full height, exclaiming, "His clothes fit me exactly, shoes and all. We were just the same height, six feet one." When in Philadelphia as Senator from Tennessee, Jackson, then about thirty, was described by Mr. Gallatin as "a tall, lank, uncouth-looking personage, with long locks of hair hanging over his face, and a cue down his back tied in an eel-skin; his dress singular, his manners and deportment that of a backwoodsman."

Other and much later writers have stated that the frontier soldier was rough and unpolished; and while there is abundant proof that he was at times harsh and vindictive, a long series of years of association with people of the better sort lay between Jackson the backwoodsman and the victor of the battle of New Orleans whom Mrs. Edward Livingston and her friends pronounced "a prince."

The various and conflicting opinions expressed about this man led Josiah Quincy to suggest that there were two Jacksons, one the person whom he himself had attempted to describe, the other "the

Jackson of comic myth." Mr. Quincy's own impressions of the General are perhaps those to be most relied upon, especially as he prefaces his description by explaining that he was not prepared to be favorably impressed by a man who was simply intolerable to the Brahmin caste of his native State.

"Although I have only a holiday acquaintance with the General," wrote Mr. Quincy, "and although a man certainly puts on his best manners when undergoing a public reception, the fact was borne in upon me that the seventh President was, in essence, a knightly personage,—prejudiced, narrow, mistaken upon many points, it might be, but vigorously a gentleman in his high sense of honor and in the natural straightforward courtesies which are easily to be distinguished from the veneer of policy."

Mr. Parton's estimate of the impression made by Andrew Jackson perfectly coincides with that of the observing Bostonian. He says that Jackson was far from handsome; only one feature of his face was not commonplace,—his eyes, which were deep blue and capable of blazing with great expression when roused. But his face, owing to the quick, distinct glance of the man, produced on others more than the effect of beauty; hence the old people, especially the women of Jackson's State, were wont to talk of him as a handsome man. He evidently possessed, as his biographer says, "that mysterious, omnipotent something which we call a *presence*. He was one of those who convey to strangers the impression that they are somebody; who naturally, and without thinking of it, *take the lead.*"

Mrs. Jackson was an exceedingly retiring, domestic woman who shrank from publicity; but it is quite evident from several of her letters which have been preserved that she was by no means the illiterate person some of the later campaign gossip and songs have represented her. Colonel Chester and other contemporaries have spoken of Mrs. Jackson as a well-bred and most exemplary woman. Her father, John Donelson, Colonel Chester said, was a proud man, and had left Virginia because one of his daughters married the hammerer in his furnace, while Bishop Meade, in speaking of the churches of Pittsylvania parishes, said that John Donelson was one of the vestrymen of the Reverend Mr. Guilliam's church, to whom a grant of land was conveyed for the church by Mr. Chamberlaine.

These circumstances and the marriage connections made by members of Mrs. Jackson's family indicate that her people held a good position among border settlers. Despite the rude, almost barbaric, simplicity of the frontier settlements, so rapid was the migration of people of standing from the Eastern and Southern States in the first quarter of the century that there soon came to be an aristocracy among the inhabitants of the border.

Nashville, which was the town nearest to General Jackson's home, the Hermitage, has been called the Philadelphia of the South. With its leading families—the Campbells, Overtons, Rutledges, Browns, Ewings, and Grundys—the Jacksons were evidently upon familiar terms.

In one of her letters Mrs. Seaton wrote,—

"Immediately on Mrs. Jackson's arrival a dilemma was presented, and a grand debate ensued as to whether the ladies would visit her. . . . Colonel Reid and Dr. Goodlet, the friends of years of General Jackson, having settled the question of propriety satisfactorily, all doubts were laid aside."

The dilemma of the Washington women was probably due to some rumors that had reached the capital of the irregularity of General Jackson's marriage. These tales were revived later and, with many variations, were made campaign issues. The explanation given by the General's friends being, as Mrs. Seaton states, accepted, the social leaders of the small society of Washington called upon Mrs. Jackson. Indeed, the General was not a man to have tolerated any lack of respect shown to his wife, to whom he was devotedly attached.

Soon after her arrival in Washington Mrs. Jackson wrote to her friend Mrs. Kingsley, of Nashville, giving her impressions of the Marquis de Lafayette and of the unaccustomed life of the capital. This letter is interesting, because of its frankness and simplicity, and for the revelation it affords of the sincerity and deep religious feeling of the writer:

"The present moment is the first I can call my own since my arrival in this great city. Our journey, indeed, was fatiguing. We were twenty-seven days on the road, but no accident happened to us. My husband is in better health than when we came. We are boarding in the same house with the nation's guest, Lafayette. I am delighted with him. All the attentions, all the parties he goes to never appear to have any effect on him. In fact, he is an extraordinary man. He has a happy talent of knowing those he has once seen. For instance, when we first came to this house, the General said he would go and pay the Marquis the first visit. Both having the same desire, and at the same time, they met on the entry of the stairs. It was truly interesting. The emotion of revolutionary feeling was aroused in them both. At Charleston General Jackson saw him on the field of battle; the one a boy of twelve, the Marquis twenty-three. He wears a wig, and is a little inclined to corpulency. He is very healthy, eats hearty, goes to every party, and that is every night.

"To tell you of this city, I would not do justice to the subject. The extravagance is in dressing and running to parties; but I must say they regard the Sabbath, and attend preaching, for there are churches of every denomination and able ministers of the gospel. We have been here two Sabbaths. The General and myself were both days at church. . . . Oh, my dear friend, how shall I get through this bustle. There are not less than from fifty to one hundred persons calling in a day. . . . Don't be afraid of my giving way to those vain things. The apostle says, I can do all things in Christ, who strengtheneth me. The play-actors sent me a letter requesting my countenance to them. No. A ticket to balls and parties. No, not one. Two dinings; several times to drink tea. Indeed, Mr. Jackson encourages me in my course."

Mrs. Jackson may have persisted in declining to "countenance the play-actors," but she was undoubtedly persuaded by her husband to accept some of the civilities offered her, as Mrs. Seaton spoke of her as being present at a ball given by General Brown in January.* At this entertainment, the result of the election by the House of Representatives not having been announced, Mrs. Seaton reported that the different candidates were delightfully jocose with one another. An amusing encounter took place at a ball at Mr. Calhoun's about this time. Mr. Adams was standing among the dancers with Mrs. Seaton, when Mr. Clay passed in high spirits, saying that he was much in the way of the dancers, or, rather, that they were troublesome to him. "Oh, that is very unkind," exclaimed Mr. Adams; "you who get out of everybody else's way, you know." This dry joke, which evidently referred to Mr. Clay's exclusion from the House of Representatives, was received in good part, and both statesmen laughed heartily.

* General Jacob Brown, of Bucks County, Pennsylvania, began his career by teaching school and surveying. During the war of 1812 he commanded a brigade with such distinction that he has been spoken of as sharing the honors in the Northern States with Scott, Porter, and Harrison.

In August, 1824, the American nation greeted with enthusiastic and sincere welcome the gallant French nobleman who when a young man had cast his lot with the struggling republic. As an additional proof of his interest and affection General Lafayette brought with him to the United States his son-in-law and his son George Washington Lafayette.

Lafayette was received in Washington in October. Mr. William Seaton was secretary of the committee of arrangements, whose pleasant duty it was to meet the guests of the hour in Baltimore and escort them to the capital. In later years, when recurring to the Marquis's appreciation of the good cheer of a city famous for its culinary triumphs, Mr. Seaton said that one breakfast in Baltimore was especially impressed upon his mind, when

"the guest was enthusiastic in his enjoyment of the fine bay perch, six of which he consumed, bread *à discretion*, all washed down with generous Bordeaux; the culmination of his enthusiasm, however, being reserved for the unsurpassed canvas-back duck and hominy; and so constantly was the General in the open air with receptions, processions, and speeches,—the excitement naturally inducing an unusual appetite,—that the consumption of a whole duck would be the tribute paid by him to the excellence of our unequalled Southern winged delicacy, the enjoyment of which a subsequent distinguished traveller, Lord Morpeth, declared to be worth a voyage across the Atlantic."

Mrs. William Seaton was selected to superintend the dress and decoration of the twenty-five young girls, representing the States of the Union and the District of Columbia, who were to welcome the French guests. Of this picturesque company of girls in uniform, with long blue scarfs, curling hair, their pretty heads adorned with wreaths of eglantine, Mrs. Seaton was the captain, or "the priestess," as she styled herself, leading her gay little troop in a gown of white muslin decorated with blue ribbons. It was the pleasant duty of a little maid representing the District, Miss Watterson, aged eleven, to deliver a message of welcome to M. le Marquis, after which each one of the twenty-five girls gave her hand to the visitor, by whom it was affectionately kissed.

In one of her letters Mrs. Seaton spoke of meeting the Marquis at General Brown's ball. This was on the evening of the 13th, after he had dined in state at the White House with Mr. Monroe. Major-General Jacob Brown, General Alexander Macomb, Commodore Tingey, and General Walter Jones, Commander-in-Chief of the District Militia, were among those who met General Lafayette and conducted him to his lodgings at the Franklin House.* General Jones also met

* The Franklin House, on the corner of Pennsylvania Avenue and Nineteenth Street, had been recently opened, and was kept by Gadsby, whose name it bore for many years.

the Marquis de Lafayette in Alexandria with a military escort, and rode with him in a coach-and-four under the floral arch that spanned Washington Street, and between lines of happy children who strewed flowers in the path of the visitor, and sang to him gay little songs of welcome.

Soon after his arrival in Washington General Lafayette begged to be excused from public ceremonials for a few hours, as he wished to pay his respects to some friends in Georgetown. The General's first visit was to Tudor Place, the home of Mrs. Thomas Peter, whom he had known as a child. He afterwards dined with Mrs. Peter and her family, and visited her brother, Mr. Custis, at Arlington, and spent an evening at the home of Colonel John Cox, Mayor of Georgetown. At Mount Vernon General Lafayette and his sons were received by Mr. George Washington Parke Custis, Mr. Lewis, a nephew of General Washington, and other gentlemen of the family, Judge Bushrod Washington being absent at this time.

This visit to the home of his old Commander-in-chief, by whom he had been treated like a son, must have stirred many pleasant memories in the mind of the sensitive and affectionate Frenchman. Lafayette and his son George had both been guests of Washington at Mount Vernon, and if

Tudor Place, Georgetown

Built by Thomas Peter

the father recalled with emotion the hospitalities of the mansion extended to him so graciously by the host and hostess forty years before, the son, now a middle-aged man, could not have revisited Mount Vernon without remembering the kindness that he had received there in the days when his father was a prisoner and the fortunes of the Lafayette family were at the lowest ebb.

After visiting the capital and the large Eastern cities, Lafayette and his suite made a tour through the Southern and Western States. In all of the cities which they visited the principal citizens welcomed the distinguished guests with speeches, processions, banquets, and rejoicings, while the most beautiful matrons and maids graced the receptions and balls, in some instances strewing flowers in the path of the "hero of two worlds." It is related that at one of these receptions Lafayette asked each young man who was presented to him whether he was married or single. If the reply was in the affirmative, the genial Frenchman would exclaim "Happy fellow!" while if in the negative, he would ejaculate, with delightful impartiality, "Lucky dog!"

In Nashville General Jackson, who had ardently supported the bill which provided for the payment of the nation's debt to Lafayette, was on the committee to receive him, and presided over one end of the table at the banquet given to the Marquis, while Judge Campbell did the honors of the other end of the table.

When Lafayette returned to Washington, in December, Mrs. Seaton gave a grand ball in his honor, which, she said,

"was attended by all of the Cabinet except Mr. Crawford who could not come, Mr. J. Q. Adams and his family, and every member of the diplomatic corps, except the Baron de Mareuil and family, the French Minister, who are *en grand deuil* for the King of France, and by court etiquette are precluded from society for three months. I regret their absence, as Madame Mareuil is an excellent and very attractive woman, superior to the generality of her countrywomen whom I have met."

The *grand deuil* for King Louis did not prevent the Marquis de Lafayette and his suite from attending the Seaton ball and many other entertainments. One especially attractive occasion was an evening at Mrs. Bomford's, when Lafayette visited her home informally. Mrs. Seaton explained that the Marquis had been intimate with Joel Barlow while he was in France, which was his reason for making an exception in favor of Mrs. Bomford, who was Mr. Barlow's sister-in-law.

"I found no company," wrote Mrs. Seaton, "but the families of Mr. Cutts (brother-in-law of Mrs. Madison) and General Dearborn, old friends of ours both; and we passed a most agreeable and charming evening, from whence we accompanied the General to the concert. We had much plain, pleasant conversation, in which the benevolent old hero participated with all the characteristic ardor of an accomplished Frenchman."

While Lafayette was in the United States a bill passed both Houses granting him a township of twenty-four thousand acres and two hundred thousand dollars,—a generous but well deserved recognition of the nation's debt to him.

During his final visit to Washington, in the autumn of 1825, the Marquis was the guest of Mr. and Mrs. Adams at the White House. In September, 1825, when the honored and beloved visitor bade his final farewell to America, all business was suspended in the capital and a vast assemblage of distinguished citizens accompanied him to the shores of the Potomac, where he set sail in a new frigate that had been named the "Brandywine" in his honor. From the first hour that the Marquis de Lafayette landed in New York to that upon which he set sail from Washington in the "Brandywine," his visit had been an emphatic and graceful refutation of the timeworn charge that republics are ungrateful.

IX

CLASSICS AND COTILLIONS

AN interesting and unique home life was that of the estimable couple who presided over the White House in 1825. Mr. Adams, despite a conscientious and painstaking performance of all official duties, found time to read several chapters of the Bible with the aid of commentaries each day, and to gather his children about him for an occasional excursion into the classics. After one of these readings, the father expressed his disappointment that his sons had no relish for literature, not having enjoyed Pope's "Messiah" as he had done in boyhood. Mrs. Adams, with charming versatility, wrote poems, sang to her harp, and translated Plato with her sons in the pauses of social duties, which had been almost as exacting while her husband was Secretary of State as when he was President.

John Quincy Adams, the only one of all the long line of our Presidents who followed his father into the Executive office, although one of the best trained officers the country has ever possessed, was the least popular of Presidents. The singular reserve and coldness of Mr. Adams's manner are well illustrated by the following anecdote in which a frontier soldier appeared to much greater advantage than the scholarly Chief Executive, whose training in diplomatic life began at the early age of fourteen. Mr. S. D. Goodrich recalled, in after-years, a meeting between Mr. Adams and General Jackson at a White House reception given soon after the election of the former to the Presidency:

"It chanced in the course of the evening that these two persons, involved in the throng, approached each other from opposite directions, yet without knowing it. Suddenly, as they were almost together, the persons around, seeing what was to happen, by a sort of instinct stepped aside and left them face to face. Mr. Adams was by himself, General Jackson had a large handsome lady on his arm. They looked at each other for a moment and then General Jackson moved forward, and reaching out his long arm, said: 'How do you do, Mr. Adams? I give you my left hand, for the right, as you see, is devoted to the fair: I hope you are very well, sir.' All this was gallantly and heartily said and done. Mr. Adams took the general's hand, and said, with chilling coldness: 'Very well, sir; I hope General Jackson is well?' It was curious to see the western planter, the Indian fighter, the stern soldier, who had written his country's glory in the blood of the enemy at New Orleans, genial and gracious in the midst of a court, while the old courtier and diplomat was stiff, rigid, cold as a statue! It was all the more remarkable from the fact that, four hours before, the former had been defeated, and the latter was the victor, in a struggle for one of the highest objects of human ambition."

Mr. Adams is described as genial and kindly in private life, combining in a marked degree a certain punctiliousness of speech and manner with extreme simplicity in daily habits. It was his custom to rise at five in the morning, in order to have a walk under the star-lit skies in winter or a swim in the Potomac when the weather was mild, and then to study the Scriptures for an hour before breakfast; after which tonic, physical and moral, the President entered upon the ordinary duties of the day.

Mrs. Adams, like her husband, was domestic in her tastes, as well as a lover of literature. The most scholarly woman who has presided over the White House, she possessed the adaptability of a Frenchwoman, or of an American, and could turn gracefully from her books or her family cares to inaugurate certain much needed reforms in official circles. By her grace, tact, and *savoir faire* Mrs. Adams did much to neutralize the effect of the President's cold and often forbidding manner.

Born and educated abroad, although of American parentage, being the daughter of Joshua Johnson, American consul in London, Louisa Catherine Adams, by her early training and her experience of the official life of several of the European courts, was admirably fitted to preside over the White House. The weekly levees, inaugurated by Mrs. Washington and continued by Mrs. Madison, were once more held by Mrs. Adams, who introduced the custom of having refreshments handed to the guests,—a service that must have required considerable skill in those days, and would be impossible in our own time.

The foreign ministers endeavored to have certain days set apart for their reception at the White House, that they might not be obliged to encounter the motley throng of Americans, so distasteful to them. To this Mr. and Mrs. Adams were too democratic in their ideas or too politic to consent, and all classes of society mingled in the throng that crowded the audience chamber and surged on into the great East Room, as in the public receptions of to-day. The hours were still early. The guests assembled at eight, the lights in the drawing-rooms were out and the house wrapped in silence before eleven o'clock.

Mr. Josiah Quincy, who visited the capital in the winter of 1826, spoke of evening-parties as features of the Washington life of the time. The company, he said, assembled at eight o'clock, and, following the wise fashion of the Executive Mansion, the entertainment was well over before midnight. Music, dancing, conversation, and card-playing enlivened the evening. Those who indulged in the latter amusement did not hesitate to play for money, and an amount of gambling that would be considered quite reprehensible in our day was carried on in the "best circles" of the capital. A story is told of a Boston lady who, in talking to Mrs. Henry Clay, asked her with remarkable frankness if it did not distress her to have her brilliant husband gamble. "Sometimes, yes," replied the ingenuous Kentucky woman, "but really he almost always wins."

Among the many graceful acts of Mrs. Adams during her official life in Washington, none appears more gracious and diplomatic in the retrospect than the ball given by her to General Jackson in January, 1824, when he was already a formidable rival of her husband. This ball was given while Mr. Adams was Secretary of State and living in the house on F Street, near Fourteenth, later known as the Adams Building. In this large double house the ball-room was on the second floor, and, according to various chroniclers, two young relatives who were staying with Mrs. Adams spent a week in preparing its elaborate decorations of tissue-paper and evergreens. In their pleasant task the two pretty girls were doubtless assisted by the two sons of the house, George and John Adams, both of whom were said to be in love with one of the girls, which was an unfair as well as uncomfortable concentration of the tender passion.

The floor of the ball-room was chalked with spread-eagles, flags, and the motto "Welcome to the hero of New Orleans." The pillars were festooned with laurel and wintergreen, while wreathings of evergreens and roses, interspersed with small, variegated lamps, with a lustre in the centre, gave what Miss Abigail Adams considered a beautiful effect. She further recorded that there were eight pieces of music, and that General Jackson, who stood beside Mrs. Adams to receive with her in the passage between the two houses, looked remarkably well. A semicircle of distinguished persons gathered around Mrs. Adams and the General, and into this choice group the guests entered two by two and made their bows, there being no handshakings in those days.

This ball, for some reason, set the muse of a certain Mr. Agg to rhyming, with the result that a number of verses were written and printed. These verses, which have been so often quoted, owe their popularity to the fact that they introduce the names of many by-gone belles and beaux.

> "Wend your way with the world to-night?
>   Sixty gray and giddy twenty,
> Flirts that court and prudes that slight,
>   State coquettes and spinsters plenty.
> Mrs. Sullivan is there
>   With all the charms that nature lent her,
> Gay McKim with city air,*
>   And winning Gales † and Vanderventer.

* Miss Ann McKim, of Baltimore, who afterwards married Mr. Samuel J. K. Handy.

† Mrs. Joseph Gales, wife of one of the editors of the *National Intelligencer*.

Forsyth * with her group of graces;
Both the Crowninshields † in blue,
The Pearces with their heavenly faces
And eyes like suns that dazzle through.
Belles and matrons, maids and madames,
All are gone to Mrs. Adams'.

"Wend your way with the world to-night?
East and West, South and North,
Form a constellation bright
And pour a blended brilliance forth;
See the tide of fashion flowing,
'Tis the noon of beauty's reign—
Webster, Hamilton are going,
Eastern Floyd and Southern Hayne,
Western Thomas gayly smiling,
Boaland, nature's protégé,
Young De Wolf, all hearts beguiling,
Morgan, Benton, Brown, and Lee,
Belles and matrons, maids and madames,
All are gone to Mrs. Adams'.

"Many a form of fairy birth,
Many a Hebe yet unwon;
Wirt a gem of purest worth ‡
Lovely, laughing Pleasanton,

* Mrs. John Forsyth, of Georgia, and her daughters. Mr. Forsyth had recently returned from the Spanish mission and was Secretary of State during the Jackson administration.

† "The Crowninshields in blue" were the daughters of Benjamin W. Crowninshield, M. C. from Massachusetts, sometime Secretary of the Navy.

‡ Mrs. William Wirt, of Virginia, wife of the Attorney-General of the United States.

Vails and Tayloes will be there,
Gay Monroe, so debonair,*
Helen, pleasure's harbinger,†
Ramsey, Cottinger, and Kerr.
Belles and matrons, maids and madames,
All are gone to Mrs. Adams'."

So wrote Mr. John T. Agg in 1824, and by some curious mental sympathy, telepathy being unknown in those days, a young Maryland lady of poetic fancy, Miss Sallie Harris, penned some lines descriptive of a ball at Wye Hall,‡ which bear a striking resemblance to those of the Washington journalist. Although no literary merit can be claimed for either of these jingles, they are not without value as illustrative of the simple habits and pleasures of an earlier time.

"Wend ye to the Hall to-night
All the belles and beaux are going,
Mary with her bright brown hair,
Hazel eyes and cheeks so glowing.
The belles of Wye, too, will be there,§
One is tall, the other winning,
Both are matchless in their forms;
They will dance like tops a-spinning.

* Miss Monroe, a niece of President Monroe.

† Miss Mary Hellen, afterwards Mrs. John Adams, Junior.

‡ Wye Hall, Queen Anne County, Maryland, the home of Mr. William Paca.

§ Miss Catharine and Sallie Carmichael, sisters of Judge Carmichael.

"Wend ye to the Hall to-night;
All the dainty dames are going,
Some in 'gigs' and some in sleighs,
Some in 'kites,' when the wind is blowing;
The maids of Woodfield will be there,
From girlhood's state to women,
Unconscious of their many charms,
So pleasing in their sex and station.

"Wend ye to the Hall to-night
All the widowers here are going,
Wishing for a change of state;
Tired of a long vacation."

* * * * *

Several allusions in the verses of the Maryland lady point to their having been written at an earlier date than those in which Mr. Agg celebrated the charms of the Washington belles who were "going to Mrs. Adams'."

Mrs. Adams's ball-room presented many interesting contrasts that would have been impossible in a later time. There was still some picturesqueness in the costumes of the gentlemen of the day, which is emphasized by the fact that the plain manner in which the President, General Jackson, and Mr. Adams dressed was commented upon as being in strong contrast to the elaborate attire of some of the guests.

Officers of the army and navy and members of the Diplomatic Corps appeared in regimentals and regalia, while plain citizens disported themselves in pumps, silk stockings, ruffled cravats, and two or even three waistcoats of different colors. The dangling fob-ribbon with gold buckles and a big seal of topaz or carnelian, regulation frock-coats of green or claret-colored cloth with huge lapels and gilded buttons, and Hessian top-boots with gold tassels completed the costume of many gentlemen of this time. Certain of the exquisites affected ultra-fashionable full dress, which prescribed coats with great rolling collars and short waists, voluminous cravats of white cambric, and small-clothes or tight trousers.

In striking contrast with the members of the Diplomatic Corps, in their gorgeous costumes blazing with orders, and with such dignified and elegant American statesmen as Mr. Clay, Mr. Webster, Mr. Crawford, Mr. Richard Rush, Judge Story, and Mr. Benjamin Ogle Tayloe, were Congressmen and Representatives from the far West of those days, who had not lost the free stride of the forest and the prairie or its freedom of speech and manner. No more remarkable was the sight of Pushmataha, the "Eagle of the Choctaws," in the White House than that of the typical backwoodsman and Indian fighter David Crockett seated in the hall of Congress beside such fellow-Representatives from Tennessee as James K. Polk and John Bell.

Mr. Josiah Quincy lodged at Miss Hyer's on Capitol Hill, where he met a delightful party of gentlemen and found much to interest him in the life of the capital. Among his daily associates were Thomas Addis Emmet and David B. Ogden, of New York; Rufus G. Amory, of Boston; Captain Zantzinger, of the army; Elisha R. Potter, of Rhode Island,—the largest man Mr. Quincy had ever seen except professional giants,—with wit and intelligence in proportion to his goodly bulk; and "Captain Stockton, a Sindbad the Sailor of unimpeachable veracity," whose tales of adventure were the delight of his messmates.

Mr. John Knapp and Justice Story, who had been Quincy's *compagnons de voyage*, were often members of Miss Hyer's circle, both excelling in "the art of conversation in days when it was considered a sort of second profession."

Mr. Quincy described an informal dinner at the White House when Mr. King and Mr. Gallatin were the only other guests. He noticed that the latter gentleman "scarcely said anything, owing perhaps to the constant and amusing utterances of the President and Mr. King, who talked as if they were under bonds to furnish entertainment for the party."

Other visitors to the White House who met Mr. Adams in familiar intercourse with his own family and a few friends have described him as an agreeable host. Mr. Adams's niece, who was often a member of his family, said that her uncle was not as cold as he appeared to the world, and was always interested in the young people around him. He was, however, an habitually taciturn man and bewailed more than once his lack of the kind of conversation that adds to the pleasure of the dinner-table or the drawing-room; adding, in his own humorous phrase, that he was "a silent animal," and that his dear mother's early dictum that "children should be seen and not heard" had wrought his social ruin.

A state dinner of forty covers at the White House Mr. Quincy found "very splendid and rather stiff," although it was enlivened for him by a *tête-à-tête* with Miss Bullitt. He was rejoiced to find that he and "this fair young lady from Kentucky" had a common acquaintance in Larz Anderson, who had journeyed all the way from his Kentucky home to Harvard College on horseback with his effects in saddle-bags. A recital of some of the young Kentuckian's exploits at college fairly broke the ice between Mr. Quincy and his pretty neighbor, and the dinner proved delightful to him. Another dinner, which this appreciative visitor described as absolutely free from stiffness or constraint, was at Mr. Webster's. The other guests who enjoyed "this feast of reason" were Mr. Henry Storrs, of New York, and Rufus Greene

Amory, of Boston. That this was not a "feast of reason" pure and simple we are led to believe from Mr. Quincy's statement that Mr. Webster carved the beef, talking delightfully all the while, telling some good lawyers' stories, and giving a graphic account of the burning of his home in Portsmouth in 1813.

"'Though I was in Washington at the time,' he said, 'I believe I know more about the fire than many who were actively at work on the spot. Besides, here is Mrs. Webster who was burned out. She will correct me if I am wrong.'

"After Mr. Webster had dwelt upon the loss of his books, which were full of notes and associations, his wife said, with an amused expression, which showed that her remark was not to be taken quite seriously: 'I think there was something in the house which Mr. Webster regretted more than his books. There was a pipe of wine in the cellar, and I am sure that Mr. Webster's philosophy has not yet reconciled him to its loss. You see we were young housekeepers in those days. It was the first pipe of wine we ever had, and the getting it was a great event.'

"'Let us be accurate, my dear,' said Mr. Webster, with one of those pleasant smiles of his, which fairly lit up the room. 'Undoubtedly it was a pipe of wine when we bought it; but then it had been on tap for some time, and our table was not without guests. If I had you upon the witness stand, I think I should make you confess that your pipe of wine could scarcely have 'een more than *half a pipe* at the time of the fire.'

"I suppose that there was nothing said at that dinner so little worth preserving as this family jest; yet the sweet and playful manner of Webster has fixed it indelibly upon my memory. That manner I cannot give, and it was everything. It somehow carried one of those side confessions of the absolute affection and confidence existing between this married pair which were so evident to those admitted beneath their roof. A congenial marriage seems to be essential to the best development of a man of genius, and this blessing rested upon that household. It was like organ music to hear Webster speak to or of the being upon whom his affections reposed, and whom, alas! he was so soon to lose. I am aware that those who knew the man only when this tenderest relation had been terminated by death never knew him in his perfect symmetry. Whatever evil speakers might choose to say about the subsequent career of Daniel Webster, he was at that time 'whole as the marble, founded as the rock.'"

The Vice-President, Mr. Calhoun, the hospitalities of whose house he enjoyed, Mr. Quincy described as

"A striking looking man, then forty-four years old, with thick hair, brushed back defiantly. He had joined the bitter opposition to the administration, and though his position prevented him from publicly assaulting the President, he ruled that John Randolph was not to be called to order for so doing."

An American who boldly announced that "*gentlemen* were the natural rulers of this country," in defiance of the principles of the Declaration, could not have been a congenial associate for Mr. Adams, who regarded that document as a sacred legacy from his own father and from those other Fathers of the Republic.

To have been in Washington at this time, and to have enjoyed the conversation of the men there assembled, was a liberal education for any young man. Mr. Quincy was an apt scholar in this early impressionist school, and in later years summed up his advantages in a few forcible lines:

"The young men of to-day who go to Washington find a city of luxurious appointments and noble buildings, very different from the capital of muddy streets and scattered houses with which I was familiar. But where is the living figure, cast in heroic mould, to represent the ideal of American manhood? Can the capital of to-day show anything so majestic and inspiring as was Daniel Webster in the Washington of 1826?"

Mr. Quincy has left descriptions of other great men whom he met: of John Randolph, whom he visited at Dawson's on Capitol Hill, who in those days appeared more like "a spiritual presence than a man adequately clothed in flesh and blood; of Robert Hayne, who in the heat of debate was so forbearing and restrained that Randolph's keenest shafts of ridicule failed to draw from him an angry retort; of the President, whose high character he revered,—yet among them all Webster shone forth to his youthful eyes like a star, as he said, completely satisfying his imagination.

Fully as he appreciated his advantages in meeting the great men of his time, it is evident from the pages of Mr. Quincy's diary that he by no means confined his observations to statesmen and orators. The first evening-party which he attended at Mrs. Wirt's, the mantle of Boston still being over him, he seems to have been more impressed by the historic lineage of the girls whom he met than by their beauty. Mrs. David Hoffman, of Baltimore, Mr. Quincy characterized as "pretty, learned and agreeable," while of the magnificent Mrs. Joseph M. White, to whose charms Mrs. Anne Royall later devoted many paragraphs in *The Huntress*, the young Bostonian has left no elaborate description.

At an entertainment given by Mrs. Johnson, of Louisiana, Mrs. Hoffman presented Mr. Quincy to Miss Cora Livingston, upon which occasion he promptly forgot his historic background and without stopping to record that she was the daughter of the Senator from Louisiana and the niece of Chancellor Livingston of New York, he joyfully wandered in the garden of the gods with this radiant young creature.

Cora Livingston, of whose birth during the eclipse of 1806 her father wrote to his sister, "God has given me so fair a daughter that the sun has hidden his face," possessed much of her mother's Southern charm and grace if not her remarkable beauty. Mrs. Livingston, in writing of her daughter at sixteen, said, "She is not a beauty, not a genius, but a good and affectionate child." Josiah Quincy upon one page of his diary recorded that "Burke's famous apostrophe to the Queen of France is none too good for the queen of American society in 1826," while upon another page he wrote that, although to describe Miss Livingston one must be able to paint the rose, "she is not handsome,—I mean not transcendently handsome. She has a fine figure, a pretty face, dances well, and dresses to admiration."

Miss Cora Livingston was evidently endowed with fine tact as well as grace and charm. After opening a public ball at Carusi's Assembly Rooms with Mr. Quincy, the young lady introduced her partner to several of the lesser belles, after which she said, "I am going to perform one of the greatest acts of heroism of which a woman can be capable. I am going to present you to my rival." That the "rival," Miss Catherine Van Rensselaer, of Albany, was "a tall genteel girl" and might be possessed of a "fine mind and a rich father" Mr. Quincy was willing to admit, but that she could be considered a rival of the incomparable Miss Livingston seemed to him entirely out of the question. Other charming girls he met, —Miss Morphin, of Kentucky, Miss Tayloe, and Miss B——, whose full name this prudent young man does not give, probably because he adds that "although pretty, she is ignorant and vain." Among all the beauties of the day who were to be met at the Mexican minister's, at the Baron de Mareuil's, or at Mr. Vaughan's, there was but one star of the first magnitude visible to the eyes of the enthusiastic young Bostonian.

Other chroniclers of this administration wrote of balls, receptions, and weddings. A White House wedding, in February, 1828, being the most notable of these, when Miss Mary Hellen was married to the President's son John, in the Blue Room. Miss Abigail Adams, following the family fashion, wrote in her diary that "the bride looked very handsome in white satin, orange-blossoms, and pearls," and that she and the other three bridesmaids had an amusing time before they joined the groomsmen in the circular room, arranging flowers and ribbons. These gay young people passed the cake through a ring, cut slices to distribute among their friends, and, the day after the wedding assembled in what Miss Adams called the "Yellow Room," which was evidently the large East Room.

Mrs. James M. Mason wrote in 1827 to invite her sister, Miss Ann Chew, of Philadelphia, to several family weddings. In her letter she gave her sister some advice about her wardrobe, which reveals the simplicity in dress and the independence of the Washington life of those happy days.

"I have absolutely fixed my heart upon your coming to us," wrote Mrs. Mason. "We have resolved to be gay, and our party will be so well selected that we must enjoy ourselves. Anne Mason and Virginia are to be Maria's bridesmaids, and Anne's sister Eliza, (who is a very clever girl) and Nanny Lloyd are to be our guests during the merry-making, also the two

Masons from Montpelier.* We shall move to the Island on Saturday, and there we shall have ample room to accommodate you and many others, all the men, married and single, (except Mr. Cooper) are to be put into the wing. Maria is to be married on the 4th, and John on the 5th, and the 6th, and 7th, are to be devoted to frolicking; on Sunday we shall go to church, and on Monday, I shall go home with my husband. I wish you would come three or four days before hand, and here I must give you a hint. Do not bring with you any display or parade of finery, you would be so singular here, as to attract observations, perhaps ill-natured ones and, maybe, a portion of envy were you to appear elegantly attired—economy is completely the order of the day amongst us. . . .

"We shall all wear the same dresses to Maria's wedding and to John's, and on Friday a nice muslin and the same on Saturday.† Let your dress for the weddings be as simple as you please,—the same dress you wore to E. Tucker's wedding will be much handsomer than any you will find here. Virginia will wear a

* Virginia Mason, here spoken of, was the sister of the bride-elect. Anne and Eliza Mason, Nanny Lloyd, and the Masons of Montpelier were cousins of the bride.

† The weddings referred to were those of Sarah Maria Mason to Lieutenant Samuel Cooper, afterwards adjutant-general, United States army, and still later adjutant-general, army of Confederate States; and of John Mason, eldest son of General John Mason, to Miss Macomb, daughter of General Alexander Macomb, United States army. It may be interesting to readers of Mrs. Mason's letters to know that Miss Chew accepted her sister's pressing invitations to enter into the wedding gayeties of the capital. The three days' journey from Philadelphia to Washington was made in Mr. Benjamin Chew's family coach, which still stands in the coach-house at Cliveden, Germantown.

white crape trimmed with large white satin ruleaus, over a white satin—the same dress which she has worn to all the parties she has attended this winter, and Teaco will wear a plain bobinet trimmed with a lace flounce she has worked for herself, I shall wear my white satin, which is still decent. Nobody here ever makes dress a matter of moment, and your wardrobe will pass unnoticed and unobserved unless you bring any thing very extravagant. . . . The prettiest dress you can wear on the grand occasion will be a white book muslin trimmed with a wreath of white flowers, or with three rows of plain bobinet quilled double thro' the middle. . . ."

Fashion decreed for the ladies of this period a scantiness of skirt that would have rendered dancing impossible, had not the narrowness of this nether garment been matched by its shortness.

"Skirts of five breadths a quarter of a yard each, of the favorite India crape, were coquettishly short for the freer display of the slipper and silk stocking, matching the color of the gown and fastened with ribbons crossed over the instep and ankle. The low baby waist, ingenuous and frank, came to an end abruptly under the arms, which were covered with gloves so fine that they were sometimes stowed cunningly in the shell of an English walnut. The hair, dressed high, was crowned with a comb of tortoise-shell, while turbans and ostrich-feathers were the peculiar ensigns of wives and matrons."

In addition to the varied social attractions of the capital there were usually a few good theatrical representations during the season, especially when a Philadelphia company stopped in Washington on its way to Savannah. In the United States

Theatre, the first playhouse of the city, and in the Washington Theatre, opened in 1820, appeared the elder Booth, Macready, and Thomas Apthorpe Cooper, whose Charles Surface and Petruchio were among the most finished representations of the day. This almost forgotten actor was only excelled in popular estimation by the English tragedian George F. Cooke and Edmund Keene, while Washington Irving said there was no one in England who could equal Cooper's Macbeth. Mr. Adams saw Edwin Forrest, when a lad, enjoying at the Washington Theatre the finished acting of Thomas Cooper, little dreaming that he was destined to dethrone Cooper, as Cooper had dethroned Fennell. Mr. William Perrine tells a charming story of the first appearance of Mr. Cooper's daughter, a lovely and accomplished girl, who had little inclination towards a theatrical life and no very marked histrionic ability. Miss Cooper undertook to play the rôle of Virginia to her father's Virginius, in the spirit of filial duty rather than from motives of professional ambition.

"The fame of the parent had caused no little interest in what might be the possibilities of 'Cooper's daughter' as an actress, and the audience greeted her with anxious sympathy. When the scene came in which Virginius says of the child, 'Send her to me, Servia,' and she appears with the loving and dutiful salutation, 'Well father, what's your will?' the audience saw only the actual father and daughter, and recognized them with an uncontrollable outburst of affectionate enthusiasm. The progress of the play was halted, and it was not until the veteran and the daughter had relieved their feelings in tears that the action was resumed."

Priscilla Cooper married Robert Tyler, son of President Tyler, and after the death of her mother-in-law presided over the White House during a portion of the fourteenth administration.

By the end of the first quarter of the century, as in later times, literary men and artists had found Washington an interesting place of resort. Washington Irving made many visits to the capital besides that first one in 1811, when he described himself as mounting with a stout heart to his room in a Georgetown inn to don his "pease-blossom and silk stockings and gird up his loins" for an effort to reach the White House at night across over a mile of bad road, from which "darkness and dirt" he finally emerged into the "blazing splendor of Mrs. Madison's drawing-room."

In addition to the large and steadily increasing corps of newspaper editors, writers, and correspondents, which included Mr. Joseph Gales and his brother-in-law William Seaton, Peter Force, founder of the *National Journal*, and such recent arrivals in Washington as Elias Kingman and James Brooks, there were in the capital two occasional writers of poetry and prose, Francis Scott Key and John Pendleton Kennedy. The fact that Mr. Kennedy's "Swallow Barn" and "Horseshoe Robinson" are little read to-day does not invalidate his claim to the distinction of being classed among early American *littérateurs*.

Two Englishmen of ability were among the journalists of this time, James Cheatham, who edited the New York *Citizen*, and resided in Washington during the session of Congress, and John T. Agg, some time editor of the *National Journal*, who "dropped into poetry" upon the occasion of Mrs. Adams's ball. Robert Fulton, artist as well as inventor, was at the capital in early days, visiting his friend Joel Barlow; and here came James Peale, who painted a number of miniatures of Washington men and women, and Washington Allston, the friend of Malbone. Although a number of Malbone's miniatures are to be found in the District, it is not probable that they were painted there, as the artist could only have visited the capital in the latter years of his life, when failing health seriously interfered with his work. Among the most charming of these miniatures is one of Mrs. Moses Poor, the ancestress of many Washingtonians. This miniature, which represents Mrs. Poor in early matronhood, was probably painted in Boston, as Mr. and Mrs. Poor did not make Washington their home until after Malbone's death.

One of the few portraits in oil executed by Malbone is to be found in the Corcoran Gallery in Washington. This picture is doubly interesting

Edward Greene Malbone

By Himself

because it represents the delicate, refined face of the artist himself, whose brilliant and promising career ended at the age of thirty.

Charles King, the limner of many Washingtonians, made this city his home early in the century, and built here the first picture-gallery. Mr. King had his studio on the east side of Twelfth Street, below F, where the Columbia Theatre was built later, and here Mr. William Dunlap, who visited him in 1824, said that he found the artist "full of business and a great painter, assiduously employed in his painting-room through the day, and in the evening attending the soirees, parties, and balls of the capital."

Those who still recall Mr. King as he appeared in later years in Washington speak of him as a picturesque figure, especially so when he appeared one evening at a fancy ball in the character of Rembrandt.

Although Mrs. Seaton wrote of Mr. and Mrs. Adams, after the election, that they were "perfectly *comme il faut* and *he* a little more gay and polite," she has left few descriptions of the social events of this administration. Mrs. Seaton's silence is perhaps due to a severe affliction that befell her in the sudden death of her little son, which naturally prevented her from entering into the gayeties of the capital.

One of Mrs. Seaton's friends, Mrs. Samuel Harrison Smith, whose husband was the original proprietor of the *National Intelligencer*, has left some interesting pictures of Washington society in the last days of the Adams administration. Through her letters Mrs. Smith kept her son, J. Bayard Smith, a student at Princeton College, *au courant* of the social and of some of the political events of the capital. In a letter written in December, 1828, she spoke of "an exhibition at the College," upon which occasion the President walked to and from the college, which Mrs. Smith considered "too great a degree of democratic simplicity," adding,—

"For my part I like a little of the pomp and circumstance of rank, and I really believe the sovereign people like it too, and mean to show their *taste* on this point on the inauguration of General Jackson. The papers already teem with accounts of the preparations making for his journey here. A superb coach and eight white horses is ready in Philadelphia. A carriage built of *hickory* is getting ready in Baltimore, and a vessel called the 'Constitution' is to be borne here *full sail* by sixteen white horses. We are threatened with a deluge of people from Virginia, Pennsylvania, Maryland, and other adjacent States. Washington will be inundated, and the papers say every house, private as well as public, will be filled to overflowing. . . . Meanwhile, the defeated party put the best face on the affair, and are more smiling and gracious and agreeable than they ever were before. At Mrs. Adams' drawing-room last week, every one attached to the administration, as well as the members of the cabinet, appeared with their best looks and best dresses. Mrs. Adams never on any former occasion was so social, attentive, and agreeable. Instead of standing in one place, making formal courtesies, she walked through the rooms conversing with every one in the most animated manner. To add to the gaiety and brilliancy of the evening, the great audience chamber was lit up, the band of musick stationed there, and dancing took place for the first time it ever was permitted in the President's house."

Mrs. Harrison Smith was doubtless quite correct in speaking of dancing as an innovation at the receptions; but that there had been dances at the White House before this time is quite evident from several letters of an earlier period. Mrs. Madison wrote to Phœbe Morris of "a small dancing frolic at the White House which would have delighted her heart, at which Mrs. Eustis, Mrs. Richard Rush, and the Hamiltons assisted."

Another time when the sounds of music and dancing were heard in the East Room was at the ball given after the marriage of Mr. Adams's son John to his cousin Miss Mary Hellen. Upon this occasion it is related that the grave and dignified President unbent for the nonce and entered with spirit into the mazes of the Virginia reel.

Referring to the unusual gayety of the last reception of the Adams administration, Mrs. Smith remarked,—

"Most people think this was going rather too far. To appear cheerful would be consistent with dignity and self-respect. But as one of the members observed they mean to march out with flying colours and all the honours of war!"

Dignified and gracious, even if her graciousness was not appreciated by men and women of different political affiliations, Mrs. Adams passed from the life of the White House to which she had added charm and distinction. Mr. Adams, who had greatly desired a proof of the people's confidence, of which his re-election would have assured him, solemnly recorded in his diary, "March 4th 1829 Genl Jackson was inaugurated as President of the U. S. . . . And the places that have known us shall know us no more."

Contrary to all precedent, Mr. Adams, instead of remaining at Quincy in the enjoyment of private life and of the Latin classics that he loved, returned to the capital as Congressman from the Plymouth district. With the manly words upon his lips, "No person could be degraded by serving the people as Representative in Congress," John Quincy Adams entered upon what has been considered by many historians the most brilliant and distinguished period of his varied and useful career.

> "Here," said Mr. Morse, "he was to attain the highest pinnacle of his fame after he had left the greatest office of the Government, and during a period for which presumably nothing better had been allotted than that he should tranquilly await the summons of death."

It was in the House that the summons finally came, but not until John Adams had served his country there ably and conscientiously for nearly a score of years. Not unfitting, it seemed that to this wise statesman and good man, then in the fulness of years, death should have come in the House of Representatives upon whose floor he had recently led a successful charge. This signal victory over unrighteous legislation John Quincy Adams humbly and devoutly recorded upon one of the last pages of his diary in the following words: "Blessed, forever blessed be the name of God!"

X

A LADIES' BATTLE

THE coach built in Philadelphia, drawn by eight white horses; the hickory carriage, Baltimore's votive offering to Andrew Jackson; and another conveyance modelled after the "Constitution," did not, it seems, occupy prominent places in the inaugural ceremonies of March 4, 1829, as, according to Mrs. Harrison Smith, General Jackson, after taking the oath of office, mounted his horse and rode home from the Capitol, having gone thither on foot.

Although the vast throng that pursued the President from the Capitol to the White House is spoken of in the newspapers of the day as a "civic procession," it appears to have consisted of a motley train of countrymen, laborers,—black and white,—carriages, wagons, and carts, a confused rabble of thousands of men, women, and children, riding, driving, and running helter-skelter, striving who should first gain admittance into the Executive Mansion, where, it was understood, refreshments were to be distributed.

"The halls," wrote Mrs. Smith, "were filled with a disorderly rabble of negroes, boys, women, and children, scrambling for the refreshments designed for the drawing-rooms! the people forcing their way into the saloons, mingling with the foreigners and citizens surrounding the President. . . . China and glass to the amount of several thousand dollars were broken in the struggle to get at the ices and cakes, though punch and other drinkables had been carried out in tubs and buckets to the people; but had it been in hogsheads it would have been insufficient besides unsatisfactory to the mob, who claimed equality in all things. . . . The confusion became more and more appalling. At one moment the President, who had retreated until he was pressed against the wall of the apartment, could only be secured against serious danger by a number of gentlemen linking arms and forming themselves into a barrier. It was then that the windows were thrown open and the living torrent found an outlet. . . . It was the People's day, the People's President, and the People would rule!"

The number of persons who offered their congratulations to the new President, or engaged in the disorderly scramble to enter the White House, was estimated by journalists of the day as upwards of ten thousand. Judge Story, who had been a warm supporter of Mr. Adams, said that after the President returned to the "palace" he was "visited by an immense crowd of all sorts of people, from the highest and most polished down to the most vulgar and gross in the nation." Some of these visitors, it is said, were so rude and lawless that in their eagerness to see the President they stood with muddy boots upon the satin damask chairs. The simplicity attending the inaugural ceremonies, the absence of military features, and the omission of the usual evening reception and ball were not simply in deference to the General's democratic ideas, but because his life was overshadowed by a great sorrow which had recently overtaken him in the death of his wife.

In a letter written soon after the inauguration, Mrs. Smith pictured the gloom and depression of the social life of the capital caused by the mourning at the White House and by a rumor of many changes to be made in official circles.*

"Never before did the city seem to me so gloomy—so many changes in society—so many families broken up, and those of the first distinction and who gave a tone to society. Those elegantly furnished houses, stripped of their splendid furniture—that furniture exposed to public sale—those drawing-rooms, brilliantly illuminated, in which I have so often mixed with gay crowds, distinguished by rank, fashion, beauty, talent—resounding with festive sounds—now, empty, silent, dark, dismantled. Oh! 'tis melancholy! Mrs. Clay's, Mrs. Southard's, Mrs. Porter's houses exhibit this spectacle—They are completely stripped—the furniture all sold—the families, for the few days they remained after the sale—uncomfortably crowded in one little room. The doors shut on company and only one or two intimate friends admitted—Nor does the entry, of the triumphant party, relieve this universal gloom—Alas! it only adds to it—Gen. Jackson's family in deep mourning—secludes them from society,—they are not known, or seen, except at formal morning visits—They quietly took possession of the *big house*,

* Unpublished letters of Mrs. Samuel Harrison Smith, written to her son, J. Bayard H. Smith, while at Princeton College. Mrs. Smith was the author of two books much read in their day, "A Winter in Washington" and "What is Gentility?"

where if they choose they may remain invisible, and as much separated from social intercourse, as if on the other side of the mountains—But what most adds to the general gloom—is the rumour of a general proscription—Every individual, connected with the government, from the highest officer to the lowest clerk, is filled with apprehension."

Mrs. Smith seems to have been a woman singularly free from prejudice. An ardent admirer of Henry Clay, who was a frequent guest at her house, she was able to find much to admire in his inveterate enemy Andrew Jackson. Regretting with Josiah Quincy the passing away of a more elegant and dignified order of ceremonies at the White House, and deploring with Mr. Rush and Mr. Clay the radical changes made in the official, diplomatic, and consular service with the incoming of a different party, this large-minded woman was pleased to record the agreeable impression made upon her mind by her own reception at the White House. As there were no levees or drawing-rooms, Mr. and Mrs. Harrison Smith called informally and were received by Miss Eastin, a niece of Mrs. Jackson. The President came into the drawing-room during the visit, and entertained his guests with courtesy and cordiality.

The presiding genius of the White House in the early years of this administration was Mrs. Andrew Jackson Donelson, whose husband, a nephew of Mrs. Jackson, was the President's private secretary.

Of this young matron, who is described as a beautiful blonde with a graceful and elegant figure, Cora Livingston wrote to her uncle, Major Daversac, then chargé d'affaires in Holland, "Mrs. Donelson, the President's adopted daughter, who presides at the White House, is a beautiful, accomplished, and charming woman, with wonderful tact and delightfully magnetic manners. Though the mother of two children, she might pass for sweet sixteen. Everybody is in love with her."

Apprehension gave place to dismay in the Washington world when the President's Cabinet appointments were announced, especially when it transpired that General Eaton had been made Secretary of War. The prevailing sentiment in social and political life may be gathered from a letter written by a woman whose husband was in constant communication with the official circles of the capital:

"Last week it was considered certainly fixed—Van Buren, for state depart—Ingham, for the Treasury, Genl. Eaton for the war, Govn. Branch for the Navy, and Mr. Berrien, Attorney Genl. Astonishment and disappointment filled the minds of friends and foes—with the exception of Van B—the cabinet was pronounced too feeble to stand and every one said such an administration must soon fall—Remonstrances were made by the Tennessee delegation in a body, (so it is said) against Genl E's appointment. . . . Every one acknowledges Genl. Eaton's talents and virtues—but his late unfortunate connection, is an obstacle to his receiving a place of honour, which it is apprehended even Genl. Jackson's firmness cannot resist—It is a pity —Every one that knows esteems, and many love him for his benevolence and amiability. Oh, woman, woman !—The rumour of yesterday was, that he was to have no place at home, but be sent abroad—so it was added (tho' evidently for the joke of it) that he was to be sent to *Hayti*, that being the most proper Court for *her* to reside in. . . . Every one thinks there is great confusion and difficulty, mortification and disappointment at the *Wigwam*—as they call the General's lodgings."

It was not thought strange that the President should have appointed an old Tennessee friend to an important office, especially as John H. Eaton had creditably represented his State in the Senate for ten years. The head and front of his offending was his giving the Bureau of War to Eaton after his marriage with the dashing Widow Timberlake.

It should be explained, in justification of the position taken by the Cabinet ladies at this time, that their objection to Mrs. Eaton was not simply that she was the daughter of an Irish tavern-keeper, but in consequence of the scandal associated with her name before and after the death of Mr. Timberlake, especially in connection with General Eaton. How fully the President understood Mrs. Eaton's character it is impossible to say. He certainly had had ample opportunities of knowing her during earlier visits to Washington, when he stopped at William O'Neill's tavern. Even if President Jackson was himself disposed to overlook the indiscretions of this brilliantly beautiful woman in consequence of her unprotected and much exposed girlhood, his attempt to command a place for her among the decorous and well-bred women of official circles in Washington was certainly arbitrary and ill-advised.

It seems a curious coincidence that the administration of one of the most independent and virile of our Presidents should have been that in which women proved a dominating force. That Peggy O'Neill, afterwards Mrs. Timberlake, and later Mrs. John H. Eaton, a beautiful, audacious, and entirely unconventional woman, should have during the early years of President Jackson's administration become an important factor in political preferment seems almost incredible. Yet so violent was the social storm raised by General Eaton's marriage and by the President's championship of the bride, that Mr. Webster wrote, "It is odd, but the consequences of this desperate turmoil in the social and fashionable world may determine who shall succeed the present Chief Magistrate."

Mrs. Calhoun positively refused to visit Mrs. Eaton, which naturally increased the strained relations already existing between the President and Mr. Calhoun. Mr. Van Buren, being a widower and unhampered by feminine *convenances*, was in a position to offer courtesies to the bride, which he promptly did, and succeeded in inducing two legation bachelors, the British and Russian ministers, Mr. Vaughan and Baron Krudener, to pay attention to the fair "Bellona," as Mrs. Eaton had been dubbed in one of the journals of the day. Balls were given by Mr. Vaughan and the Russian minister, assisted by Mr. Van Buren, at which it was arranged that Mrs. Eaton should be accorded the place of honor at supper and in the dance. These amiable gentlemen, however extensive may have been their knowledge of international diplomacy, were quite unversed in feminine finesse, and great was their consternation when they beheld substantial Cabinet dames float away and vanish into thin air upon the approach of the radiant and faultlessly attired "Bellona," while cotillion after cotillion dissolved into its original elements when she was given the place at its head. At a very elegant ball, given by the Russian minister, the *coup de grace* was given when Mrs. Huygens, wife of the Dutch minister, upon being conducted to a seat at the supper-table beside Mrs. Eaton, took her husband's arm and with great dignity left the room.

That the anti-Calhoun faction magnified the importance of the Cabinet ladies' opposition to Mrs. Eaton there can be no doubt. How much Mr. Van Buren's championship of the fair Bellona influenced his promotion cannot be so readily ascertained, as he had already rendered the President valuable service in the campaign of 1828. In accordance with a carefully arranged plan, Mr. Van Buren resigned the portfolio of State in 1831, and was promptly appointed minister to the Court of St. James, from which he returned later to serve as a candidate for Vice-President on the Democratic ticket of 1832. His election to this office was a stepping-stone to the Presidency in 1837.

Mrs. Calhoun persisted in her refusal to recognize Mrs. Eaton, who, with all her beauty and vivacity, seems to have possessed no attraction for refined and cultivated women. The other Cabinet and diplomatic ladies upheld her. The President expostulated in vain with the members of his Cabinet, who, retreating behind the aphorism so convenient in social matters, *place aux dames*, declared themselves quite powerless to alter the decree of their rebellious partners. In this dilemma their chief might have been expected to sympathize, as his niece, Mrs. Donelson, maintained the same uncompromising attitude towards the wife of the Secretary of War.

To have been the cause of Mrs. Donelson's leaving the White House, while she remained, in high favor, championed by the President, the Secretary of State, and the foreign ministers, was no small triumph for this most audacious Peggy. With her Irish love of adventure and broil, she was like a war-horse scenting the fray from near and from afar. Rejoicing in the clash of arms and tongues that she had stirred up, with a keen zest of the humor of the situation, and all unhampered by any feeling of delicacy on account of the publicity of her position, Mrs. Eaton entertained herself and her zealous champions by enacting for them graphic and highly colored scenes from this *Bataille aux Dames*, of which she herself was the *casus belli*.

A curiously undignified picture was presented by the President of the United States during the Eaton imbroglio. At one moment he exhausted eloquence and invective in trying to persuade or command his Cabinet officers to use their influence upon their refractory consorts; and when both arguments and threats failed he was heard swearing by the strong oath to which he was addicted, "By the Eternal, the spiteful cats who plagued the life out of my patient Rachel shall not scratch this brave little Peggy!" An undignified picture was this, and yet one most characteristic of this man of the people, dominating, hot-headed, often wrong-headed, obstinate, impulsive, and at the same time generous, unselfish, and always tender and chivalrous in his devotion to womankind.

By no stretch of the imagination could Andrew Jackson have been considered a carpet knight, although a certain courtly deference in the presence of women invariably won for him their friendship and affection; and no knight of the days of chivalry was more ready to champion the cause of maid or matron in distress than was this frontier soldier. Jackson's attitude towards women, which was much more than an external and superficial deference, had been a marked characteristic from early years, when the fate of an heroic and devoted mother who met her death on her way to Charleston to care for the wounded soldiers there, had, as he revealed to several intimate friends, consecrated all womankind for him.

It is impossible to understand the position taken by the President at this time without recurring to some earlier incidents of his career. The events that preceded his marriage have been so little understood and so grossly misrepresented by partisan journals that it seems far more just to this man to repeat the explanation given by contemporaries than to gloss over the affair. Judge Overton, in his account of Jackson's marriage, written in 1827, says that when he decided to settle in what was then called West Tennessee he solicited Mrs. Donelson, the mother of Mrs. Lewis Robards, to give him board in her house, good accommodations being rare in that part of the country. About the same time Andrew Jackson entered the family, of which Mr. and Mrs. Robards were also inmates.

"Here," says Judge Overton, "we lived in the same cabin room and slept in the same bed as young men of the same pursuits and profession, and with few others in the country with whom to associate, besides sharing, as we frequently did, common dangers, such an intimacy ensued as might reasonably be expected.

"Not many months elapsed before Robards became jealous of Jackson, which, I feel confident was without the least ground. Some of his irritating conversation on this subject, with his wife, I heard amidst the tears of herself and her mother."

Judge Overton says that Jackson was very much disturbed by the thought that he had caused trouble between Robards and his wife, who is described as a gentle, sensitive woman, while of Jackson his friend wrote, "in his singularly delicate sense of honor, and in what I thought his chivalrous conception of the female sex, it occurred to me that he was distinguishable from every other person with whom I was acquainted."

Instead of leaving Mrs. Donelson's home, as Jackson was advised to do by Judge Overton, he, with lamentable want of tact and understanding of human nature, undertook to remonstrate with Lewis Robards upon his treatment of his wife. It is said that Jackson's chivalrous feeling towards the persecuted wife so far overcame his judgment that he exclaimed, "If I had such a wife, I would not willingly bring a tear to her beautiful eyes!" To which Robards wrathfully retorted, "Well, perhaps it is a mistake, but she is not *your* wife." From this beginning the domestic infelicities of the Robards family rapidly passed from bad to worse. Lewis

Robards seemed to have been possessed of a moody and revengeful disposition. A member of Mrs. Jackson's family, in writing of this episode, says of Mr. Robards,—

"He was handsome, well educated, polished in manner and conversation, far superior to any man of her acquaintance in those attributes supposed to have fascination for women; but, high-tempered, jealous-hearted, he proved a cruel, tyrannical husband.

"There are men—and men not altogether bad—with whose affections there mingles a strain of singular perverseness. If they have pets—cats, dogs, birds and horses—they tease and torment them, and their wives and children are alternate victims and idols. Robards belonged to this category. He doubtlessly loved his wife, but with a passion that blighted, violent love scenes would end in jealous wrangles, cruel taunts and upbraidings follow flattering endearments."

Robards continued to foster his jealous wrath against his wife and young Jackson until it gained the mastery over his common sense and led him to apply to the Legislature of Virginia for a divorce. The romantic and emotional side of Andrew Jackson's nature was evidently dominant in these early days, to the exclusion of prudence and good judgment. His sympathy was excited by the misfortunes of a charming young woman, and he was too frank and unguarded in his expressions of interest and friendship, in view of the jealous nature of her husband. It is quite possible that Jackson did not realize how deeply his affections were engaged until, at Colonel Stark's request, he had set forth as one of the little party which had been gathered together to protect Mrs. Robards upon her journey from Nashville to Natchez. Colonel Stark, a valued friend of the Donelsons, had asked Jackson to accompany the party, feeling that he needed a stronger force, in view of some disturbances among the Indians in that part of the country. Mrs. Robards was making this journey to some friends in Natchez, with her mother's knowledge and consent, in order to escape a command of Mr. Robards to return to him.

Soon after Jackson's journey to Natchez he heard that Robards had applied for a divorce from his wife, and, without waiting to assure himself that it had been granted, he asked Mrs. Donelson for permission to marry her daughter. To the mother's query, "Mr. Jackson, would you sacrifice your life to save my child's good name?" the young man answered, with characteristic fervor, "Ten thousand lives, madam, if I had them!"

The following summer Jackson returned to Natchez, married Mrs. Robards, and brought her back to Nashville.

Judge Overton, in writing upon this much-discussed question, says that he himself was under the impression that the Virginia Legislature had granted the divorce applied for by Lewis Robards, and did not learn anything to the contrary until December, 1793, when Jackson and Mrs. Robards had been married for two years, and were living near Nashville, beloved and esteemed by all classes. He adds that, upon learning that the divorce had not been granted in 1791 by the Legislature of Virginia, but had been granted by Mercer Court in Kentucky two years later, he informed General Jackson of this circumstance, which greatly surprised and distressed him.

Acting upon Judge Overton's advice, Jackson immediately obtained a license, and, in the presence of a number of persons, had the marriage ceremony again performed.

Jackson's carelessness in not investigating the legal bearings of the case seems absolutely unpardonable; yet Judge Overton, according to his own statement, was equally ignorant that the Virginia court applied to had not the power to grant a divorce.

"The circumstances of the marriage were such," says Mr. Sumner, "as to provoke scandal at the time, and the scandal, which in the case of a more obscure man would have died out during thirty years of honorable wedlock, came up over and over again during Jackson's career. It is plain that Jackson himself was to blame for contracting a marriage under ambiguous circumstances, and for not protecting his wife's honor by precautions, such as finding out the exact terms of the act of the Legislature of Virginia. Having put her in a false position, against which as a man and a lawyer, he should have protected her, he was afterwards led by his education and the current ways of thinking in the society about him to try to treat the defects of his marriage certificate by shooting any man who dared to state the truth, that said certificate was irregular."

This was literally true, as the famous duel with Charles Dickinson, fought in 1806, was the result of some disparaging remark made about Jackson's marriage with Mrs. Robards.

The campaign of 1828 was full of bitter personalities. Against Jackson were brought up the irregularity of his marriage and every salient feature of his strenuous frontier life and more or less despotic military governorship that could be discovered or invented, while Mr. Adams was charged with having made a corrupt promise to Mr. Clay, with being a monarchist and an aristocrat, with having married an English woman, with being rich, with being in debt, with receiving large sums of public money, with quarrelling with his father, with corruping the public confidence, with having a billiard-table put in the White House at the public expense, and with many other accusations equally absurd or equally false. These, a few among many charges made against President Adams, are cited to show that General Jackson was not the only sufferer from malicious tongues and journals in this campaign, although he, being as deeply hated by one party as he was enthusiastically beloved by the other, suffered more at the hands of his enemies than the rival candidate.

When the news of her husband's nomination was communicated to Mrs. Jackson, she remarked, with evident sincerity and a keen appreciation of the sacrifice of domestic happiness that this step involved, "Well, for Mr. Jackson's sake I am glad; for my own part, I never wished it."

One tale that has been related of Mrs. Jackson is that during a shopping expedition to Nashville, soon after the election, she picked up a paper while resting at an inn, and read some of the scurrilous charges made against her husband and herself. As the story runs, the poor lady, from whom the papers had been carefully secreted, was so shocked and distressed that she never recovered from the blow, and died soon after. The story told by a member of Mrs. Jackson's family is somewhat different, and is probably the correct version of a very sad experience. After the election, when preparations were being made for leaving the Hermitage for Washington, Mrs. Jackson was obliged to go to Nashville to have some dresses fitted. The occasion of "Mistus" going to town was always quite an affair among the colored people. They gathered around her as she left the house, each one asking her not to forget him or her. One was to have a ribbon, others a kerchief, a bandana, or some little gift. Mrs. Jackson drove away from her home in good spirits, accompanied by her husband, who always rode beside his wife's carriage as far as Stone's River. After she reached Nashville and attended to her dress-making and shopping, Mrs. Jackson, being very much fatigued, went to the principal inn to rest before starting upon her twelve-mile drive to the Hermitage. Reclining on a sofa in the back parlor, the folding doors between it and the front room being closed, she heard her name spoken, followed by a repetition of campaign slanders, many of them heard by her for the first time, cruel suggestions as to the practicability of getting rid of her, remarks upon her appearance and manner, and unkind predictions of the impression she would make in Washington society. Before she was able to escape from the room the poor lady had heard enough to make her very unhappy. When asked afterwards why she did not make her presence known, she answered, with characteristic amiability, "I supposed they did not know I heard them, and would be hurt if they found out I had." All through the long drive home the cruel words kept ringing in Mrs. Jackson's ears. When her husband met her at Stone's River he noticed that she looked tired and spiritless, and said to her, "What is the matter, my love?" but could draw nothing from her. Mrs. Jackson afterwards told her niece what had happened. Mrs. Donelson begged her not to think again of the words of the ill-natured gossips, to which she answered, sadly, "I cannot help thinking of it, Emily, because it is true. I will be no advantage to my husband at the White House, and I wish never to go there and disgrace him. You will go and take care of his house for him, and I will stay here and take care of everything until he comes back, as often before in Mr. Jackson's absences."

In the weeks that followed, Mrs. Jackson often seemed feeble and depressed without being actually ill. On the day of a grand ball to be given in Nashville in the General's honor, the date chosen being the anniversary of the battle of New Orleans, Mrs. Jackson urged her husband to go and rest before dressing for the ball. He left her, telling the family to send for him if his wife wanted him. A few minutes after he had left the room, Mrs. Jackson called her niece and said that she felt ill, and had difficulty in getting her breath. The General was summoned, and in a few moments she died in his arms. Her husband and those who were with her constantly said that Mrs. Jackson had never been the same since her visit to Nashville, and one of the old servants who met her on her return declared that "Mistus looked like she'd been shot in the heart." It seemed, indeed, as if the tender heart of this gentle, affectionate creature had been wounded past healing. To an intimate friend she had said, in view of the unpleasant gossip about her marriage, "To think of my bringing trouble to the good man who released me from wretchedness and has made my life so happy!"

Mrs. Jackson was unquestionably ailing for some months before her death. Grief and depression of spirits may have hastened the end, without being the actual cause of her death, as her husband, in the bitterness of his anguish, seems to have believed. With this fresh grief in his heart, feeling that his gentle Rachel's life had been shortened by the tongue of slander, it is not strange that the warm-hearted and chivalrous Jackson, to whom the traditions and conventionalities of society were as nothing in comparison with the happiness of one fellow-creature, was ready to champion the first woman in distress whom he chanced to meet. The fact that the woman in question, the dashing Widow Timberlake, was as different from his gentle, innocent-minded Rachel as night from day made no difference to him. Peggy was persecuted, his friend Eaton was about to marry her, and, right or wrong, she should have her place in the society of the capital. If this woman's walk and conversation had not been above reproach, there was reason the stronger for defending her and starting her again in the right direction. So argued, with rare clemency, this man who at certain periods of his military and political career had shown himself implacable towards his foes, tyrannical in the use of power, and at times overbearing and cruel.

The merits of this curious episode in the social life of the capital are still discussed by old inhabitants. Warm admirers of President Jackson contend that he had a right to insist that the Cabinet ladies should treat Mrs. Eaton with civility when they met her in official circles, which was all that he demanded, while others consider his position arbitrary and unreasonable.

General Eaton finally cut the Gordian knot by tendering his resignation. The President soon after appointed him governor of the recently acquired Territory of Florida, from which he was advanced to the more congenial position of minister to Spain. At the Court of Madrid Mrs. Eaton spent the happiest years of her life.

General Eaton died in 1859, and his widow, who retained her remarkable beauty to an advanced age, distinguished herself by eloping with the young dancing-master who was engaged to instruct her grandchildren. That this marriage was one of convenience to the dancing-master was proved soon after by his appropriating to himself all of the bride's jewels and available money, with which he retired from the scene, accompanied by the young and beautiful granddaughter of his elderly consort.

Mrs. Donelson, who had retired to her Tennessee home during the Eaton imbroglio, returned to the White House, and again presided over its dinners and drawing-rooms. Another woman who sometimes received the President's guests in the "Round Room," as the Blue Room was then called, was Mrs. Andrew Jackson, the wife of General Jackson's adopted son. This young woman, a daughter of Peter Yorke, of Philadelphia, is described as lovely and attractive in manners and conversation. The General became very much attached to young Mrs. Jackson. Upon one occasion, when receiving a deputation from the Keystone State, he met its members with the pleasant remark, "Gentlemen, I am very glad to see you, for I am much indebted to Pennsylvania. She has given me a daughter who is a great comfort to her father."

Mrs. Edward Livingston and her daughter were frequently at the White House, Mr. Livingston being Secretary of State under the Jackson administration. A warm friendship had existed between these two families ever since the eventful winter of 1815 in New Orleans, when the General had sworn his favorite oath that he would hang an English officer, who was his prisoner, "as high as Haman" if the British dared to touch a hair of Edward Livingston's head. Cora Livingston had been a favorite of the old soldier from her childhood, and when Mrs. Donelson's little girl, Mary Emily, was born, she stood as godmother to the White

House baby, at the especial request of the President. Miss Livingston married Mr. Thomas Pennant Barton in 1833, and her father being given the English mission about this time, the President sent Mrs. Barton an appointment for her husband as secretary of legation at Paris, that she might have the pleasure of presenting it to him with her own hands.

Other guests who were frequently at the White House were Mrs. John Macomb, Mrs. Rives, Mrs. Watson and her daughters, Miss Rebecca McLane, and Miss Blair. Mrs. Wilcox speaks of Miss Mary Tutt, afterwards Mrs. Thorndyke, of New York, as often at the White House with Mrs. Donelson, and of Miss Mary Eastin, who was married there to Lucius J. Polk, a cousin of the future President.* Lucius Polk, a man of fine presence and much dignity, when asked in later years whether he was a member of the family of President Polk, was wont to reply, with consider-

* Mary Eastin, afterwards Mrs. Lucius J. Polk, was one of Mrs. Jackson's many nieces. Mrs. Wilcox was a great-niece. This little girl, the third child born in the White House, was the daughter of Mr. and Mrs. Andrew Jackson Donelson. The President's family was confusing at this time, as Mrs. Jackson's nephew, Andrew Jackson Donelson, and another nephew and adopted son, Andrew Jackson, both lived with their uncle. After his marriage Andrew Jackson spent most of his time at the Hermitage.

Mrs. Lucius J. Polk   Madame Pageot

able impressiveness of manner, "No; the President belongs to my family."

A friend of Mrs. Lucius J. Polk was Mary Lewis, a Tennessee girl and a daughter of William B. Lewis, one of the President's associates. Miss Lewis afterwards married M. Alphonse Pageot, secretary to the French legation and chargé d'affaires for a number of years.

Major William B. Lewis, who had taken a long journey to Washington to witness the inauguration, after a visit of a few days told the President that he must leave him, as it was planting time, and his farm required his attention. "Why, Major," exclaimed his host, "you are not going to leave me here alone after doing more than any other man to bring me here?" The General clung to his Tennessee friends, and was lonely in the great house without their familiar faces. He offered Major Lewis a position in the Treasury, urging him to stay, to which he consented, and became a member of the President's family. The other men who were credited with having most influence over Jackson during the early years of his administration were General Duff Green, editor of the *United States Telegraph*, the Jackson organ, Isaac Hill, from New Hampshire, and Amos Kendall. These three journalists, with Major Lewis, formed what the enemies of the administration were pleased to call "the kitchen cabinet," which was supposed to exert much more influence in public affairs than the actual Cabinet. Another of the President's warm friends and adherents was Francis Preston Blair, of Kentucky, who established the *Globe*. Mr. Blair was a speaker and writer of marked ability, whose name has been creditably represented in the later political life of the nation by his son, General Frank P. Blair.

Mrs. Lee, a daughter of the elder Blair, recalls to-day the charm and courtesy of General Jackson's manner, especially towards women and children. It sometimes seems as if the roughness and extreme plainness of Jackson's life and surroundings before he came to the Presidency must have been exaggerated, perhaps in order to please the popular fancy for tales of sudden elevation from low birth and surroundings to the highest place in the gift of the nation. A certain directness of speech and simplicity of daily habits he never lost. His cob pipe was dear to his heart and horse-racing a favorite pastime. Yet, in the presence of women no more courtly gentleman could be found than this pioneer soldier.

An amusing account is given by a relative of Mrs. Jackson of the reception at the White House of an English traveller, soon after General Jackson's first inauguration. Lady E. was making a visit to Washington, and being known to Mr. Buchanan, she expressed a desire to be received by the President. Mr. Buchanan offered his services to arrange an interview. Going to see the General, he found him enjoying his dishabille and cob pipe in his study. Mr. Buchanan made his request for an interview, to which the President replied that he would receive Lady E. in an hour's time. Before going to acquaint the lady of the engagement which he had made for her, Mr. Buchanan paused to remind Jackson that his expected visitor was an English lady of rank, accustomed to all the refinements of the social life of her time. The President listened with some impatience, and then turning to the Pennsylvania Senator, said, " Jeemes Buchanan, when I went to school I read about a man that I was much interested in. He was a man who minded his own business and he made a large fortune at it."

It is needless to say that the dignified statesman retired in some confusion, anathematizing the unlucky star that had led him to proffer Lady E.'s request for an audience on this particular day, when the President seemed so ill prepared to receive her. Mr. Buchanan's confusion gave place to surprise an hour later, when he drove up to the White House with the expected visitor, and found the President waiting to receive her in an irreproachable costume. He descended to the coach, and escorted Lady E. up the broad steps with the grace of a Chesterfield.

When the visitor was leaving the house, after a pleasant interview with the President, she said to Mr. Buchanan, "Why did you not prepare me for this? In all my travels I have not met a more elegant gentleman."

Mrs. Lee, who was often at the White House in her girlhood, and, in consequence of her father's intimacy with the President, spent an entire summer with the family near Fortress Monroe,* says that "when Mrs. Donelson and Mrs. Andrew Jackson were at the White House with their young children, and the babies were restless and fretful at night, the President, hearing the mother moving about with her little one, would often rise, dress himself, and insist upon having the child, with whom he would walk the floor by the hour, soothing it in his strong, tender arms, while he urged the tired mother to try to get some rest." Mrs. Lee remembers the General's great kindness to the children at the White House table, where he sometimes insisted that they should be helped first, saying that they had "better appetites and less patience, and so should not be expected to wait until their elders were served." This indulgent fondness, injudicious as it may have been and subversive of any regular discipline, plainly reveals the tender and affectionate

* This was when the fort, then called the Rip Raps, was being built.

nature of a man who in his early life had known many hardships and little tenderness.

It is not strange that men and women, who were in their childhood the guests of General Jackson, should in old age remember him with affection, and count among the happiest hours of their lives those spent with him in the White House.

A woman still living in Washington, who was a child of eleven or twelve at the time of the General's second inauguration, still vividly recalls the ball given at Carusi's, which her parents allowed her to attend at the earnest solicitation of the President, with whom she was a great pet. Attired in a green silk dress, with green shoes to match, the gifts of her elderly admirer, this child "tagged after her mother," as she expressed it, full of delight and wonder over her entrance into what seemed like fairy-land.

Mrs. Wilcox has written her recollections of happy days spent at the White House, especially of one golden Christmas Day that shines forth in memory luminous and fair, different from any other festival of her after-life.* These favored children of the President's family, two little Jacksons and five Donelsons, hung up their stockings in "Uncle's room," while one of the boys, with great glee, tied

* "Christmas under Three Flags," by Mary Emily Donelson Wilcox.

one of the President's socks to the tongs, saying, "Now, let's see how Santa Claus will treat you, Mr. Uncle Jackson, President of these United States." It is needless to say that the stockings were not allowed to suffer from neglect. Little Mary Emily Donelson seems to have received a lion's share of gifts, among them a miniature cooking-stove from her godfather, the Vice-President, and a charming doll from Madame Serurier. "A big doll, wearing the red brass-button jacket, gray gold-striped pants, plumed chapeau, spurs, and sabre worn by French postillions. I had had many handsome dolls," says the vivacious narrator, "but never a boy doll before, and like other foolish mothers welcoming a son after a succession of disappointing daughters, I clasped him in my arms and crowned him lord and master of my heart."

There was a gay party in the great East Room that year, to which the little Woodburys, Blairs, Macombs, Joneses, Pleasantons, Lees, and many other Washington children were invited by a note, which said,—

> "The children of President Jackson's family request you to join them on Christmas Day, at four o'clock P.M., in a frolic in the East Room.
>
> "WASHINGTON, December 19."

A few older guests were invited, says Mrs. Wilcox, among them "Mrs. Madison, bringing her grand-niece, Addie Cutts, Mrs. Lee, with little Custis, the

Baroness Krudener, Mesdames Huygens and Serurier, and Sir Edward Vaughan, who joined the President and members of the family in the Red Room and served as spectators of a novel and delightful entertainment."

The Vice-President, being also among the spectators, was not long content to merely look on, and joining Miss Cora Livingston, fair mistress of the revels, entered with great spirit into "Blind Man's Buff," "Puss in the Corner," and a game of forfeits, while the children, doubtless instigated by their elders, tried to catch the Vice-President and Miss Livingston under the mistletoe bough that was suspended from the chandelier. The failure of this mischievous scheme was, says Mrs. Wilcox, the only disappointment of the evening.

To the music of the "President's March" the happy little guests were ushered into the supper-room, where a feast was served, in whose preparation Vivart, prince of chefs, had excelled himself. Amid the many dainties which loaded the beautiful table was a pyramid of snowballs, surmounted by a gilt game-cock, with head erect and outspread wings. The snowballs, which were made of non-combustible, starch-coated cotton, were distributed among the children, who were allowed to have a royal game of snowballs in the East Room after supper. At the close of the evening the happy children marched around the room, kissing their hands as they passed the President, and saying, "Good-night, General." Mrs. Madison, who stood by the side of the genial host enjoying the gay scene, exclaimed, "What a beautiful sight it is! It reminds me of the fairy procession in the 'Midsummer Night's Dream.'"

A lady who was frequently at the White House during General Jackson's administration has left a pleasant picture of the happy domestic life of this childless widower:

"A large parlor, scantily furnished, lighted from above by a chandelier; a bright, blazing fire in the grate; around the fire four or five ladies sewing, say Mrs. Donelson, Mrs. Andrew Jackson, Mrs. Edward Livingston, and another one or two; five or six children, from two to seven years of age, playing about the room, too regardless of documents and work-baskets. At a distant end of the apartment the President, seated in an arm-chair, wearing a long, loose coat, smoking a long, reed pipe, with a red clay bowl, exhibiting the combined dignity of a patriarch, a monarch, and an Indian chief. A little behind the President, Edward Livingston, Secretary of State, reading to him, in a low tone a dispatch from the French Minister for Foreign Affairs. The President listens intently, yet with a certain bland assurance, as though he were saying to himself, 'Say you so, Monsieur? We shall see about that.' The ladies glance toward him, now and then, with fond admiration expressed in their countenances. The children are too loud occasionally in their play. The President inclines his ear closer to the Secretary, and waves his pipe, absently, but with an exquisite smiling tenderness toward the noisy group, which, Mrs. Donelson perceiving, she lifts her finger and whispers admonition."

XI

THROUGH SEVERAL ADMINISTRATIONS

EDWARD LIVINGSTON was in 1833 appointed minister to France by President Jackson, and Andrew Stevenson, of Virginia, who had been Speaker of the House for seven years, was in 1836 sent to represent the United States at the Court of St. James. By means of these appointments two women were introduced to the social and diplomatic circles of Paris and London who were admirably fitted to grace the salons of those cities. Mrs. Livingston's vivacity, intelligence, and charm made her very popular in the society of the French capital. Greatly as she enjoyed Parisian life, she was always loyal to her own country, declining upon one occasion to assist at a state banquet because she considered that the American representatives were not accorded their proper position. In the matter of precedence this Louisiana woman had always been somewhat punctilious. To go into dinners and receptions after "*Madame le ministre d'Etat* or *Madame de la Guerre*" did not offend her ideas of propriety; but, as she expressed it in her fascinating Creole English, "to walk in to dinner behind Madame Poze-offeese, *jamais!*"

Mr. and Mrs. Andrew Stevenson reached London soon after the death of William IV., and were present at the coronation of Queen Victoria. Mrs. Stevenson's letters, still preserved in the family, give vivid and interesting descriptions of this ceremonial, as well as her own impressions of the womanly grace and *bonté de cœur* of England's young Queen. At the time of the jubilee celebration in 1887, a relative of Mrs. Stevenson's copied one of these letters written fifty years before and sent it to Queen Victoria. Through her secretary, Lord Ponsonby, the royal lady thanked the owner of the letter for the pleasure she had given her in allowing her to read what the young American matron had written of her coronation so many years before.

As the wife of the American minister, Mrs. Stevenson was sometimes invited to Windsor Castle, and often amused her friends by telling them how the Queen had prescribed for her upon the occasion of one of these visits. Learning that Mrs. Stevenson was indisposed, the Queen sent for some black pellets, which she insisted that her visitor should take, assuring her that they were most efficacious and cured all of her ailments.

While in London Mr. and Mrs. Stevenson frequently entertained Mr. Richard Vaux, of Phila-

Mrs. Andrew Stevenson

By G. P. A. Healy

delphia, who for a time acted as private secretary to the American minister. At a state ball, when Mr. Vaux and the Honorable George M. Dallas were present, these two handsome Philadelphians are said to have attracted the attention of the Queen. While dancing a quadrille, the royal lady lost her partner, either by accident or intention, and graciously extending her finger-tips to Mr. Vaux, gave him an opportunity to tread a measure with the ruler of one of the greatest empires in the world. This incident of his early life in London, Mr. Vaux was wont to relate with great spirit in later years.

Mrs. Stevenson, who was a woman of ability, tact, and intelligence, made many friends among English people of rank and learning. Those who remember her, as she appeared in later years in her home near Richmond, describe her as a striking-looking person, tall and commanding, as in her portrait, with clear, penetrating eyes, attractive manners, and great conversational ability.

John Van Buren, a son of the President, was in London with the Stevensons, while another bond was established between the two families by the marriage of Mrs. Stevenson's niece, Angelica, to Abraham Van Buren. Soon after their marriage the young couple visited the Stevensons in London, and the pretty and graceful bride entered with her aunt into some of the gayeties of the English capital during the season after the coronation. This period was made especially brilliant by the presence in London of the Emperor of Russia, Prince Henry of Orange, and many foreigners of rank.

Mrs. Van Buren, under the chaperonage of the wife of the American minister, enjoyed peculiar advantages, while her charming, unassuming manners made an agreeable impression and drew around her a circle of warm friends. "In the court circles of England," says a writer of the time, "she made herself most agreeable and maintained in the salons of royalty the simplicity and dignity of her republican education."

President Van Buren is described, by an acquaintance still living in Washington, as graceful and sympathetic in manner and unusually clever and charming in conversation. His son Abraham was extremely handsome, while John Van Buren was exceptionally brilliant and witty, with attractive manners and marked ability as a speaker and *raconteur*. Mr. R. R. Wilson, writing of John Van Buren, says that after being attorney-general of New York

> "He left the Democratic party with his father, and when the latter was nominated by the Free Soil party, the son's oratorical abilities were most effective in securing converts for the new departure. John Van Buren afterwards returned to the Democratic fold, and whenever taunted by his associates as a

renegade, his sole excuse for his former action was a quaint allusion to the barnyard anecdote, 'Dad was under the hay.'" *

Although Mr. Van Buren in politics followed in the footsteps of his predecessor and retained most of General Jackson's Cabinet officers, his social ideas were much more in accord with those of Madison, Monroe, and John Quincy Adams. In carrying out his plans for a restoration of the more dignified social usages of the White House, the President found an able assistant in his daughter-in-law, Mrs. Abraham Van Buren. This young woman had been introduced to the gayeties of the capital the winter before her marriage by her cousin Mrs. Madison. Connected by ties of kinship and association with the more aristocratic element in Washington life, which was led by Mrs. Madison and Mrs. Alexander Hamilton, young Mrs. Van Buren was by birth and natural gifts admirably fitted to draw into harmonious relations the varied elements of the cosmopolitan city. In addition to the advantages of youth and beauty, she possessed tact and adaptability. In describing the impression made by Mrs. Van Buren when she assisted the President in receiving his guests at a New Year's levee a few weeks after her marriage, one of the newspapers of the day recorded that

* "Washington: The Capital City," by Rufus Rockwell Wilson.

"She was universally admired, and is said to have borne the fatigue of a three hours' levee with a patience and pleasantry which must be inexhaustible to last one thro' so severe a trial."

If there was less promiscuous entertaining in the White House during Mr. Van Buren's term than in that which preceded it, a greater sociability prevailed in official circles. The President not only gave many delightful dinners at the White House, but encouraged his Cabinet officers and their principal subordinates to follow his example. Consequently, fortnightly dinners were given at a number of houses at which the resident society of the capital and the members of the official and diplomatic circles were brought together. Weekly levees were held at the White House, which, if less popular and democratic than those of the previous administration, were more elegant and dignified. It was pleasant to have a genial host and a graceful hostess in the Executive Mansion once more. The old house looked bright and cheerful with carriages constantly driving to its door, often filled with gayly dressed visitors, as Washington women, even those of its most exclusive circles, warmly welcomed young Mrs. Van Buren.

Mrs. Madison was living in the capital during Mr. Van Buren's administration, having returned thither the year following the death of her husband, bringing with her a favorite niece, Anna Payne.

The square, gray house, still called the "Dolly Madison house," which in those days had its entrance on Lafayette Square, soon became a favorite resort of the Washington world, and no sojourner in the capital considered his visit complete without a call upon Mrs. Madison. Despite advancing years, physical infirmities, and the shadow of a great sorrow in the loss of a husband to whom she was devotedly attached, this woman still possessed a charm of manner and conversation that drew to her side young and old alike. Mrs. Fremont, writing of Mrs. Madison as she appeared in the forties, said that in those happy times, "when character outranked appearances," no person thought of criticizing the short-waisted, puff-sleeved, gored velvet gowns of an earlier period, which were still worn by the mistress of the gray house on Lafayette Square. Poverty came to Mrs. Madison in later years, chiefly through the extravagance of her son; and when the choice lay between relinquishing the pleasures of society or appearing in old gowns, the genial lady speedily decided in favor of the social life that she loved. And so cheerfully and gracefully were the old dresses worn that many persons, even critical young girls, testified to their suitableness, and said that no other costume would have become her as well.

Afterwards, through the exertions of Mr. Webster and other friends, some of Mr. Madison's papers were bought from Mrs. Madison, and President Tyler urged upon Congress the propriety of purchasing Mr. Madison's library for a sum that would make his widow comfortable in her declining years. This was done, and a Washington woman, in speaking of these plans for Mrs. Madison's relief, says, that Mr. Corcoran and Mr. J. Bayard Smith induced her to make a will and leave the little property that she still possessed to her faithful niece, Anna Payne, rather than to her undutiful son.

On public holidays, such as the Fourth of July and New Year's Day, Mrs. Madison's doors always stood open, and the throng of people who paid their respects to the President at the White House trooped across Lafayette Square to offer their greetings to "the young lady of fourscore years and upwards," as Philip Hone described Mrs. Madison in 1842. A great-niece, recalling her impressions of her aunt, speaks of crossing with her mother and brother "the ragged little square opposite the White House" to be received by a "very sweet looking lady, tall and erect, with eyes that were blue and laughed when she smiled and greeted her friends, who seemed so glad to see her."

At this reception, which was during the administration of President Polk, the young narrator says:

"A throng of people passed in and out, among them some old ladies, whom I have since heard of as the wives of men known to fame. There was Mrs. Decatur, who at that time lived in a little cottage near Georgetown College, and never went out except to call on Aunt Madison. She wore a little close bonnet, and had great, sad, dark eyes. Mrs. Lear (Mrs. Tobias Lear, whose husband was Washington's secretary) was another most beautiful old lady whom we all called aunt, I suppose because all the children loved her; Mr. Bancroft, who lived in the Ogle Tayloe house, next door; Mr. and Mrs. Webster, whom I saw for the first time; also Mrs. Polk, who was always so gracefully attentive to Mrs. Madison, and was then a tall, handsome, young-looking person, and much beloved in society."

A social event of this administration, still recalled by many older Washingtonians, was the marriage of Miss Williams, of Georgetown, to the elderly Russian minister, Baron Bodisco. Mrs. Fremont, in her "Souvenirs," tells of the beauty and grace of Harriet Williams, who was among her companions at the fashionable school of Miss English in Georgetown. One year Miss Williams, who was a great favorite with her schoolmates, being amiable as well as beautiful, was chosen by them to be Queen of the May at their annual celebration. Mrs. Fremont relates, with great spirit, a sad tale of the setting aside of the beloved candidate for the very poor reason, according to youthful judgment that the young lady's standing in her classes was not satisfactory to the principal and teachers. Another and more studious scholar was crowned Queen of the May in the place of Harriet Williams; and then, as if in defiance of the retributive justice of Sunday-school literature and "Parents' Assistants," this pretty maid who did not attend to her tasks was soon after invited to walk into fairy-land *à la Russe.* The fact that the Prince of the tale was in this instance short and stout, with a broad Kalmuck face, much wrinkled, surmounted by a shining brown wig, did not much concern those gay school-girls, or the bride either, for the matter of that. Beautiful, placid, and smiling, she accepted the good gifts that came to her as if engaged in a lottery in which she drew all the prizes, while her friends enjoyed with her the balls, dinners, *bonbons*, and fine feathers. Baron Bodisco, who seems to have had a great liking for young people, gave a famous Christmas party for the boys and girls of his acquaintance at his large house on O Street, in Georgetown. The entertainment was in honor of the Baron's nephews, who lived with him, and the preparations, which were in Russian style, were for days the wonder of the quaint old town. The house was illuminated, and great fires burned in the vacant square in front of the mansion, which were, according to a kindly Russian custom, for the comfort of the coachmen; but upon this stormy Christmas night they served as beacon-lights to guide the young people "to the haven where they would be." One of these happy guests, writing of the party, said that inside the doors fairy-land began, as everything was provided that children, little and big, could fancy. The balconies of the house had been enclosed and hung with curtains and mirrors. In one of these improvised rooms were wonderful red and gold swings; in another gifts galore,—toys, picture-books, boxes of kid gloves, fans, ribbons, and bags of *bonbons*, "all these," adds the narrator, "for us to take home." There were elaborate refreshments at this party, dancing, and games; but what most impressed the young guests was the generosity of the Russian Kriss Kringle, who had provided so many gifts for them to carry away, in which the elderly host showed a genuine appreciation of the loot-loving tendencies of the average child.

In issuing invitations for this entertainment, which seems to have included young persons from ten to sixteen and upwards, by some mischance an invitation was not sent to little Miss Williams, who lived on U Street. Learning of the omission, the Baron himself wrote a very polite note of apology and an invitation to the young lady, who gracefully accepted both.

The night of the ball, the Baron asked his nephews to be sure to present him to Miss Williams, as he wished to make amends for his apparent neglect. So well did the host act his part and so gracefully did the young girl accept the *amende* that in a short time the diplomat of sixty was seen meeting sweet sixteen and carrying her books to school, which encounters were followed by a proposal, made to Mr. Williams in due form, and a betrothal.

"The Bodisco wedding," as it was always called, was the talk of the Washington world for some weeks. The ceremony was performed at the home of the bride's father, Mr. Brooke Williams, but the feast was spread at the Baron's house on O Street.* Among the guests at this wedding were the President and his Cabinet, members of the Diplomatic Corps in full regalia, officers of the army and navy in uniform, and many ladies in attractive visiting costume. "It was a lovely day in early spring, fortunately," wrote one of the bridesmaids, "for though it was a wide and roomy house the company overflowed into hall and piazzas and the grounds, while out in the road the crowd of carriages was swarmed around by a throng of outsiders. It was like a gay country fair with its cheery, moving crowd." Mrs. Fremont, then Jessie Benton, aged fourteen, was one of the bridesmaids selected by Miss Williams, her attendant being the dignified and handsome Senator Buchanan, who had recently returned from the Court of St. Petersburg. The Chevalier de Martini, minister from

* The Williams house, on U Street, near Observatory Place, the scene of this wedding, and the Bodisco house at No. 3322 O Street, both standing, are among the interesting landmarks of old Georgetown.

The Hague, waited with a lovely sixteen-year-old daughter of Commodore Morris, whose sister Louise afterwards married Mr. William W. Corcoran. The bridesmaids were all young, to harmonize with the bride, the groomsmen of an age and dignity suited to those of the groom. "Consequently," says Mrs. Fremont, "it was May and December all through."

Among the groomsmen was the English minister, Henry Stephen Fox, older and more withered and gray than when Byron met him at Naples and wrote home, "I met, the other day, Henry Fox, who has been dreadfully ill, and, as he says, is so changed that his oldest creditor would not know him."

Mr. Fox was a familiar figure upon the streets of the capital, in his nankeen trousers, blue swallow-tailed coat with brass buttons, high shirt collar, wide brimmed hat, and an inevitable green silk umbrella. Upon the occasion of Baron Bodisco's wedding, says one of the guests, "he appeared, resplendent in a court suit of scarlet and gold, his rough gray eyebrows frowned over his half-shut eyes, and his whole attitude a protest." Perhaps the English minister's protest was not so much against the matrimonial venture of the elderly diplomat as against the early rising necessitated by a morning wedding. It was currently reported of Mr. Fox, who went to bed at dawn and rose at three in the afternoon, that upon the occasion of the funeral of a member of the Diplomatic Corps, he turned to the wife of the Spanish minister, and said, "How very odd we all look by daylight!" it being the first time he had seen his colleagues except by candle-light.

A bustling, anxious master of ceremonies was the Baron, giving orders right and left, and up to the last moment engaged in arranging the wedding party in the approved horseshoe curve of the day. The bride, who was to be given away by Henry Clay, was beautiful in a gown of white satin and silver lace, which was fashioned after the costume of a Russian bride, a coronet of red velvet blazing with diamonds resting upon her golden hair. Gay, happy, and apparently unconscious of her own attractions, she was busied in distributing flowers to her bridesmaids and pearl rings from the groom; complaining one moment of the elegant but oppressive wrap of satin and swansdown which had to be worn as a part of the ceremony, and the next wishing that she might satisfy her school-girl appetite upon the delicacies of the wedding feast that was to be served at "Bodisco's house."

"When we were arranged quite to his (Baron Bodisco's) taste," says Mrs. Fremont, "in a horseshoe curve, the glistening white dresses and young faces and flowers thrown into higher relief by the age and court dress of the men, while Bishop Johns in full canonicals, and Mr. Clay, tall and dignified, made the contrasting touch, Bodisco gave a last reviewing look, then ordered the doors to be rolled back. Certainly the guests saw a beautiful tableau,—whether painful also it was for each one to judge. But of this we had no thought. To go through our parts with ease and dignity, to remain in position during the ceremonious congratulations, and only speak *in answer*, to group around the bridecake with its ring, and offer it to those coming to its special flower-dressed table, these were our limit."

Among the entertainments given in honor of the Baron Bodisco and his bride was a dinner at the White House. One of the guests speaks of crossing the windy hall from the dressing-room to the drawing-room, which Mr. Van Buren later had protected by glass screens.

Around the pretty, youthful bride were grouped her girl bridesmaids, while the elderly groomsmen made a sombre background for the gay tableau.

"The old mirror plateau on the dinner-table has never reflected such an odd company," says one of the guests, "but with such a host, in such a house, the dinner and the invited reception that followed had to be beautiful and a success. Mr. Van Buren had great tact and knew how to make each one show to advantage. He was also very witty, but he controlled this, knowing its danger to a man in public life."

The sequel proves this apparently ill-assorted union between sixty and sixteen to have been a happy one. The Baron was a kind and indulgent husband, generous to his wife's family as well as to herself. The monotony of a Georgetown residence was varied by several visits to Russia, when the beautiful young Baroness was received at the court of St. Petersburg, where her children and grandchildren afterwards occupied positions of distinction.

After ten or twelve years of married life the good old Baron died, having expressed an amiable desire that his wife might marry again and be as happy as she had made him. The still young and beautiful Madame Bodisco fulfilled this last, as she had every other request of her husband, and soon after became the wife of an English officer named Scott. This second wedding was solemnized in St. John's Church, Lafayette Square; many of the guests were present who had assisted at "the Bodisco wedding," and Mr. Buchanan again occupied a prominent position, as he was called upon to give away the bride.

The refurnishing of the White House soon after Mr. Van Buren's inauguration was severely criticized, as was the greater formality of the weekly receptions and the absence of hard cider at these gatherings. Some writers have even stated, in all seriousness, that the lack of the favorite beverage, the redecoration of the White House, and rumors of a silver service and gold spoons in use upon the President's table cost him his re-election in 1804.

Upon one occasion, when Mr. Ogle, who had been a frequent guest at the White House, made some campaign speeches in which the gold spoons figured prominently, a friend asked Mr. Van Buren if Ogle was right about the "gold spoons." "He ought to know," replied the President, "he has often had them in his mouth." Although the unpopularity of the thirteenth administration was chiefly due to the financial depression consequent upon the carrying out of General Jackson's favorite banking schemes, every social innovation at the White House was magnified and criticized as indicative of a dangerous and unrepublican tendency towards the luxury and extravagance of foreign courts. Exaggerated contrasts between rude and luxurious living, which had been employed with considerable success in the campaigns of 1828 and 1836, were carried to an extreme by the Whig party in 1840. The blessings of rustic simplicity, the advantages of life in a log cabin over that in an ordinary dwelling-house—the Whig candidate having spent much of his life upon the frontier—were extolled in political speeches, editorials, and songs. During this campaign, which was one of banners, emblems, and jingles, verses ending in "Tippecanoe and Tyler too," with allusions to "Van, a used-up man," were sung everywhere, and doubtless contributed much to the overwhelming defeat of the conservative Van Buren and to the triumphant election of General Harrison.

A soldier who had served in the Indian wars with Wayne, and had received his commission from the hands of Washington, was a figure well calculated to arouse the enthusiasm of the American people. In the brief term of one month granted to him as Chief Executive, William Henry Harrison fully vindicated the confidence reposed in him by his countrymen.

An heroic figure was that of the old soldier surrounded by his Cabinet and advisers, battling manfully against the encroachments of the spoils system, opposing even such giants in the political arena as Webster and Clay, and when brought to bay, turning upon them with the unanswerable argument that whatever pledges they may have ventured to make, he, William Henry Harrison, was the President.

It has been said that General Harrison died from the effects of a cold contracted while delivering his inaugural address from the east portico of the Capitol upon a chill March day. Dangerous as such exposure may have been to an elderly and not very strong man, the President's fatal illness may perhaps with more justice be attributed to the unaccustomed exertions of the campaign and the inauguration, and more especially to the fatigue and strain caused by the importunities of office-seekers and the purveyors of places, who crowded about him. During his illness the President's mind wandered, but always turned back to the same familiar subject; and the last words that were heard by those who surrounded him were such as did honor to the righteous man and the good citizen. "It is wrong—I won't consent—it is unjust," he murmured, as if speaking to some one. "These applications, will they never cease? Sir, I wish you to understand the true principles of the government. I wish them carried out. I ask nothing more."

The death of President Harrison placed in the office of Chief Executive the Vice-President, John Tyler, a veteran politician and a Virginia gentleman of the old school.

Although the inauguration of President Tyler brought some dissension into the House and Senate, peace and happiness reigned within the walls of the Executive Mansion, where open-handed Virginia hospitality was once more extended. The dinners and receptions, if less ceremonious than those of the previous administration, were characterized by a warmth and graciousness that are inherent in the sons and daughters of the Old Dominion. Mrs. Tyler was in delicate health, and frequently unable to appear at the weekly levees; but her two daughters, Mrs. Lightfoot Jones and Mrs. Semple, and her daughter-in-law, Mrs. Robert Tyler, were fortunately at hand to take her place.

Mrs. Semple, a bride at the time of her father's inauguration, was beautiful and distinguished in appearance and manners. Still living in Washington,

Mrs. Semple recalls the brilliant and varied life of the White House in the early forties, or the simpler and more congenial delights of a drive or walk with her father through woods or over the unclaimed common that, in days when the living district did not extend north or west beyond Thomas Circle, lay near the heart of the city.

Mrs. Robert Tyler, a clever and charming young matron, presided over many of the White House entertainments. Once, when receiving Mr. Joseph Nourse, an old friend of her father, whom she had not seen since her childhood, she exclaimed, "Ah, Mr. Nourse, truth *is* stranger than fiction, which is exemplified by my receiving you here in the White House."

The children of Mr. and Mrs. Robert Tyler were often with them in Washington, and a fancy ball, given by the President to his eldest granddaughter, Mary Fairlie Tyler, is still recalled by men and women who were among the guests of the evening. Little Mary Tyler, representing a fairy, with gossamer wings, a diamond star on her forehead and a silver wand in her tiny hand, stood at the door of the East Room to welcome into Queen Titania's realm her delighted young friends. At this beautiful ball there were the usual number of flower-girls and gypsy fortune-tellers, Miss Adéle Cutts appearing as one of the former, and Miss Rosa Mordecai in the latter interesting rôle, while the Senorita Almonte, daughter of the Mexican minister, represented an Aztec princess, and young Master Schermerhorn, of New York, an Albanian boy.

The sociable Tyler family introduced the custom of having music in the White House grounds on Saturday afternoons, which made a pleasant rallying-point for the Washington world. The beautiful grounds around the Capitol furnished another attractive meeting-place, and here the band played on Wednesday afternoons during the spring and summer. A Washington woman, in recalling the persons to be met at the White House and in the Capitol grounds, speaks of the handsome, soldierly figures of General Winfield Scott and General May, both destined to rise to distinction in the war with Mexico; of John C. Calhoun and the Reverend Park Addison, the latter dressed like a college-man of the old time, in long, black silk stockings, and shoes with buckles. Dr. Addison, of Georgetown, known as the blind parson, was usually accompanied by his young granddaughter. Here, also, were to be met General Edmund P. Gaines and his wife, he known as the hero of Fort Erie, and she as the heroine of a prolonged and interesting law-suit. The small, slight figure, and keen dark eyes of Myra Gaines were familiar to Washingtonians even in the latter years of the century.

Mr. Webster, says the narrator, was often present

at these Wednesday and Saturday promenade concerts *en plein air*, in blue swallow-tailed coat with brass buttons, open vest, and expansive white ruffled shirt-front, in company with a legal colleague, General Walter Jones. This latter gentleman, although as brigadier-general of the District militia he was known by a warlike title, had distinguished himself in a profession which is supposed to herald the dawn of peace and good-will upon the earth. General Jones was one of the lawyers retained by the heirs of Stephen Girard when their case to recover his bequest to the city of Philadelphia was tried before the Supreme Court of the United States.

A brilliant galaxy of wit and learning appeared upon both sides in this celebrated trial,—General Jones, senior lawyer, Mr. Stump, of Maryland, and Mr. Webster appeared on behalf of the Girard heirs, while the city of Philadelphia sent, to plead the cause of the orphan, two of her greatest lawyers, Horace Binney and John Sargent.

One of the strong points made by the counsel for the heirs was "that the college was an un-Christian institution, inasmuch as one of the provisions of the will was that no minister of the Gospel should enter its walls." Mr. Binney said, with some asperity, that they had made religion a stalking horse to stalk off with the orphan's bread; to which Walter Jones replied, in allusion to the vast sum consumed in erecting the costly and beautiful building, that "the orphans had asked for bread, and that they had given them a stone, a very beautiful stone indeed, but still a stone." *

Many witty sallies and clever passages of arms marked the sessions of the court during this trial. When all the evidence had been taken on both sides, Mr. Webster presented the case for the heirs. "The concluding argument belonged of right to Walter Jones as senior counsel in the case, who courteously waived his right to his colleague, Daniel Webster. Up rose great Dan, immaculate in white shirt bosom, blue cloth coat and brass buttons, his deep-set eyes kindling with more than their wonted fire, and delivered one of the most beautiful and powerful arguments in defence of the Christian religion ever uttered."

Says a witty narrator of the event, "It was perhaps the one instance in the history of the world when the law should have taken precedence of the Gospel.

* By a provision of the will of Stephen Girard, no ecclesiastic missionary or minister of any sect whatever was to hold communication with the college, or be admitted to the premises as a visitor. The reason for this restriction was, according to the testator, that "the tender minds of the orphans" who were to derive advantage from this institution should be "unprejudiced, and upon their entrance into active life free to choose such religious tenets as their mature reason may enable them to prefer."

"The case was decided against the heirs, although it was said in thus deciding, the Supreme Court had reversed three of its previous decisions. Walter Jones said with regard to it that the judges had 'swallowed their own opinions like hearty fellows.' "*

It should perhaps be added, in justice to the great lawyers who appeared in behalf of the defenceless orphans, that their arguments, and perhaps also the righteousness of their cause, triumphed, even in the face of three days of the great Webster's marvellous, impassioned pleading.

Other distinguished lawyers often to be seen upon the streets of Washington were Henry D. Gilpin and George M. Dallas, of Philadelphia, the latter destined to be Vice-President under Mr. Polk, a picturesque figure with his crown of snow-white hair, as was that of his learned townsman, Charles Jared Ingersoll, who still wore the Revolutionary buff and blue. Here also was Levi Woodbury, who, after representing New Hampshire in the Senate for a number of years, and acting as Secretary of the Treasury under President Jackson, was appointed by Mr. Tyler to succeed the venerable and honored Joseph Story as a justice of the Supreme Court. On the street, at the Capitol,

* "Walter Jones," written for the Columbia Historical Society by Fanny Lee Jones.

and at every place of general resort, "a chiel amang them takin' notes" was Mrs. Anne Royall. In her paper, *The Huntress*, appeared what she doubtless considered pen-pictures of the great and little folk of the Washington world. Yet, despite her opportunities for the observation of individualities among men and women of the day, there was a notable sameness in Mrs. Royall's portraitures. The women who pleased the writer's fancy were described as beautiful, with oval faces, Grecian features, raven or golden locks, as the case might be, and forms of the Venus mould; while the men whom she honored with her friendship were invariably intellectual giants, with penetrating eyes and expansive brows.

When Mrs. Anne Royall established her office on Capitol Hill, in 1836, and announced that *The Huntress* would be published every Saturday, she became the ancestress and forerunner in journalism of a long line of men and women of the pen who have since then written of the sayings and doings of people of their day. Prior to this time there was little to be found in the Washington papers of social events, or of the people who entered into the gay life of the capital. Mrs. Anne Royall, in her *Huntress*, Mr. N. P. Willis, in his Washington letters written for the New York *Mirror*, and Mr. James Gordon Bennett, in his correspondence to the *Courier* inaugurated a departure in journalism, whether for good or ill is still a question open to discussion.

If Mrs. Royall described her favorites with a pen dipped in honey, gall and wormwood were not wanting when dealing with those who had been so unfortunate as to incur her disapproval, which frankness of expression led Mr. John Quincy Adams to bestow upon the journalistic free-lance the title of the "virago-errant in enchanted armor."

True to her own sex and profession, Mrs. Royall announced in her paper, of February, 1847, that "Washington City was honored with the presence of three of America's most talented authoresses,—Mrs. L. H. Sigourney, Mrs. A. L. Phelps, and Mrs. Ann S. Stephens."

Another literary visitor to Washington in the early forties was Charles Dickens, who was *fêted* at the capital, as in other cities, and was received at the White House by President Tyler, his daughter-in-law, and his daughter, Mrs. Semple. Mr. Dickens spoke of the official reception at the Executive Mansion as extremely dignified, informal, and well managed. The usual number of visitors had been augmented in consequence of the presence of two literary lions, Washington Irving having accompanied Mr. Dickens, and the English visitor expressed himself as greatly surprised that this vast concourse of over three thousand persons created no disorder or confusion. Mrs. Dickens was with her husband in

Washington, and afterwards in Richmond, as appears from some letters which passed between Mr. William Seaton and the English novelist, in which Mrs. Seaton and Mrs. Dickens exchanged pleasant messages.

An interesting guest who was welcomed to the capital in 1841 by President Tyler was the young Prince de Joinville. The President, in addition to the usual dinner of ceremony, gave a ball in the Prince's honor. It is said that when members of the Cabinet remonstrated against dancing in the White House as undignified, Mr. Tyler replied that a dance would best please a young navy man and a Frenchman.

"Accordingly," says a young girl who was present at this entertainment, "we had a charming and unusually brilliant ball. All our army and navy officers were in uniform, as the Prince and his suite wore theirs, and, for the son of a King, the Diplomatic Corps were in full court dress. Mr. Webster, as Secretary of State, was, next to the President, the chief person. For fine appearance, for complete fitness for that representative position, both Mrs. Webster and himself have never been surpassed.

"The Prince was tall and fine-looking, and Miss Tyler and himself opened the ball, while those of us who knew French well were assigned to his officers.

"We had remained in the oval reception-room until the company was assembled, and then, the President leading, the whole foreign party were taken through all the drawing-rooms, ending by our taking places for the *Quadrille d'honneur* in the East Room; that ceremony over, dancing became general, and we were free to choose our partners."

This young prince carried away many pleasant memories of social and also of rural life in America. After travelling through the West and staying in the family of a farmer, in order to see the harvesting, he was greatly impressed by the fact that the families of working-people had meat on their tables three times a day, and by the intelligence of this class in the community. "The farmer, and even his wife," he said, "talked politics, although she made excellent bread and of so many kinds."

The winter succeeding the inauguration—that of 1842—was an eventful one in the White House. In January of this year Elizabeth Tyler, the President's third daughter, was married in the East Room to William Waller, of Williamsburg, Virginia, and in the following September lovely Mrs. Tyler, wife of the President, was removed from the joys and sorrows of earth.

Mrs. Robert Tyler presided over the White House during the years that intervened between the death of her mother-in-law and Mr. Tyler's second marriage to Miss Julia Gardiner, of New York.

Mrs. Tyler was many years younger than the President, and was handsome and youthful in appearance. Although, as Mrs. Fremont says, the new mistress of the White House was somewhat commented upon by old-fashioned people, "because she drove four horses (finer than those of the

Russian minister), and because she received seated, her arm-chair on a slightly raised platform, in a velvet gown with three feathers in her hair," young Mrs. Tyler made numerous friends during her eight months of official life, and left the Executive Mansion regretted by many. It is said that even political enemies of the President had only words of praise for his charming young wife.

XII

MID-CENTURY GAYETIES

THE Washington life of the days of Presidents Van Buren, Polk, Taylor, and Fillmore presented many of the characteristics that distinguish it to-day. Although the city has spread out upon lines of beauty, and muddy streets and inadequate sidewalks, over which cows and pigs rambled at will, no longer annoy the visitor, as they did M. de Bacourt in 1840, the capital still retains a certain simplicity and homelike charm that belonged to it in earlier times. Then, as now, the presence of many foreigners in the diplomatic service gave to this city a cosmopolitan character, while a generous, warm-hearted hospitality which belonged to its social life, being distinctly American, has not disappeared amid the growth and expansion of the larger city, with its stricter code of social and diplomatic etiquette. In addition to the official circles and the changing population of Washington, it has always possessed an attractive and interesting society, composed of the old families of the District and of those who, having gone there upon business, have yielded to its attractions and made it their home.

Lady Emmeline Stuart Wortley, who visited Washington in 1849, while keenly alive to certain crudities and incongruities in its life, found much to admire in the beauty of its public buildings and the graceful hospitality and intelligence of its citizens. M. de Bacourt, on the other hand, looking always through glasses dimmed by prejudice, saw nothing but the defects of the rambling village-like capital, which he was pleased to call his prison. After being hospitably received at the White House by Mr. Van Buren, whom he had met on the Continent, the French diplomat had nothing more favorable to say of the President than that "his politeness was finished and in perfect imitation of a gentleman;" while of Daniel Webster and Henry Clay he recorded that one was pompous to a degree, and the other of the gentleman farmer type. The Washington ladies whom M. de Bacourt met at Mrs. Meade's, at Mrs. Woodbury's, at the Baron Bodisco's, and at the various weddings and assemblies of the season he described as "badly dressed, badly trained, and badly combed, in fact, like third-rate English people," while, if possible, their dinners and suppers were more execrable than themselves. Mrs. Abraham Van Buren the critical Frenchman alone excepted in his sweeping and adverse criticism of the belles and beauties of the capital. "The daughter-in-law of President Van Buren would," he said, "in any country pass for an amiable woman of graceful and distinguished manners and appearance."

Lady Wortley was in Washington during the brief administration of General Taylor, to whom she and her little daughter were presented by Madame Calderon de la Barca, wife of the Spanish minister. Of "the hero-President," as the English lady was pleased to call him, she has left an interesting and sympathetic description:

"Mrs. Bliss, the charming daughter of the President, was in the drawing-room when we first went in. Mrs. Taylor has delicate health, and does not do the honors of the Presidential mansion. Mrs. Bliss received us most cordially and courteously, saying her father would come as soon as his presence could be dispensed with. Presently after, the President made his appearance: his manners are winningly frank, simple, and kind, and though characteristically distinguished by much straightforwardness, there is not the slightest roughness in his address. There was a quick, keen, eagle-like expression in the eye which reminded me a little of the Duke of Wellington's. . . . He was so exceedingly good-natured as to talk a great deal to my little girl about roses and lilies, as if he had been quite a botanist all his life. This species of light, daffydowndilly talk was so particularly and amiably considerate and kind to her, that it overcame her shyness at once, and the dread she had entertained of not understanding what he might say to her. . . . General Taylor spoke very kindly of England, and, adverting to the approaching acceleration and extension of steam communication between her and America (the contemplated competition about to be established by 'Collins's line'), he exclaimed, 'The voyage will be made shorter and shorter, and I expect England and America will soon be quite alongside of each other, ma'am.'

"'The sooner the better, sir,' I most heartily responded, at which he bowed and smiled.

"'We are the same people,' he continued, 'and it is good for both to see more of each other.'

"'Yes,' I replied, 'and thus all detestable old prejudices will die away.'

"'I hope so,' he continued; 'it will be for the advantage of both.'

"He continued in this strain, and spoke so nobly of England that it made one's heart bound to hear him. And he evidently felt what he said; indeed, I am sure that honest, high-hearted, true-as-steel old hero could not say anything he did not feel or think."

Mrs. Polk proved a graceful and accomplished hostess during her four years' residence in the White House, and made many friends in Washington; but Mrs. Zachary Taylor, who succeeded her, was less ready to meet the demands of society. This good lady, who had endured without complaint the hardships of army life upon the frontier, and was, as the General said, as much of a soldier as himself, was too ill at the time of the inauguration to enjoy with her husband the crowning triumph of his life. Upon Mrs. William W. Bliss, the daughter of General and Mrs. Taylor, devolved the social duties of the White House.*

* Mrs. Bliss afterwards married Mr. Dandridge, and in her Virginia home still recalls for the entertainment of her friends the pleasures of her life in the White House. Her sister was the first wife of Jefferson Davis, his second wife was a Miss Howell, of the New Jersey family of that name.

Mrs. Bliss—Betty Bliss, as her friends called her—brought to her task charm, tact, and the enthusiasm of youth. Many persons still recall this young matron as she appeared at the White House dinners and receptions,—a beautiful, gracious, attentive, and self-forgetful hostess. The President's son, afterwards known as General Dick Taylor, a dashing Confederate officer, and his daughter, Mrs. Jefferson Davis, were often in Washington. All the young people of the President's family were at the capital in March, 1849, and entered with him into the gayeties attending the inauguration. One of the merriest of this family group was Rebecca Taylor, a niece of the President, who at her uncle's request was taken from the Convent School at Emmetsburg and brought to the capital to enjoy the festivities of the White House. This sixteen-year-old *débutante*, who was attractive and witty, made many friends, and entered into all the social pleasures of her uncle's brief administration.

A day long to be remembered in Washington was that upon which was laid the corner-stone of the beautiful monument which to-day

> "High from the city's heart, a lifted spear,
> In its straight splendor makes the heavens seem near."

On July 4, 1850, the corner-stone of the Washington Monument was laid with appropriate ceremonies, in which the President and his Cabinet took part, in the presence of many distinguished residents of the capital and a large number of invited guests. Upon the evening of the Fourth, President Taylor was taken ill of a malady which proved fatal, and on the 8th of July following he breathed his last.

The sudden death of President Taylor brought to the White House a man and woman of simple domestic tastes and habits, whose intelligence and tact enabled them to enter acceptably into the social life of the capital.

President Fillmore, a handsome man, distinguished in appearance, with dignified and courtly manners, had been Comptroller of his own State, and had represented her interests in the nation's councils for a number of years. Mrs. Fillmore, whose maiden name was Abigail Powers, like another Abigail who had first presided over the White House, was a descendant of the Puritans, and, like her, was a woman of intellectual ability and cultivation. The President and his wife were accompanied by their son and daughter. Powers Fillmore acted as his father's secretary, while Miss Fillmore assisted her mother, who was extremely delicate, in her duties as mistress of the White House. Friends of Miss Abigail Fillmore, who still remember her with fond affection, speak of her as a cultivated, studious girl, an exceptionally brilliant musician, and a hostess of great tact and charm.

Mr. Benjamin Ogle Tayloe and other persons living in Washington at this time have described the winter succeeding the inauguration of Mr. Fillmore as one of unusual gayety and attractiveness. Mr. and Mrs. Tayloe entertained with a generous yet discriminating hospitality in their beautiful house, which is still standing on Lafayette Square; while Mr. and Mrs. Webster, who occupied the Swann house on the north side of the square, inaugurated a series of evening receptions which brought together the most distinguished and charming residents of Washington, and such visitors as Washington Irving, Horace Greeley, Mrs. Lippincott, better known as "Grace Greenwood," Charlotte Cushman, Louis Kossuth, Mr. and Mrs. Edward Everett, and many interesting members of the Diplomatic Corps.

If, as Lady Emmeline Wortley cleverly remarked, Washington reminded her of "a vast plantation with the houses kept far apart as if to give them room to grow and spread," these oases scattered over the plain were all centres of a delightful hospitality. Capitol Hill was in the middle of the century and even later a favorite residence district. One of the most attractive homes in this neighborhood was that of Senator Benton, where the presence of his lovely wife, four charming daughters, and the delights of good music and brilliant conversation drew to his fireside many interesting men and women of the day. Here General Dix, then Senator from New York, the Prussian minister Baron von Gerolt, Mr. Sumner, Mr. Buchanan, and Samuel F. B. Morse were all frequent and informal visitors. The Ellsworths, like their neighbors the Bentons, were warm friends of Mr. Morse, the women of the family being ever ready to lend a sympathetic ear to his so-called visionary schemes in the days when he was laughed at in Congress, his funds exhausted, and his health threatened. It is not strange that the first message sent over the electric wire by the inventor was to Miss Ellsworth,—"See what God hath wrought;" to which Mrs. Fremont says he might well have added, "And what mountains are moved by the patient, tender faith of women!"

Near neighbors of the Bentons were General Dix and Francis Scott Key, the latter a lawyer of considerable distinction, although known to-day chiefly as the author of the "Star-Spangled Banner." General Walter Jones, who was associated with Mr. Key in the celebrated Gaines case, lived in a square brick house still standing at the corner of Second and B Streets, on the old turnpike road to Baltimore, within a stone's-throw from the Capitol. The building used while the Capitol was being rebuilt, and ever after known as the "Old Capitol," was a famous boarding-house, where Mr. Calhoun and other politicians lived, while in another house near by, kept by the Misses Harrington,

Mr. Buchanan and Mr. William King made their home.

Another pleasant social centre was the square on F Street between Thirteenth and Fourteenth, where ex-President John Quincy Adams and his family long resided. Here also lived Dr. Robert K. Stone and Mrs. Thornton, whose house was afterwards the residence of Dr. Thomas Miller, a distinguished physician, who attended so many Presidents that he well deserved the title of "court physician" laughingly accorded him by his friends.

Many fine, substantial old mansions on F, E, G, H, and I Streets were the residences of the Jesups, Kearneys, Macombs, Meades, Hobans, Porters, Rigges, and Markoes. Pennsylvania Avenue was a favorite place of residence in the middle of the century. One of the Six Buildings, still standing, between Twenty-first and Twenty-second Streets, was the home of the Honorable Richard Rush, while in another lived Dr. Johnston, a celebrated physician of old Washington. Opposite the Six Buildings lived Dr. Magruder, Mr. and Mrs. Henry Clay, and Mrs. Tobias Lear, a niece of Mrs. Washington, who had stayed with her at Mount Vernon, and, living beyond the middle of the last century, is still remembered as the beloved "Aunt Fanny" of many Washington children.

A short distance east of the Six Buildings, on I Street, was William O'Neill's famous inn, the

Franklin House, among whose patrons were the most distinguished statesmen of the last century; while upon the triangular space in front of the tavern, which was formerly occupied by a market-house, the witty and eccentric, but always earnest, itinerant preacher, Lorenzo Dow, frequently discoursed to large audiences. Several blocks east of the Six Buildings Mr. Francis Preston Blair, editor of *The Globe*, lived for many years in a house still occupied by his descendants. This house, No. 1651 Pennsylvania Avenue, was during Mr. Blair's lifetime the resort for many prominent men of the day,—General Jackson, Thomas H. Benton, Levi Woodbury, and President Van Buren being among its frequent visitors. Here resided Mr. Bancroft, the historian, while he was Secretary of the Navy under President Polk. Near neighbors of Mr. Blair, around the corner on Jackson Place, were Commodore Stockton, and the Livingstons, who leased the Decatur house for some years. Here afterwards lived Mr. James Gore King, whose daughter, Mrs. Bancroft Davis, distinctly remembers seeing Mr. Webster go in and out of the Swann house opposite. The long, low building at the corner of H Street and Jackson Place, built by Commodore Decatur, was afterwards the residence of Mr. and Mrs. Beale for so long a term of years that it is often spoken of as the Beale house. The Swann mansion, on the square, in which Mr. Webster resided while Secretary of State was afterwards for many years the home of Mr. William W. Corcoran, the generous and judicious benefactor of Washington City. Mrs. Bancroft Davis says that Mrs. Madison was often to be seen at the Websters' evening receptions, wearing her old-time turban and kerchief, smiling and gracious, courted and beloved by every one.

Mrs. Madison's home was on the east side of the square, at the corner of H Steeet, on what is now known as Madison Place. Her neighbors were Mr. and Mrs. Benjamin Ogle Tayloe, while beyond them lived Commodore Rodgers, whose residence occupied the site of the Lafayette Theatre.

West of St. John's Church, and next to Mr. William W. Corcoran's house, was the home of Mr. Thomas Ritchie, editor of the *Richmond Inquirer*. Here Mr. Ritchie lived for many years with his family of charming daughters, until one by one they flew away to nests of their own.* East of the church is a house built by Matthew St. Clair Clarke, in which Lord Ashburton lived during the discussion of the treaty of 1842. Sir Henry Bulwer resided in this house in the middle of the

* This house was afterwards the home of the Honorable Gideon Welles, Secretary of the Navy under President Lincoln. On the same side of H Street, at the corner of Connecticut Avenue, lived Commodore Shubrick, in a house still occupied by his descendants.

century, and here his nephew, Robert Bulwer, afterwards Lord Lytton, is said to have written his narrative poem "Lucile." Lady Bulwer, a daughter of Lord Cowley, had spent her early years in Paris, and was charming, cultivated, and a thorough musician. The Bulwers' Tuesday evenings and musical parties drew around them the most interesting people in the Washington world, as did the entertainments of Sir Henry Bulwer's successor, Sir John Crampton, which added not a little to the attractions of the Fillmore administration.

The interest of the Washington seasons in the early fifties was greatly enhanced by the happy circumstance that Jenny Lind, Parodi, Sontag, and Albani sang to crowded houses, that Lola Montez danced for the entertainment of the gay world, while Miss Cushman, Miss Davenport, Lester Wallack, Burton, and Brougham appeared in tragedy and comedy.

To the capital, with its many pleasures and interests, social, political, and literary, there came in the winter of 1852, by a singular turn of the wheel of fortune, a young girl who was well fitted to appreciate all its varied attractions. The story of her introduction to the life of Washington and to that of the White House is gracefully and sympathetically told by the fortunate young visitor, Miss Julia F. Miller, of Buffalo. After explaining that she and Abigail Fillmore were schoolmates and dear friends, and that Mr. Fillmore, who seemed to her like a king or a prince in a fairy-tale, was the kindest and gentlest of men, and ready to take any amount of trouble to gratify his daughter and her young friends, Miss Miller relates a prophetic conversation which occurred between herself and her schoolmate.

"One day Abbie said that when she was grown up she meant to teach school.

"'Oh, no, you won't,' said I, 'my father says that your father will be President some day, and you won't be allowed to teach school. You will be the President's daughter and live in the White House.'

"'What nonsense,' she said, 'I am going to be a teacher and earn my own living.'

"'Well, I don't believe any such thing. But if you do teach school I'll come to your school as a pupil even if I'm an old woman and married.'

"'All right,' said Abbie, laughing, 'you'll look well doing it. And if my father ever gets to be President, you shall visit me in the White House.'

"'Sure?'

"'Sure.'"

These words, uttered lightly by girlish lips, would have been quite forgotten, like many similar predictions, had not both prophecies and promises been literally fulfilled.

After completing her course at the famous school conducted by Miss Catharine Sedgewick, at Lenox, Massachusetts, Miss Fillmore attended the State

Abigail Fillmore
By Le Clear

Mrs. Alexander Hamilton
Painted by Charles Martin in 1851
Page 317

Normal School at Albany. One of the rules of this institution was that each graduate should teach at least three months; and, although after Miss Fillmore's entrance into the school Mr. Fillmore was elected Vice-President of the United States, his daughter remained in Albany and fulfilled the conditions of her contract. True to her promise, Miss Miller attended her friend's classes, which she says were admirably conducted.

About a year later, when Mr. Fillmore became President of the United States, the other half of the prophecy was fulfilled. Miss Fillmore went to the White House with her parents, and an invitation to Miss Miller to visit her there followed in due time.

> "It came at last, the longed-for invitation to the White House," says Miss Miller. "In the summer of '52 Abbie paid a visit to Buffalo and spent part of the time with me at my father's house and pleaded hard with my father and mother to let me go. . . . It was a fine thing for Miss Miller, and much to the credit of Miss Fillmore that her head was not so turned by the situation in which she found herself that she forgot old friends and neighbors. . . . Finally, consent was given. My modest preparations were soon made, my two trunks packed, and I went to Washington under the escort of Hon. S. G. Haven to be the guest of the President. We arrived there the Saturday before the first Monday in December, that Mr. Haven, Member for Erie County might be present at the opening of Congress."

Miss Miller's record, which has been supplemented by recollections written out for the amusement of the young people in her family, abounds in animated descriptions of the pleasures that filled her days, of official and social entertainments, of receptions and balls, of state dinners at the White House, and of quiet evenings in the Library with the Fillmore family and a few intimate friends. "After dinner," she says, "we sometimes spent a few minutes in the Red Room, but usually went upstairs to the Library. The Library was an oval room, over and exactly corresponding to the Blue Room."

It was during Mr. Fillmore's administration that this room was fitted up and used as a library. Mrs. Fillmore, with her scholarly tastes and pursuits, felt the need of books in the White House, and at the President's suggestion Congress was induced to supply them as part of the furniture of the Executive Mansion. As the appropriation granted was for books solely, and as there was no fund for refurnishing, Mrs. Fillmore used her own ingenuity in making the room habitable. Being a good housekeeper, like most intellectual women, she soon discovered that the new carpet in the Blue Room had been put down over the old one. Both were taken up and cleaned, and the old carpet put down in the Library. A few pieces of furniture were borrowed from other rooms of the White House, which, with the addition of some comfortable chairs, favorite books, and Miss Fillmore's piano and harp, made the room homelike and attractive. In this pleasant Library, with its cheerful wood fire, the President and his family spent their evenings and received intimate friends.

Miss Miller recalls many delightful hours in the Library, before the gay season began, when there was reading aloud, interesting conversation, and always Miss Fillmore's charming music. Sometimes Powers Fillmore would join his sister in singing such old-time melodies as "Sweet Vale of Avoca," "In the Desert a Fountain is Springing," or "Old Folks at Home," which, as Miss Miller says, "was new in those days."

In the Washington of that day, as in a later time, the gayeties of the season did not begin with the 1st of January. There was, however, a ball at the home of Mr. George W. Riggs, the banker, and a number of dinners were given by the President to the members of his Cabinet, to the Judges of the Supreme Court, to Senators, to Congressmen, and to the *Corps Diplomatique*.

"At all of these dinners," says Miss Miller, "I had my place and a more or less distinguished escort. I was invited to one or two Cabinet dinners where there were young ladies in the family, and one at the house of the Honorable John P. Kennedy. I got to know Miss Kennedy and Miss Dulany very well. At this dinner I was escorted by the Honorable Thomas Corwin of Ohio, Secretary of the Treasury, one of the most agreeable talkers I ever met, and the darkest white man I ever saw."

The description given by Miss Miller of a New-Year's reception proves that much the same etiquette was observed in 1853 as that which marks the levees of the twentieth century.

" The President and his wife and family stood together. The Cabinet ladies and guests of the house in the second row, a little to one side where their acquaintances could speak to them without interrupting the procession. Mrs. Fillmore wore wine-colored velvet, Honiton lace and diamond brooch. Abbie wore a silk ot a changeable green and red, a pattern brocade with three flounces and fine French muslin embroideries in waist and sleeves. Mrs. Cyrus Powers wore black velvet. She had magnificent black hair, four feet long, made into a rope coil at the back of her head. I wore a Napoleon blue silk with black velvet trimming and embroidered muslin sleeves.

" First of all came the *Corps Diplomatique*, the gentlemen in regular court dress, stiff with embroidery and gold lace. The ladies were dressed in the style of the winter, all very handsomely, of course, but I only remember one clearly. It was Mme. Bodisco, the American wife of the aged Russian Minister. He was past seventy and she twenty-eight. He married her when she was sixteen. She was very beautiful, not at all flirtatious nor unhappy, and was the mother of seven boys. There was a pretty story afloat how M. Bodisco used to walk with her to school and carry her books. When she was sixteen he would wait no longer and they were married. On this New-Year's day she wore a heavy white silk with three richly embroidered flounces, a lovely little white mantilla to match and a white velvet bonnet and plumes.

" It was a beautiful sight. The President received in the Blue Room. Persons entered the Red Room and passed into the Blue, thence through the Green Drawing-Room and into the great East Room from which there was an exit built from the windows. The Blue Room was full of these richly dressed men and women. One of the ladies of the English legation, Mrs. Corbett, wife of a secretary of Minister Crampton, was a granddaughter of the original Minna Troil in Scott's novel of the *Pirate*. I often saw her. She was very pretty, and lively, danced a good deal and dressed always in white.

"After the *Corps Diplomatique* came the Cabinet members, the Judges of the Supreme Court and their wives. Some of the ladies remained during the whole reception. Those who remained did so by invitation and were unbonneted. Everybody else came in handsome street costume.

"Then anybody and *everybody* came in, and were without exception sober, decent and well behaved. One little street waif was caught in the current and drawn into the crowd. She had on a calico frock, a little red shawl and a red knit hood, and was much frightened. But the President shook hands, smilingly, with her and whispered to the Marshall to take care of her. At three o'clock the reception was over, and we were glad enough to get up-stairs."

One of the most interesting events of the holiday season was an old-fashioned Twelfth-night party, where Miss Miller met Commodore Wilkes, of Japanese fame, and some of his officers. One of them, Captain Ringgold, drew the ring in the cake, which made him King of the revels. He very gallantly presented the ring to Miss Fillmore, which made her Queen of the evening.

"This he should not have done," says the critical chronicler; "it should have been given to the lady who drew the bean, who happened to be the daughter of the hostess; but he would not allow Abbie to return the ring, which she offered to do when she heard of the rule. 'Keep it as a souvenir of the evening and of me.' So she did, and we had quite a jolly little evening."

Among the many noted persons whom Miss Miller met were General Winfield Scott, who she says was head and shoulders above all the rest, and nearly always in uniform, brave, handsome, and frankly vain; Judge Butler, from South Carolina; and the Honorable Thomas L. Clingman. Mr. Clingman was small, with gray eyes and a dark skin, and limped. "It is said," adds Miss Miller, "that he carried a bullet from a duel, which was very interesting. He told every lady that he was in love with her, and kept on doing it, and nobody paid any attention to it."

Another famous beau of the Washington world in those days was Mr. John Barney, of Baltimore. Odd, humorous, and gallant, Miss Miller still recalls the quaint figure of this seventy-year-old gentleman, his necktie ornamented with a spread-eagle in diamonds, and his hand and heart at the disposal of each new belle.

The women whose beauty most impressed Miss Miller were Miss Chalfont, of Cincinnati; Mrs. Stannard, a lovely dark-eyed widow from Richmond; Miss Adèle Cutts, Miss Carroll, and Miss Dulany. Adèle Cutts, who afterwards married the Honorable Stephen A. Douglas, Miss Miller describes as "a dark-haired beauty with skin like the petals of a water-lily.* Miss Violetta Carroll (not of Carrollton, but of Washington) was a tall, fair blonde, who attracted the attention of every one to herself as she entered the room."

Miss Mary Dulany, whom Miss Miller found so beautiful and charming, was a daughter of Grafton Lloyd Dulany, of Baltimore. A great favorite of Washington Irving was this young girl, whom he frequently met at Mr. John P. Kennedy's house in Washington. Miss Dulany married Gardiner G. Howland, of New York. After the marriage a large reception was given to the beautiful bride by her mother-in-law, upon which occasion Mr. Irving, then in his seventy-fifth year, came down from Sunnyside to offer his congratulations to the young couple. Mr. Irving, when speaking of Miss Dulany's great beauty, was wont to add, thoughtfully, that she was "such a good girl."

An English man of letters who visited Baltimore in the middle of the last century wrote of Miss Dulany,—

"I have never seen a countenance more faultlessly lovely. The pose of the small head and the sweep of the neck, resembled the miniatures of Guilia Guisi in her youth, but the lines were more delicately drawn and the contour more refined.

* Mrs. Stephen A. Douglas, in 1866, married General Robbert Williams, and lived for many years in Washington, admired and beloved by all who knew her.

The broad, open forehead, the brows firmly arched without an approach to heaviness, the thin, chiselled nostril and perfect mouth cast in the softest feminine mould, reminded you of the First Napoleon. Quick mobility of expression would have been inharmonious there. With all its purity of outline, the face was not severe or coldly statuesque, only superbly serene. Not lightly to be ruffled by any sudden revulsion of feeling; a face of which you never realized the perfect glory 'till the pink coral tint flushed fairly through the clear pale cheeks, while the lift of the long, trailing lashes, revealed the magnificent eyes."

Another beauty of this time who charmed the Washington world was Miss Gabriela Chapman, of Virginia, who married the Marques de Potestad Fornari, attaché to the Spanish legation in the United States. Madame de Potestad was tall and distinguished in appearance, with dark hair, a dazzling complexion, and eyes of sapphire blue. A Washington woman, in speaking of her, says, "Every one who knew Madame de Potestad adored her. I remember her as a most beautiful and brilliant woman. I have never seen any one who compared with her except her friend Mrs. Edward Beale." *

At the foreign courts which the Marquesa de

* Mrs. Edward Fitzgerald Beale was a daughter of the Honorable Samuel Edwards, for many years a member of Congress from Chester, Pennsylvania. When Mr. Beale was appointed minister to Austria Mrs. Beale accompanied him and was greatly admired at the Court of Vienna.

Mrs. Gardiner G. Howland
(Mary Dulany)

Marquesa de Potestad Fornari
(Gabriela Chapman)

Potestad visited with her husband, who was in the diplomatic service, she gracefully and charmingly represented her country. In Paris the central figure of a gay and brilliant circle, which included the most distinguished Frenchmen of the day, Madame de Potestad was always known as a good wife and mother, as well as a brilliantly beautiful, attractive, and witty woman.

At one of the fairy-like *fêtes* given by the Empress Eugenie, at the Hotel d'Albe, which she had bought for her mother, Madame de Potestad is described as radiantly beautiful, " in a costume created by Worth, called *clair de lune dans un bois*," which was well suited to the lovely gardens with their picturesque *bosquets* in which the Empress entertained her guests.

Although Miss Miller entered into many gay scenes and received quite enough attention from distinguished men and women to have turned so young a head, the fact that the most lasting impressions were made upon her mind by a visit to Mrs. Alexander Hamilton and by a day spent at Mount Vernon speaks much for her taste and discrimination.

Of the visit to Mrs. Hamilton Miss Miller writes:

" She was ninety-two years of age at this time and died two years after. She was a tiny little woman, most active and interesting, although she could never have been pretty in her life.

She kept me by her side, holding me by the hand, telling me of the things most interesting to me. How she knew Washington (with whom she was a great favorite), and Lafayette, who was 'a most interesting young man.' How they were often at the house of her father, Gen. Philip Schuyler. How when she was a child she was free of the Washington residence, and if there was company Mrs. Washington would dress her up in something pretty and make her stay to dinner, even if she came uninvited, so that she was presentable at table. She showed me the Stuart portrait of Washington, painted for her, and for which he sat; the old Schuyler chairs and tiny mirrors; most interesting to me. This tiny dot of a woman and of such a great age, happened to think of something in her room which she wanted to show Abbie. Her granddaughter, Mrs. Hamilton Holley, offered to get it for her. 'Sit down, child, don't you think I can get it myself?' and up she went and got it, whatever it was."

Of the manner in which the Mount Vernon visit was arranged Miss Miller gives the following account:

"One day the statue, which stands in the centre of Lafayette Square, was unveiled, and a large party of the President's friends was invited to see the ceremony from the windows of the White House and to lunch afterwards. While we were at lunch, Mr. Andrew Kennedy sat by me. 'Now do you know, Miss Miller,' said he, 'I've been thinking that although it is a grand house, some other scenes might be livelier ones for a young lady, and Miss Fillmore and all of them are very busy and a good deal taken up with cares and so forth, and there might be things you'd like to see and do, and here is an old fellow with grown-up daughters and nothing on earth to do but what you and they want him to do for them. Now then what is it?'

"'Oh, how good you are,' I cried. 'I have spoken of going to Mt. Vernon, and somehow we have never gone. Of course they have all been there, but I really don't feel that I ought to leave Mecca without seeing the tomb of the Prophet.'

"'Why of course not, of course not. Well, well, we'll manage it. My girls want to go too.'

"About a week after this, as I had begun to wonder why I did not hear from Mr. Kennedy, Abbie and I had been at the Capitol, and when returning down Pennsylvania Avenue the carriage was suddenly stopped and two gentlemen, hats in hand, stood at the door to speak with Miss Fillmore, Mr. Andrew Kennedy and Mr. John Washington, the proprietor of Mt. Vernon, and in brief this was the conversation :*

"Said Mr. Kennedy, 'Mr. Washington is a sort of cousin of ours, and is stopping with my brother John. Mr. Washington wants us all to come down to Mt. Vernon to spend the day with him, and Washington Irving is with us now, and I hear that Miss Miller has never been there, and can't you all join us and go down to-morrow? We are going to the theatre to-night, and if it is not too late, we could stop at the White House on the way home and arrange it.'

"There was a grand dinner at the White House that night. Just as the last guest departed, Mr. Kennedy and Mr. Washington came in, Mr. and Mrs. Fillmore were duly enlightened as to the plan, and I stood by and begged with my eyes. Mr. Fillmore did not offer the slightest objection, and invited the whole party from the Kennedy house to breakfast at nine o'clock.

---

* Mount Vernon was at this time the home of Mr. John A. Washington, the estate having been inherited by him from his uncle, Judge Bushrod Washington. The daughter Lulu, of whom Miss Miller speaks, was Louisa Washington, who married Colonel R. P. Chew.

Mr. Washington had chartered the steamer, and it would start at our pleasure, probably about ten o'clock. . . .

"It was a very jolly breakfast party indeed, although Mr. Fillmore was a most stately host, and Mr. Irving was rather quiet but genial, even in silence. There were Mr. and Mrs. Fillmore, Powers, Abbie and myself of the household. Mr. Andrew Kennedy, Mr. John Kennedy, and his niece, Mary Kennedy, Miss Dulany of Baltimore, Washington Irving and John Washington.

"At table the talk naturally turned upon General Washington.

"'Did you ever see Washington?' said Mr. Fillmore.

"'Only once,' said Mr. Irving. 'I shall never forget it. I was about five years old, and was being led along Broadway by my Scotch nurse. She spied the General just going into a shop. She caught me up in her arms and rushed after him, calling out, "General, General, here's a bairn that's called after you. Give him your blessing and he shall be blessed." And he turned around and laid his hand on my head and said, "God bless the little boy." I seem to feel it now sometimes,' said Irving, reverently, 'and I know that I have been blessed.'

"This rather quieted down the party, and we soon left the table and drove to the steamer dock. When we landed Mr. Irving offered me his arm, and we walked up the hill together and were met by Mrs. Washington and her daughter Lulu a girl of twelve or so. They showed us all the relics, the swords of Washington, the old copying books, antedating the days when he made his mark on the cherry tree, and some other writings of his; the famous 'pitcher portrait,' a chance likeness caught by some foreigner, sketched and carried to Delft and being used as the decoration of a Delft pitcher, was found to be one of the best likenesses of Washington ever taken. This unfortunately was the only copy that could be procured. There was also the key of the Bastille, and some few prints of the French King and Queen, presented by Lafayette. We were not shown the upper rooms, as it was then a family residence. We visited the tomb of Washington, and I gathered a few pebbles which I kept for years. Mr. Irving plucked a branch of holly from the tree overhanging the tomb, which he gave me, saying 'It is immortal.' Lulu Washington gave me the twig of a lemon-tree in the conservatory which George Washington had planted with his own hands, so she said. We enjoyed the beautiful prospect from the porch, and I discovered that the house was built of finely hewn logs, bevelled to look like cut stone.

"It was a beautiful, clear, warm day. I had my full share of happiness. On the way back all of the men devoted themselves to the beautiful Miss Dulany, whom I discovered to be one of the prettiest girls I ever saw. Her beauty is now historical, as Mr. Irving said of her, 'She is one of the loveliest and sweetest girls I have ever seen.' And just so she seemed to me. . . .

"There was to be a levee that evening and the Chubb ball to come after it and many were going there from the levee. Then it had come out all about our little excursion, and that Washington Irving would be there, and many came for a glimpse of him. He was there and escorted Miss Kennedy and Miss Dulany, who each wore a spray of the famous holly which he had given them. At this time Mr. Irving was seventy-two years old. A placid, sweet, lovable old gentleman, not tall, rather stout, with large, soft brown eyes, rather quiet, and gave the impression of being a listener rather than a talker, and a quiet observer rather than an actor on the world's stage."

Although Miss Miller enjoyed the Chubb ball and danced until two o'clock in the morning, which was considered extreme dissipation at that time, she says that the visit to Mount Vernon was glory enough for one day, long to be remembered as "a spotless white day" in her life.

The young girl who left Washington in 1853 did not revisit it until the boundary-line of the new century had been crossed.* While appreciating the greater beauty of the capital of to-day, with its wide avenues and charming circles, the glamour of early association still glorified the narrow streets and simpler dwellings of the older and far less attractive city. It was with pleasure that she turned from the superb residences upon Dupont Circle and Massachusetts Avenue to rest her eyes upon such familiar landmarks as the Van Ness mansion, the Octagon, and the French Embassy on H Street. Kalorama no longer crowned the heights above Rock Creek; the house of Mr. Riggs, the banker, and of Mr. Chubb, the scenes of brilliant entertainments, were both torn down or modernized beyond all recognition; but the White House, filled with memories of a happy past, was little changed, except that a conservatory had been added on the side next to the old banquet-room, and Lafayette Square in front of it presented many familiar façades.

Lafayette Square, or Jackson Square, as it was called for a time, is the most interesting in its asso-

* Miss Julia F. Miller, as Mrs. Frank M. Snow, of Buffalo, revisited Washington in the spring of 1901.

ciations of any square in the United States, with the exception of Independence Square in Philadelphia and the Boston Common and its surroundings. This park, in whose centre General Jackson and his charger perform feats of horsemanship and agility that have not been surpassed in any succeeding decade, has been crossed by all the great statesmen and patriots of the past century; while St. John's Church, on its north side, has been attended regularly or occasionally by a long line of Presidents, Congressmen, soldiers, and sailors, from the days of Monroe, Adams, Marshall, Story, Webster, Clay, Brown, Barney, Porter, and Bainbridge to those of Lincoln, Grant, Sherman, Sheridan, and Farragut.

In the houses that surround Lafayette Square, and in those nearby on Pennsylvania Avenue and on H Street, much of the history of the last century has been made,—for here lived Daniel Webster, Chief Justice Taney, Edward Livingston, William H. Seward, James G. Blaine, Thomas Ritchie, the Blairs, Commodores Decatur, Rodgers, Stockton, Wilkes, Porter, and Shubrick, Gideon Welles, and George Bancroft.

Lafayette Square, or President's Square,—for so it was called by the gracious lady who lived in the gray house at the corner of Madison Avenue,—as it stands to-day, girt about by houses rich in associations of the past, is a spot loved and honored by the citizens of Washington. A never-failing centre of interest is this beautiful square to those who visit the capital, and bringing their children, point out to them on all sides the houses where the great men of the country lived, and the paths they trod daily on their way to the home of the nation's chief,—that low, wide-spread White House, the home of many Presidents, which from the days of John Adams to those of William McKinley and Theodore Roosevelt has been the scene of simple, dignified hospitality, and of a domestic life of which the nation may well be proud.

INDEX

INDEX

INDEX

INDEX

INDEX

INDEX

INDEX

H

INDEX

I

J

INDEX

R

S

INDEX

THE END